Using Multicultural Literature
to Teach K–4 Social Studies

Related Titles

Cultural Diversity and Education: Foundations, Curriculum, and Teaching, 4/e
James A. Banks
ISBN: 0-205-30865-1

Portraits of Teachers in Multicultural Settings: A Critical Literacy Approach
Lettie Ramírez and Olivia Gallardo
ISBN: 0-205-30575-X

Because We Can Change the World: A Practical Guide to Building Cooperative, Inclusive Classroom Communities
Mara Sapon-Shevin
ISBN: 0-205-17489-2

Learning in Living Color: Using Literature to Incorporate Multicultural Education into the Primary Curriculum
Alora Valdez
ISBN: 0-205-27446-3

For further information on these and other related titles, contact:

Allyn and Bacon
75 Arlington Street
Boston, MA 02116
www.ablongman.com

Using Multicultural Literature to Teach K–4 Social Studies

A Thematic Unit Approach

Barbara Edwards

University of North Carolina at Charlotte

J. Allen Queen

University of North Carolina at Charlotte

Allyn and Bacon

Boston ■ London ■ Toronto ■ Sydney ■ Tokyo ■ Singapore

Series Editor: *Traci Mueller*
Editorial Assistant: *Bridget Keane*
Manufacturing Buyer: *Suzanne Lareau*
Executive Marketing Manager: *Stephen Smith*
Cover Designer: *Jenny Hart*
Production Coordinator: *Pat Torelli Publishing Services*
Editorial-Production Service: *Lynda Griffiths, TKM Productions*
Electronic Composition: *TKM Productions*

Copyright © 2002 by Allyn & Bacon
A Pearson Education Company
75 Arlington Street
Boston, MA 02116

Internet: www.ablongman.com

Library of Congress Cataloging-in-Publication Data

Edwards, Barbara.
 Using multicultural literature to teach K-4 social studies : a thematic unit approach/ Barbara Edwards, J. Allen Queen.
  p. cm.
 Includes bibliographical references and index.
 ISBN 0-205-27379-3
  1. Social sciences--Study and teaching (Primary)--United States. 2. Multicultural education--United States. 3. School children--Books and reading--United States. I. Queen, J. Allen. II. Title.

LB1530 .E39 2002
372.83'044--dc21   2001053570

Printed in the United States of America

10 9 8 7 6 5 4 3 2 1   05 04 03 02 01

For Chandler and Ashlin, who asked long ago,
"Why aren't there kids like us in these books?"
                                                    B. E.

To all the higher-level consciousness teachers who have risen
above the pettiness of individualism to embrace humanity
and all its diversity and to my wonderful son, Alex.
                                                    J. A. Q.

CONTENTS

Unit No.	Grade Levels	Book(s)	Thematic Focus	Cultural Group(s)	NCSS Strands	Page
1	K–1	Multiple books	Work Is Important!	Multicultural	IV, VI, VII	123
2	K–2	*Thundercake*	Getting Rid of Fears	European American	IV	142
3	1–2	Multiple books	Family Helpfulness	Multicultural	I, IV, VII	151
4	2–3	Multiple books	Overcoming Barriers	Multicultural	II, IV, V	170
5	3–4	*The House on Maple Street*	Cultural Change and Differences	Multicultural	II, III	184
6	3–4	Multiple books	Respecting the Earth	Multicultural	I, III, VIII, IX	199
7	3–4	*Freedom Train*	Courage and Leadership	African American	II, VI	219
8	4–5	*Felita*	Overcoming Prejudice	Hispanic/Latino American	IV, V	234
9	4–5	*Nightjohn*	Courage and Commitment	African American	II, X	240
10	4–5	*Missing May*	People, Places, and Environments	European American	I, II, III	248

PREFACE

This book is intended primarily for classroom use by practicing teachers who are seeking means and materials to use multicultural literature with their students more effectively, particularly through integrating literature with social studies. Those teachers might be searching for more compelling stories, strategies for integrating lessons in their busy daily schedules, reasons to share their choices of materials with parents and principals, or entire units to implement. They may also be looking for questions and answers that put words on impressions, worries, perceptions, or concerns that they've not quite articulated—concerns about diversities among their students that they either don't recognize or don't understand, worries about unsuccessful students who don't seem to find their niches in the classroom, fears that students' lives are far more difficult and chaotic than anyone would wish, and a growing apprehension that school curriculum may be viewed as less relevant and that academic achievement may be valued less by increasing numbers of students and their families. We support, encourage, and trust you.

Using Multicultural Literature to Teach K–4 Social Studies is also intended as a supplementary text for undergraduate or graduate courses in language arts, social studies, children's literature, curriculum development, and multicultural education. Grounded in theory and research, it is a practical tool for moving forward into multicultural education through curriculum integration of thematic social studies units with fine multicultural children's literature at the core. It provides tools for translating academic depth of learning into confident educational practice.

Acknowledgments

We thank the following reviewers for their helpful comments: Patricia Ann Baltz, University of California at Los Angeles; M. Lee Manning, Old Dominion University; and Richard Peters, Texas A&M University, Corpus Christi. We also acknowledge with appreciation the many suggestions and observations of our undergraduate and graduate students as they read and thought about multicultural literature with us, shared their surprises and upsets, brought new books to us, field-tested activities, participated in classroom simulations, voiced their concerns about lack of time to teach social studies and lack of time to find and read children's books, expressed chagrin about their insufficient awareness of cultural differences, and reaffirmed their outstanding commitment to continued growth so that they can assure successful learning for every student. We especially acknowledge and thank Maureen Gillen, an outstanding teacher and excellent principal-to-be, for her assistance in the final days of preparation. You kept us going, Maureen!

Barbara Edwards
J. Allen Queen

PART ONE

Setting the Context

The fact that you picked up this book may mean that Part One is going to "preach to the choir," or that you're skeptical, or that you're perhaps mildly curious. A number of questions beginning with *Why?* are targeted here. Parts Two and Three provide tools for *how*. We hope that the brief answers to the questions of this section will stimulate, support, or satisfy you.

Choose a question below that intrigues you, and read on! Use our resources and recommendations for further reading when you want more. All children's books mentioned throughout the narrative portions of this book are listed in Chapter 9's annotated bibliography. The sequence of questions below worked for us, but you are free to choose the best order for you. If you don't need the answers we offer, skip this whole section and dive into the rest of the book immediately.

CHAPTER 1

Why should I make any changes in my teaching? It works for most of my students.

Many very fine instructional methods and materials do work for most students. However, in a nation of growing diversity, there are children in the United States not responding in expected ways to these methods and materials. If you have been puzzled by one or more children in your classroom, consider this cluster of questions:

- Who are the students *not* included in that group of "most" of your students? Is that portion of your class growing? Those children will grow up to be productive or nonproductive adults—what is your prediction if they've never been a part of "most" of someone's class?
- What are the predictions for the near future in your area concerning business, industry, and population changes? Are you prepared to make rapid revisions when your classroom suddenly has a much larger number of non-English-speaking immigrant children because of a new internationally owned factory or the settlement efforts of a church in your community?
- Within your school district, when housing patterns change or school boundaries shift, will your teaching methods and classroom organization still work for "most" children if your next class is different in major characteristics such as economic status, primary language and preferred dialects, family structure, and racial and ethnic composition?
- How will your classroom be affected if your community experiences change in rates of unemployment, layoffs, natural disasters, violence, or teenage pregnancy? Are you ready for hungry, abused, or homeless children?

My dad and I live in an airport. That's because we don't have a home and the airport is better than the streets. We are careful not to get caught.

Mr. Slocum and Mr. Vail were caught last night. "Ten green-bottles, hanging on the wall," they sang. They were as loud as two moose bellowing.

Dad says they broke the first rule of living here. Don't get noticed. Dad and I try not to get noticed. We stay among the crowds. We change airlines.

> "Delta, TWA, Northwest, we love them all," Dad says.
>
> He and I wear blue jeans and blue T-shirts and blue jackets. We each have a blue zippered bag with a change of blue clothes. Not to be noticed is to look like nobody at all.
>
> —Excerpt from *Fly Away Home* by Eve Bunting (1991, pp. 5–8)

Following are examples of conflicts to expect and to explore further if some of the preceding questions are related to your situation, or if the excerpt from *Fly Away Home* affects you.

School Practices and Family Conflict

Long-Standing Practice in Schools

Homework: The child is expected to read orally to a parent 30 minutes every evening.

Intended Benefit: Levels of reading proficiency will increase.

Assumption: Time at home with mother begins as soon as school is out at 2:00 or 3:00.

School Hours and Calendar: School is in session 6 or 7 hours a day for 9 months of the year.

Intended Benefit: Match the child's energy and concentration levels; provide time for family activities and vacations; historically, provide time for children to help with farm work.

Assumption: Mother is home before and after school and during the summer months.

Holidays: School activities (e.g., stories, decorations, performances) and vacation schedules are related to Christmas and Easter (e.g., social studies units on "Christmas around the World").

Intended Benefit: Promote interest in school activities; provide extra practice in reading, writing, speaking; match family vacation times; show a connection between school and family celebrations.

Assumption: All students are either Christian or celebrate these holidays in a secular manner.

Possible Current Conflict for Families

For working parents with school-age children, there may not be enough 30-minute slots for every child that can be scheduled between picking children up at day care at 5:00 or 6:00, dinner, clean-up, baths, and bedtime.

For working parents, the school day and calendar are significantly different from the work schedule, necessitating additional day care or resulting in latch-key practices.

Students in U.S. schools represent many religious communities besides Christianity.

Many parents must work during religious holiday vacations.

School is often in session during the focal holidays of non-Christian faiths. Those children must either miss important family worship or celebrations or be absent from school.

With those examples of common practices and possible conflicts to consider, think about the following issues as well. You've undoubtedly seen many facts and figures about changes in families, poverty, violence, and other areas of concern in today's twenty-first-century society. Just looking at recent U.S. census data is unsettling (www.census.gov), but educators must accept that discomfort and face the possibilities of transforming their classrooms through asking some difficult questions, such as the following:

Critical Changes in Society

Single-Parent Families, 1990–2000

- Nearly 30 percent of school-age children live in single-parent homes.
- Median income level in single-parent families is 35 percent of that of two-parent families.

Working Mothers, 1990–2000

- Fifty-nine percent of mothers with children under age 6 work.
- Seventy-eight percent of mothers with children age 6 or older work.

Demographic Changes

- The population is growing and is increasingly mobile.
- The percentage of white children has declined.
- The percentage of ethnic minorities, especially Latino Americans and Asian Americans, has increased.
- There is an increase in the percentage of immigrant children.
- The movement is toward a nation of multiple minorities with no one majority group.

Poverty

- More than 20 percent of African American, Hispanic American, and Native American school-age children live in poverty, compared to 11 percent of Asian American and 8 percent of European American school-age children.
- The largest single related variable is the single-parent home—over 50 percent of impoverished children come from single-parent homes.

Questions for Teachers

- Do my instructional materials and unit plans respect diverse family structures?
- Do I expect more homework supervision than one parent can possibly provide?
- Am I willing to teach parents, too?

- Do I incorrectly assume that mothers read to children, teach common manners, require chores, have bedtime rituals?

- Do I have systems for helping newcomers adapt to classroom procedures at any time?
- Do I have genuine interest in, respect for, and knowledge of other cultures, including their politeness conventions?
- Do my lessons include perspectives of the many cultural groups in the United States?

- Does my school have personnel who help families obtain emergency medical and dental care, food, and housing?
- Are my K–4 students cooking for and babysitting younger siblings?
- What everyday experiences am I incorrectly assuming to be in everyone's background?

Violence

- Approximately one-fourth of U.S. communities report school violence that results in death or injuries requiring hospitalization.
- More children are witnesses to and victims of violence in their communities each year.

- Will "cute" stories and activities reach my students, provide a temporary distraction, or be offensive in their shallow simplicity?
- Will any curriculum content help children grow into nonviolent teenagers and adults?
- Will my curriculum help children heal?

Child Development

- Half the children under age 4 are at risk.
- At-risk factors include poverty, welfare, one-parent families, unwed mothers, undereducated parents, and lack of health insurance.

- Am I ready for children who aren't ready for my school's social and intellectual demands?
- How effective am I with exceptional children?
- Am I prepared to teach an ever-widening variety of exceptional and diverse learners?

Whatever your particular surprises and frustrations may be, whether more or less disconcerting than the examples just given, think about the word *social* for a moment. Consider how important the *social* part of *social studies* should be when educators reflect on the complex social interactions affecting children today—inside and outside the school setting. Consider how *social* the drive should be to read, write, listen, and speak in order to communicate with others. Then consider the following quotations contrasting traditional classrooms with those we envision and many teachers are creating:

> "In traditional classrooms, the classroom is the teacher's and students are simply renters for the school year" (Tompkins, 2001, p. 8).

> In a *classroom community*, students are "a 'family' in which all the members respect one another and support each other's learning. Students value culturally and linguistically diverse classmates and recognize that all students can make important contributions to the classroom" (Wells & Chang-Wells, 1992, in Tompkins, 2001, p. 8).

If any of these data or questions trigger new concerns for you or point to a problem that has been nagging you, we recommend the following additional resources.

READINGS ABOUT CHANGES, CHILDREN, AND CRISES IN THE UNITED STATES

Berliner, David. (1996). *The manufactured crisis: Myths, fraud, and the attack on America's public schools.* Reading, MA: Addison Wesley–Longman.

Berman, Sheldon, & LaFarge, Phyllis (Eds.). (1993). *Promising practices in teaching social responsibility.* Albany: State University of New York Press.

Boyer, Ernest. (1994). *Ready to learn: A mandate for the nation.* Princeton, NJ: Carnegie Foundation for the Advancement of Teaching.

Brendtro, L., Brokenleg, M., & Van Bockern, S. (2000). *Reclaiming youth at risk: Our hope for the future.* Bloomington, IN: National Educational Service.

Bryson, Ken. (2001). *Census briefs: America's children at risk.* Washington, DC: U.S. Department of Commerce. (*Note:* for additional census briefs, go to www.census.gov.)

Bullough, Robert. (2001). *Uncertain lives: Children of hope, teachers of promise.* New York: Teachers College Press.

Children's Defense Fund. (1996). *The state of America's children: Yearbook 1996.* Washington, DC: Author.

Clinchy, E. (2001). Needed: A new educational civil rights movement. *Phi Delta Kappan, 82,* 492–498.

Cogan, J., & Dericott, R. (Eds.). (1998). *Citizenship for the 21st century: An international perspective on education.* Sterling, VA: Stylus Publishing.

Cortés, Carlos. (2000). *The children are watching: How the media teach about diversity.* New York: Teachers College Press.

Dunn, R. (1997). The goals and track record of multicultural education. *Educational Leadership, 54,* 74–77.

Hamburg, David. (1994). *Starting points: Meeting the needs of our youngest children.* New York: Carnegie Corporation.

Hamburg, David. (1992). *Today's children: Creating a future for a generation in crisis.* New York: Times Books.

Hernandez-Sheets, Rosa, & Hollins, Etta. (1999). *Racial and ethnic identity in school practices: Aspects of human development.* Mahwah, NJ: Erlbaum.

Hodgkinson, H. (2001). Educational demographics: What teachers should know. *Educational Leadership, 58,* 6–11.

Kozol, Jonathan. (2000). *Ordinary resurrections: Children in the years of hope.* New York: Crown Publishers.

Kozol, Jonathan. (1995). *Amazing grace: The lives of children and the conscience of a nation.* New York: Crown Publishers.

Kozol, Jonathan. (1991). *Savage inequalities: Children in America's schools.* New York: Crown Publishers.

National Center for Children in Poverty. (1995). *National center for children in poverty: A program report on the first five years.* New York: Columbia University School of Public Health.

Powell, Timothy. (2000). *Ruthless democracy: A multicultural interpretation of the American renaissance.* Princeton, NJ: Princeton University Press.

Roberts, T. (1994). *A systems perspective of parenting: The individual, the family, and the social network.* Pacific Grove, CA: Brooks/Cole.

Slavin, R. (1997). Can education reduce social inequity? *Educational Leadership, 55,* 6–11.

Van Horn, R. (1999). Inner-city schools: A multiple-variable discussion. *Phi Delta Kappan, 81,* 291–297.

Watkins, William. (2001). *Race and education: The roles of history and society in educating African American students.* Boston: Allyn and Bacon.

R E A D I N G S   A B O U T   C R E A T I N G   C L A S S R O O M   C O M M U N I T I E S   F O R   A L L   L E A R N E R S

Au, K. (1993). *Literacy instruction in multicultural settings.* Fort Worth, TX: Harcourt Brace.

Ballenger, Cynthia. (1998). *Teaching other people's children: Literacy and learning in a bilingual classroom.* New York: Teachers College Press.

Barr, Robert, & Parrett, William. (2001). *Hope fulfilled for at-risk and violent youth: K–12 programs that work* (2nd ed.). Boston: Allyn and Bacon.

Boyer, E. (1995). *The basic school: A community for learning.* Princeton, NJ: Carnegie Foundation for the Advancement of Teaching.

Carger, C. (1997). Attending to new voices. *Educational Leadership, 54,* 39–43.

Crawford, Leslie. (1993). *Language and literacy learning in multicultural classrooms.* Boston: Allyn and Bacon.

Cullinan, B. (Ed.). (1993). *Children's voices: Talk in the classroom.* Newark, DE: International Reading Association.

Dyson, Anne. (1997). *What difference does difference make? Teacher reflections on diversity, literacy, and the urban primary school.* Urbana, IL: National Council of Teachers of English.

Dyson, Anne. (1993). *Social worlds of children learning to write in an urban primary school.* New York: Teachers College Press.

Freedman, Sarah, Simons, Elizabeth, & Kalnin, Juli. (Eds.). (1999). *Inside city schools: Investigating literacy in multicultural classrooms.* New York: Teachers College Press.

Garcia, Eugene. (1999). *Student cultural diversity: Understanding and meeting the challenge.* Boston: Houghton Mifflin.

Gregory, Eve (Ed.). (1997). *One child, many worlds: Early learning in multicultural communities.* New York: Teachers College Press.

Handel, Ruth. (1999). *Building family literacy in an urban community.* New York: Teachers College Press.

Harris, Karen, Graham, Steve, & Deshler, Donald. (1998). *Teaching every child every day: Learning in diverse schools and classrooms.* Cambridge, MA: Brookline Books.

Hayes, Curtis, Bahruth, Robert, & Kessler, Carolyn. (1998). *Literacy con cariño: A story of migrant children's success.* Portsmouth, NH: Heinemann.

Henkin, Roxanne. (1998). *Who's invited to share? Using literacy to teach for equity and social justice.* Portsmouth, NH: Heinemann.

Hollins, Etta, & Oliver, Eileen (Eds.). (1999). *Pathways to success in school: Culturally responsive teaching.* Mahwah, NJ: Erlbaum.

Holman, L. (1997). Meeting the needs of Hispanic immigrants. *Educational Leadership, 54,* 37–38.

Kuykendall, C. (2000). *From rage to hope: Strategies for reclaiming Black and Hispanic students.* Bloomington, IN: National Education Service.

Lehr, Judy, & Martin, Craig. (1994). *Schools without fear: Group activities for building community.* Minneapolis: Educational Media Corporation.

Miramonte, Ofelia, Nadeau, Adel, Commins, Nancy, & Garcia, Eugene. (1997). *Restructuring schools for linguistic diversity: Linking decision making to effective programs.* New York: Teachers College Press.

Morrow, Lesley Mandel. (1996). *Motivating reading and writing in diverse classrooms: Social and physical contexts in a literature-based program.* Urbana, IL: National Council of Teachers of English.

Nieto, Sonia. (1999). *The light in their eyes: Creating multicultural learning communities.* New York: Teachers College Press.

Pang, Valerie. (2001). *Multicultural education: A caring-centered, reflective approach.* Boston: McGraw-Hill.

Perry, Theresa, & Fraser, James (Eds.). (1993). *Freedom's plow: Teaching in the multicultural classroom.* New York: Routledge.

Rothstein-Fisch, C., Greenfield, P., & Trumbull, E. (1999). Bridging cultures with classroom strategies. *Educational Leadership, 56,* 64–67.

Saravia-Shore, M., & Arvizu, S. (1992). *Cross-cultural literacy: Ethnographies of communication in multiethnic classrooms*. New York: Garland.

Tompkins, Gail. (2001). *Literacy for the 21st century: A balanced approach*. Upper Saddle River, NJ: Merrill Prentice-Hall.

Weiner, Lois. (1999). *Urban teaching: The essentials*. New York: Teachers College Press.

Wells, G., & Chang-Wells, G. L. (1992). *Constructing knowledge together: Classrooms as centers of inquiry and literacy*. Portsmouth, NH: Heinemann.

CHAPTER 2

Why should I move toward something called multicultural education? What is that, anyway?

> I hugged the wall and peeked around the corner.
>
> A boy with fire-colored hair pointed his finger. "Pajamas!" he shouted. "They wore white pajamas to school!" The American children tilted back their long noses, laughing.
>
> I turned away. "I want to go home to Father and Little Quang," I said.
>
> Chi Hai's hands curved over my shoulders. "Children stay where parents place them, Ut. We stay."
>
> Somewhere, a loud bell jangled. I lost my sisters in a swirl of rushing children.
>
> "Pa-jaa-mas!" they teased.
>
> —Excerpt from *Angel Child, Dragon Child*
> by Michele Maria Surat (1983, p. 7)

The bottom line? Schools must move toward multicultural education because the United States is becoming more multicultural every year. Even in some areas that are basically monocultural, regardless of what the culture is, children and families move, travel, and enter a workforce that is likely to be multicultural. Few people lead truly monocultural lives. Educators must teach *all* students, and children must learn to respect each other and work together if they are going to grapple successfully with the societal concerns affecting the general population. More immediately, teachers must not only teach but also learn with children how to get along in their classrooms so that learning can occur in a safe, disciplined environment.

What do we mean by culture? Rituals, costumes, art, music, foods? That view shortchanges too many of the complexities of human beings. Traditions, relationships, a common history, geography, language, social class, race? Well, that's closer, but it still seems more like a viewpoint of looking *at* people instead of trying to look through their eyes at the rest of the world, thereby better understanding them, ourselves, and others. We like a third possibility provided by Saravia-Shore and Arvizu (in Hollins, 1996) that defines culture in terms of thinking, feeling, and acting, or, as Hollins expands, the understandings, values, perceptions, behaviors, language, beliefs, customs, traditions, and knowledge of accomplishments held in common by a group of people (pp. 8–9).

So, if all of those elements make up "culture," what's multicultural? The United States is multicultural. It has many identifiable groups of people who share ways of thinking, feeling, and acting that differ in some interesting and/or problematic ways from other groups of people.

And what's multicultural education? Banks and Banks (2001), longstanding leaders in promoting multicultural education, define it as "an education reform movement, and a process whose major goal is to change the structure of educational institutions so that male and female students, exceptional students, and students who are members of diverse racial, ethnic, language, and cultural groups will have an equal chance to achieve academically in school" (p. 1). Multicultural education, then, is a way of teaching and learning that

- acknowledges and respects cultural differences through varied teaching and organizational methods;
- promotes the achievement of all ethnic, immigrant, racial, socioeconomic, and linguistic groups, as well as children of both genders and those with exceptionalities; and
- has curriculum content that honors the experiences and perspectives of different cultural groups.

"Multicultural education represents a way of rethinking school reform because it responds to many of the problematic factors leading to school underachievement and failure.... Multicultural education can transform and enrich the schooling of all young people" (Nieto, 2000, p. 319).

The purposes of multicultural education are readily interwoven with the purposes of social studies and children's literature, as reflected in the work of many writers:

> "To help all children—regardless of ethnicity, gender, disabilities, or social class—understand and appreciate events and people from various points of view ... and to develop the knowledge, perspectives, and frames of reference that build mutual respect between and among all peoples" (Welton & Mallan, 1999, pp. 65–67).

> "Now multicultural education is conceived more as a particular ideological and methodological approach to the entire educational enterprise" (Gay, 1999, p. 354).

> "Cultural diversity should be an integral part of the total educational experiences of all students in all school settings [and] the contexts and structures of teaching and learning, as well as their content and text" (Gay, 1999, p. 356).

"When students are exposed exclusively to literature in which they see reflections of themselves and their own lives, they are miseducated to view themselves and their lives as 'normal,' to interpret their own cultural attitudes and values as 'human nature,' and to view other people and other lives as exotic at best, and deviant at worst. Students who retain such a perspective, because they have learned to take their privilege as a given and have not been taught to question the status quo, are likely to perpetuate the discrimination and oppression that multicultural education is supposed to help eliminate" (Bishop, 1999, pp. 4–5).

To ensure that "students from all social class, gender, racial, and cultural groups will have an equal opportunity to learn" (Banks & Banks, 2001, p. 3).

We agree with the many writers who claim that calling the United States a "melting pot society" no longer works. Americans are many peoples with different histories, and those stories overlap and interact. The United States is and always has been composed of a multitude of cultures—cultures that sometimes clash with the "national culture" deeply ingrained in most schools. Hollins (1996, pp. 19–22) identifies the following six aspects of the "national culture." Can you already see children in your classroom (or their parents) whose culture clashes with one or more of these six aspects?

1. *Individualism* a drive toward self-reliance, independence, and autonomy; however, this drive is tempered by the need to "fit in" with a group
    - Do you have students who always seek to fit in, go along with a group, function well in cooperative group activities, show little signs of moving toward independence, or expect you to give them directions and follow your lead respectfully?
2. *Freedom* the right to live in dignity and security and to seek fulfillment as an individual or group member without arbitrary constraints or sanctions from the government or other citizens
    - Do you have students who chafe at school or class rules, seem to question your authority constantly, or want reasons for what seem to you to be quite customary school rules?
3. *Equality* the belief that all citizens should have equal rights economically, legally, politically, and socially
    - Do you have students who yield their rights to students of other cultural groups?
    - Do you have students who act as if their rights take precedence over the rights of others?
    - Do you have students who never seem to "stand up for themselves"?
4. *Justice* a sense of fairness and respect for the legal and personal rights of others
    - Do you have students and parents whose sense of fairness is vastly different from yours? For example, do you teach students not to hit back, and that rule seems ludicrous to some students and their parents?

5. *Competition*   a focus on individual achievement and success
   - Do you have students who seem to shy away from praise, or who avoid competition?
6. *Diversity*   the belief that citizens have rights to be different and to choose their own lifestyles, group memberships, and personal preferences within the law; a respect for laws that are intended to provide personal and group freedom, yet maintain relative peace and order
   - Do you have students who seem embarrassed by their cultural differences or who make fun of others' differences, as did the boy with fire-colored hair in *Angel Child, Dragon Child*?

If you identified students in response to any of these questions about aspects of the "national culture," you may be noticing behaviors influenced by either obvious or subtle cultural differences rather than behavior problems caused by laziness, poor attitudes, defiance, shyness, lack of interest, or other negative characteristics. Multicultural education seeks to use teaching styles and materials that respect, interest, and meet the learning style needs of students from a variety of cultural backgrounds. Students who see their culture reflected in the curriculum typically develop more positive attitudes toward school and education.

Banks and Banks's (2001) model of multicultural education is the one that we find most useful and that we will apply to our suggestions and structures for using multicultural literature. The following briefly describes the *dimensions* of their model, which will be referenced again in the next chapter.

Banks and Banks's Dimensions of Multicultural Education

Content Integration
Logical and authentic infusion of ethnic and cultural examples and content into various subject areas to "illustrate key concepts, principles, generalizations, and theories" (p. 21)

Knowledge Construction Process
How teachers help students realize that "implicit cultural assumptions, frames of references, perspectives, and biases" within any field of study influence the ways people have constructed and presented the knowledge base within that field (p. 21)

Prejudice Reduction
Lessons, instructional units, and activities that teachers use "to help students develop positive attitudes toward different racial, ethnic, and cultural groups" (p. 22)

Equity Pedagogy
Modifying teaching methods to address the range of learning styles within various ethnic and cultural groups in order to facilitate academic achievement (pp. 22–23)

Empowering School Culture

A restructured school culture and organization that promotes gender, racial, and social-class equity through multiperspective examination and change of such variables as grouping practices, sports participation, and enrollment in exceptional children's programs (p. 23)

To make a conscious effort to develop and implement curriculum that is multicultural is one of the primary responsibilities of an educator in a country claiming to be democratic. If teachers fundamentally accept the framework of the six aspects of U.S. national culture listed earlier, then they must consider Shannon's (1996) challenge:

> Teachers must remember that students do not speak only for themselves; rather social groups also speak to one another through individual students. Conflict within and among voices in a classroom is a fact of life because we are not a homogeneous society with one set of values, mores, and interests. And we are better for our diversity. How teachers (and all of society) choose to handle these conflicts and our diversity makes all the difference in how we will live together in and out of schools. To assert privilege for one type of voice among all others in a classroom promotes and maintains a hierarchy among social groups based on nationality, gender, race, economic class, and ethnicity. Unless teachers and students are allowed and willing to listen to each other, to explore the variety and historical and social origins of their differences, and to use their multiplicity of voices in any classroom, there is little hope for democratic development in our society. (pp. 291–292)

If this chapter has raised new questions or concerns for you, there may be materials in the references that are useful. You may wish to turn to Chapter 9 to skim the annotated bibliography organized by major U.S. cultural groups to develop a sense of the richness of the country's diversity shown in children's literature. You may wish to examine some of your own (and other teachers') difficulties in seeing prejudice, question some of your own beliefs about students from other cultures, or identify some of the hidden hurdles of prejudice by reading sections of Pang's new book, *Multicultural Education: A Caring-Centered, Reflective Approach* (2001). You may wish to read more about multicultural education from several of the references here or from those listed at the end of Chapter 1 before moving ahead to making curriculum changes in social studies.

READINGS ABOUT MULTICULTURAL EDUCATION

Au, K. (1993). *Literacy instruction in multicultural settings*. Fort Worth, TX: Harcourt Brace.
Banks, James, & Banks, Cherry (Eds.). (2001). *Multicultural education: Issues and perspectives* (4th ed.). New York: Wiley & Sons/Jossey-Bass.

Bishop, Rudine Sims. (1999). Selecting literature for a multicultural curriculum. In V. Harris (Ed.), *Using multiethnic literature in the K–8 classroom* (pp. 1–19). Norwood, MA: Christopher Gordon.

Carlson, Dennis. (1997). *Making progress: Education and culture in new times.* New York: Teachers College Press.

Davidman, Leonard, with Davidman, Patricia. (1994). *Teaching with a multicultural perspective: A practical guide.* New York: Longman.

Dunn, R. (1997). The goals and track record of multicultural education. *Educational Leadership, 54,* 74–77.

Evans, Ronald, & Saxe, David. (1996). *Handbook on teaching social issues.* Washington, DC: National Council for the Social Studies.

Gay, Geneva. (1999). Briding multicultural theory and practice. In Ornstein and Behar-Horenstein (Eds.), *Contemporary issues in curriculum* (2nd ed.). Boston: Allyn and Bacon.

Glazer, Nathan. (1997). *We are all multiculturalists now.* Cambridge, MA: Harvard University Press.

Gorski, Paul. (2001). *Multicultural education and the Internet: Intersections and integrations.* Boston: McGraw-Hill.

Heath, Shirley Brice. (1983). *Ways with words.* Cambridge: Cambridge University Press.

Heath, Shirley Brice. (1982). Questioning at home and at school: A comparative study. In G. Spindler (Ed.), *Doing the ethnography of schooling: Educational anthropology in action* (pp. 102–131). New York: Holt, Rinehart and Winston.

Hollins, Etta. (1996). *Culture in school learning: Revealing the deep meaning.* Mahwah, NJ: Erlbaum.

Hollins, Etta, & Oliver, Eileen (Eds.). (1999). *Pathways to success in school: Culturally responsive teaching.* Mahwah, NJ: Erlbaum.

Kendal, Frances. (1996). *Diversity in the classroom: New approaches to the education of young children* (2nd ed.). New York: Teachers College Press.

King, Joyce, Hollins, E., & Hawman, W. (1997). *Preparing teachers for cultural diversity.* New York: Teachers College Press.

McMahon, Susan, & Raphael, Taffy. (1997). *The book club connection: Literacy learning and classroom talk.* Newark, DE: International Reading Association.

de Meléndez, Wilma, & Ostertag, Vesna. (1997). *Teaching young children in multicultural classrooms: Issues, concepts, and strategies.* Albany, NY: Delmar.

Michaels, Sarah. (1981). "Sharing time": Children's narrative styles and differential access to literacy. *Language in Society, 10,* 423–442.

Miller-Lachman, Lyn, & Taylor, Lorraine. (1995). *Schools for all: Educating children in a diverse society.* Albany, NY: Delmar.

Morrow, L., Tracey, D., & Maxwell, C. (Eds.). (1995). *A survey of family literacy.* Newark, DE: International Reading Association.

Nieto, Sonia. (2000*). Affirming diversity: The sociopolitical context of multicultural education* (3rd ed.). New York: Longman.

Pang, Valerie. (2001). *Multicultural education: A caring-centered, reflective approach.* Boston: McGraw-Hill.

Philips, Susan. (1972). Participant structures and communicative competence: Warm Springs children in community and classroom. In C. Cazden, V. John, & D. Hymes (Eds.), *Doing the ethnography of schooling: Educational anthropology in action.* New York: Teachers College Press.

Saravia-Shore, M., & Arvizu, S. (1992). *Cross-cultural literacy: Ethnographies of communication in multiethnic classrooms.* New York: Garland.

Shannon, Patrick. (1996). Developing democratic voices. In R. Robinson, Michael McKenna, & Judy Wedman (Eds.), *Issues and trends in literacy education* (pp. 287–297). Boston: Allyn and Bacon. (Reprinted from *The Reading Teacher, 47,* 1993.)

Welton, David, & Mallan, John. (1999). *Children and their world: Strategies for teaching social studies.* Boston: Houghton Mifflin.

CHAPTER 3

Why should I teach social studies when so many children are struggling with literacy achievement?

We'll start to answer that question with a perspective on social studies, then we'll address the literacy issue. Some of the reasons children are struggling with literacy achievement are related to their lives outside of school—their lives in a complex and often troubled world—the very *stuff* of social studies. If social studies at a school is relegated to paper costumes of Pilgrims and Native Americans at Thanksgiving, obligatory summaries of a newspaper's current event each week, or a disappointingly dry textbook study of your state in fourth grade, it's no wonder that teachers are tempted to forget it and to concentrate only on those areas to be tested at the end of the year.

That said, we do not mean that you should eliminate the reality that you may teach a Pilgrims and Native Americans unit that is wildly successful, or that your method of handling current events is stimulating, or that your text is remarkably interesting. For many students and teachers, however, such a reality does not exist. In the three major conceptual approaches to social studies education described by Welton and Mallan (1999) and discussed next, many students still do not make connections between the school learning called "social studies" and their own lives within the social context of family, neighborhood, community, and society. Without such a connection, social studies remains merely a school subject to be ignored or merely tolerated by students and teachers alike as each group responds to more pressing demands.

The *cultural heritage* model focuses on the basic historical approach to social studies education, where the elements and events of the traditional, white, middle class are highlighted as the dominant perspective of history. In the elementary grades, the concepts found in the expanding environment of family, neighborhood, community, state, and nation are centrally focused in social studies lessons grounded on traditional history and geography.

Often, children from different cultural backgrounds feel confused or disconnected when instruction is focused on so-called traditional values, events, expectations, and environments. For example, how do Native American children view the study of Thanksgiving with the customary Pilgrims and Native Americans activities, when that event was soon followed by years of assaults on their ancestors' environment and traditional ways of life?

The use of this model may directly interfere with the *prejudice reduction* dimension of Banks and Banks's (2001) model of multicultural education (discussed in the previous chapter) unless teachers are able to expand beyond the traditional perspectives and accurately include the current and historical perspectives of all the diverse peoples who contributed to the development of this nation.

The *social sciences* model divides social studies into specific disciplines of geography, anthropology, political science, history, sociology, and economics for instruction. In this approach for the lower elementary grades, the major focus is on concepts in sociology. In the upper elementary grades, the emphasis expands to include geography, political science, economics, and history.

Generally, children have difficulty integrating concepts from various social science disciplines; this problem can be further complicated if the child is a member of a nonmainstream cultural group. For example, when teaching the sociological concept of neighborhoods, teachers often show houses that are single dwellings in upscale areas. Children living in apartments, motels, trailer parks, and rooming houses may feel particularly disenfranchised.

To combat the difficulty of this model for young children, teachers may wish to consider the *content integration* dimension of Banks and Banks's (2001) model of multicultural education. That is, even within a specific social science discipline, logical and authentic examples may be added to illustrate key concepts within that discipline. For example, the study of community helpers today typically includes more females in male-dominated careers and African Americans in more professional roles. However, examples from numerous other minority cultures in the United States are often omitted.

In the *reflective inquiry* model, students are expected to focus on issues or concerns in a problem-solving format. Although most social studies teachers agree that this is the best model for teaching, many teachers lack the time or experience to use this approach effectively. Teachers using this model often present appropriate background information and then a problem to be solved, usually in a cooperative group format.

The cooperative group and peer-run problem-solving discussion may provide a varied teaching method needed by some children, and thereby approach Banks and Banks's (2001) *equity pedagogy,* but problems may remain because of the very content chosen for problem solving. For example, if the issue is how to handle a class bully, students from some cultures may feel disconnected when the emerging preferred answers clearly point to telling the teacher or avoiding the bully. If the issue is how best to use an allowance, many children will be unable to make the connection between the economics lesson and their own lives.

What a different perspective on social studies your children might develop if they saw themselves at the center of such study—how they think, feel, act, and perceive similarly to and differently from others, and how those similarities and differences affect them, their families, their communities, and the world in which they are growing up. If it is not themselves as the center of the social studies lesson, then a compelling character and problem in literature allows them a chance for a strong vicarious experience.

For those who have recently immigrated to the United States—and for those who may show discomfort at their presence—there's a different social studies lesson or unit to be taught at Thanksgiving, perhaps with literature, such as the following:

> It was the next day, the tomorrow, that we sighted land again. I was afraid to hope.
>
> A boat came. My mother clasped her hands and bent her head. Was she afraid to hope too?
>
> The boat circled us twice and then a line was thrown and we were pulled toward shore.
>
> There was such a silence among us then, such an anxious, watchful silence.
>
> People waited on the dock.
>
> "Welcome," they called. "Welcome to America."
>
> That was when our silence turned to cheers.
>
> "But how did they know we would come today?" my father asked.
>
> "Perhaps people come every day," my mother said. "Perhaps they understand how it is for us."
>
> —Excerpt from *How Many Days to America? A Thanksgiving Story* by Eve Bunting (1988, p. 26)

For those children whose families have never been accused of stealing something that the police didn't believe a person of their cultural group could possibly afford, what shocking new economic and *social* awareness could be developed from reading and discussing this next book:

> We reached the Mississippi state line and soon after we heard a police siren. A police car came up behind us. My father slowed the Cadillac, then stopped. Two white policemen got out of their car. They eyeballed the Cadillac and told my father to get out.
>
> "Whose car is this, boy?" they asked.
>
> I saw anger in my father's eyes. "It's mine," he said.
>
> You're a liar," said one of the policemen. "You stole this car. Turn around, put your hands on top of that car and spread eagle," said the other policeman.
>
> —Excerpt from *The Gold Cadillac* by Mildred Taylor (1987, pp. 73–74)

For the students who are avid sports fans, who have cheered Michael Jordan's baskets or celebrated the record-breaking homeruns of Sammie Sosa and Mark McGuire, what a social studies lesson there is in realizing how people had to fight laws and traditions in order to integrate the sports teams. Reading about the integration of baseball by Jackie Robinson will shock and startle many youngsters as they realize what being *Teammates* really meant:

> The Reds played in a small ballpark where the fans sat close to the field. The players could almost feel the breath of the fans on the backs of their necks. Many who came that day screamed terrible, hateful things at Jackie when the Dodgers were on the field.
>
> More than anything else, Pee Wee Reese believed in doing what was right. When he heard the fans yelling at Jackie, Pee Wee decided to take a stand. With his head high, Pee Wee walked directly from his shortstop position to where Jackie was playing first base. The taunts and shouting of the fans were ringing in Pee Wee's ears. It saddened him, because he knew it could have been his friends and neighbors. Pee Wee's legs felt heavy, but he knew what he had to do.
>
> —Excerpt from *Teammates* by Peter Golenbock (1990, pp. 24–26)

The National Council for the Social Studies (NCSS) has developed a model for K–12 social studies education that emphasizes 10 strands or themes (http://www.socialstudies.org/standards/exec.html#Themes). The model promotes the application of social studies concepts to children's immediate lives so that they become effective citizens of the world. It expects teachers to respect the multicultural perspectives and values of the nation's diverse citizenry, while guiding children toward acceptable common ground for their lives together.

The 10 NCSS strands, or themes, of social studies cut across grade levels and political/geographical areas of the United States. This design for social studies assumes that teachers will tailor thematic instruction to the developmental levels of their students and to specific local or state requirements. Some strands deserve more emphasis at lower or upper grades, but all 10 should be woven into the curriculum each year. The specific K–4 performance objectives for each strand and recommended multicultural literature are shown in Chapter 8.

These 10 themes, as shown here, were chosen because there was a need for integration of social studies content to exceed the limited focus of "expanding environments," "chronological history," and "isolated events." The themes cover every area from all aspects of the social studies, using an organized, correlated, and integrated approach to instruction that allows for a wider lens on diversity and multiculturalism.

The NCSS Themes of Social Studies

    I. **Culture**   experiences that provide for the study of culture and cultural diversity

    II. **Time, Continuity, and Change**   experiences that provide for the study of the ways human beings view themselves in and over time

    III. **People, Places, and Environments**   experiences that provide for the study of people, places, and environments

    IV. **Individual Development and Identity**   experiences that provide for the study of individual development and identity

    V. **Individuals, Groups, and Institutions**   experiences that provide for the study of interactions among individuals, groups, and institutions

    VI. **Power, Authority, and Governance**   experiences that provide for the study of how people create and change structures of power, authority, and governance

    VII. **Production, Distribution, and Consumption**   experiences that provide for the study of how people organize for the production, distribution, and consumption of goods and services

    VIII. **Science, Technology, and Society**   experiences that provide for the study of relationships among science, technology, and society

    IX. **Global Connections**   experiences that provide for the study of global connections and interdependence

    X. **Civic Ideals and Practices**   experiences that provide for the study of the ideals, principles, and practices of citizenship in a democratic republic

In grades K–4, the fact that social studies doesn't have to be taught as a separate subject is an incredible opportunity. It can be integrated; it can permeate the day through other subjects, through classroom organization and management, through grouping practices, through guidelines for behavior, and through the fair and equitable treatment of all learners.

And now, here's a different way of answering the chapter's question: Why should I teach social studies when so many children are struggling with reading, writing, and math? This answer is very practical and highly focused on literacy development: Greater gains in literacy achievement across the various cultural groups in the United States occur when there is greater engagement of the learners. Among other aspects of teaching and learning, greater engagement is related to *learner-centered instruction* and to *social interaction among learners* (Guthrie & Wigfield, 1997, p. 10). Such engagement certainly should occur when multicultural materials, meaningful content, and inclusive, collaborative instructional activities are chosen to integrate social studies and literacy instruction.

READINGS ABOUT SOCIAL STUDIES

Banks, James, & Banks, Cherry (Eds.). *Multicultural education: Issues and perspectives* (4th ed.). New York: Wiley & Sons/Jossey-Bass.

Brophy, Jere, & Alleman, Janet. (1996). *Powerful social studies for elementary students*. Orlando, FL: Harcourt Brace.

Chapin, June, & Messick, Rosemary. (1999). *Elementary social studies: A practical guide* (4th ed.). New York: Longman.

Cogan, J., & Dericott, R. (Eds.). (1998). *Citizenship for the 21st century: An international perspective on education*. Sterling, VA: Stylus Publishing.

Ellis, Arthur K. (1998). *Teaching and learning elementary social studies* (6th ed.). Boston: Allyn and Bacon.

Evans, Ronald W., & Saxe, David W. (1996). *Handbook on teaching social issues*. Washington, DC: NCSS.

Farris, P., & Cooper, S. (1997). *Elementary and middle school social studies: A whole language approach* (2nd ed.). Chicago: Brown & Benchmark.

Garcia, Jesus, & Michaelis, John. (2001). *Social studies for children: A guide to basic instruction* (12th ed.). Boston: Allyn and Bacon.

Grant, S. G., & VanSledright, Bruce. (2001). *Constructing a powerful approach to teaching and learning in elementary social studies*. Boston: Houghton Mifflin.

Guthrie, John, & Wigfield, Allan (Eds.). (1997). *Reading engagement: Motivating readers through integrated instruction*. Newark, DE: International Reading Association.

Martorella, Peter. (1998). *Social studies for elementary school children: Developing young citizens* (2nd ed.). Upper Saddle River, NJ: Prentice-Hall.

Maxim, George W. (1998). *Social studies and the elementary school child* (6th ed.). Upper Saddle River, NJ: Merrill-Prentice-Hall.

Parker, Walter, & Jarolimek, John. (1997). *Social studies in elementary education*. Upper Saddle River, NJ: Merrill-Prentice-Hall.

Seefeldt, Carol. (2001). *Social studies for the preschool/primary child* (6th ed.). Upper Saddle River, NJ: Prentice-Hall.

Staudt, K. (2001). Democracy education for more than the few. In R. Soder, J. Goodlad, & T. McMannon (Eds.), *Developing democratic character in the young* (pp. 45–68). San Francisco: Jossey-Bass.

Tyree, C. (1997). Teaching values to promote a more caring world: A moral dilemma for the 21st century. *Journal for a Just and Caring Education, 3*, 215–226.

Welton, David, & Mallan, John. (1999). *Children and their world: Strategies for teaching social studies* (6th ed.). Boston: Houghton Mifflin.

Zarrillo, James. (2000). *Teaching elementary social studies: Principles and applications*. Upper Saddle River, NJ: Prentice-Hall.

INTERNET RESOURCES FOR THE SOCIAL STUDIES

Description of the 10 NCSS themes: http://www.socialstudies.org/standards/exec.html#Themes
Intercultural email classroom connections: http://www.stolaf.edu/network/iecc
Homepage for the NCSS: http://www.ncss.org
Resources and lesson plans for the NCSS thematic strands: http://www.socialstudies.org/links/
Teaching responsibility, civility, and respect: http://www.responsiblediscipline.com
Varied lesson plans for multicultural social studies:
    http://www.lessonplanspage.com/SS.htm
    http://www.curry/edschool/virginia.edu/go/multicultural/sites/education.html
    http://www.mcps.k12.md.us/curriculum/socialstd/MBD/lesson_index.html
    http://www.edel.edu/sine/educ/multicult.htm

CHAPTER 4

Why should I emphasize multicultural literature? What's wrong with *Charlotte's Web* or *Brown Bear, Brown Bear*?

There's absolutely nothing wrong with *Charlottes's Web* or *Brown Bear, Brown Bear*, but they're not enough. If you've been teaching 5, 10, 20, or 30 years, you've seen phenomenal changes and upheavals in the teaching of literacy. Children's literature has played a larger and larger role in literacy instruction since Bill Martin Jr. challenged teachers and the traditional basal reader approach with his alternative basal series, *Sounds of Language*, in the late 1960s and early 1970s. Teachers from kindergarten to graduate school, across many content areas, are discovering and using literature to provoke thinking and to enrich the learning of their students. We strongly agree with Judith Langer (1995), who said, "Literature plays a critical role in our lives, often without our notice. It sets the scene for us to explore both ourselves and others, to define and redefine who we are, who we might become, and how the world might be" (p. 5).

There is a far greater abundance of children's literature selections today as compared to 20 and 30 years ago. Both familiar and new titles are available as affordable individual paperbacks, hardcover, and big books, and as selections within literature anthologies now published by basal reader companies. If you taught during the 1980s or 1990s, you've seen how the line has blurred between using a story *as a tool* to teach the skills and strategies of reading and using that story *as literature* to promote aesthetic, intellectual, and emotional benefits.

For years, teachers didn't really expect children to read books such as E. B. White's *Charlotte's Web* (1952) or Lynd Ward's *The Biggest Bear* (1952) on their own; rather, teachers read such selections *to* students. Children read the stories in the basal readers with their carefully controlled introduction of new vocabulary, sounds, prefixes, suffixes, contractions, and compound words. Children checked out library books after teachers had read them aloud, but teachers typically did not hold students accountable for reading those books with accuracy or understanding.

For the sake of perspective, the chart on the next page outlines some critical differences in the uses of children's literature in the last three decades.

Changes in the Use of Children's Literature

Traditional Purposes for Children's Literature

- To provide aesthetic experiences for children
- To provoke intellectual and emotional responses to the universal problems of humankind

Current Purposes for Children's Literature

- To provide aesthetic experiences for children
- To provoke intellectual and emotional responses to the universal problems of humankind
- To stimulate oral language development as well as reading and writing proficiency

Former Common Instructional Strategies

- The teacher read aloud as children rested after lunch; questions of fact were minimal; and emphasis was on pleasure.
- The teacher read aloud from a literature anthology separate from the basal reader; emphasis was on discussions and interpretations about characters and their problems; attention was given to the beauty of the language.
- Artistic responses were encouraged, such as drawing, painting, constructing, and dancing.
- Basal readers and reading instruction were not connected to literature until Bill Martin Jr.'s controversial *Sounds of Language* series (Holt, Rinehart and Winston) became available in the late 1960s and early 1970s.

Current Common Instructional Strategies

- The teacher reads aloud from a big book; the children follow pictures and. text, and begin to "read" familiar or repetitive parts.
- The teacher reads aloud from a novel; the children follow in their own paperback copies and read excerpts silently or aloud.
- Children read picture books, novellas, and novels independently, keeping response journals and/or taking computerized tests about what they've read.
- Teachers conduct guided reading/listening lessons with literature selections; the focus is on comprehension and personal response.
- Teachers search for ways to integrate phonics skills and vocabulary development into reading/literature lessons.
- Children study elements of literature, such as archetypes, imagery, and linear and circular journeys.

Literacy Achievement Measures Then

- Reading achievement tests focused on word recognition and basic comprehension of short passages; literature was not involved.

Literacy Achievement Measures Now

- Reading achievement tests measure knowledge of literary elements and genres as well as comprehension of long passages taken from literature—that is, passages with complex ideas and without controlled vocabulary.
- Writing tests measure children's ability to compose in a particular mode, such as personal narrative or descriptive writing.

Now, in this new century, you face several dilemmas when choosing and using children's literature for the multiple expected purposes today, including the integration of literature with social studies instruction that we promote. Consider the following:

- If you choose meaningful stories to captivate youngsters as they practice reading strategies and skills, how do you balance compelling content with necessary skill?
- If you read favorite stories frequently to emerging readers so that they memorize the stories and appropriately experience what it is like to "read" fluently, when will they acquire and apply the skills and strategies for independent reading?
- If the material children can read independently quickly pales in comparison to the more "meaty" literature they want, how can you assist them in bridging the gap between their actual reading ability and their thirst for literature?
- If most of your third- or fourth-graders can be guided through a book study using novellas, such as *The Gold Cadillac* (Taylor, 1987), or novels, such as *Stone Fox* (Gardiner, 1980), and can read sections independently, what do you do with those who can't?
- If a social studies concept is taught through studying the problems and resolution in a compelling story instead of listening to a lesson, reading a text, or viewing a videotape, will children realize they have learned an important concept to be applied beyond that book?

In a balanced literacy program, in an integrated curriculum, and in separate-subject organizations, teachers choose a variety of stories for different purposes. For example, stories with greater literary value—such as *Amazing Grace* (Hoffman, 1991), *Angel Child, Dragon Child* (Surat, 1983), and *How Many Days to America?* (Bunting, 1992)—may naturally involve more practice in the comprehension strategies of making and changing predictions about characters and plot development. Such strategies will evoke aesthetic, intellectual, as well as emotional responses.

Books such as Slobodkina's classic *Caps for Sale* (1947) or Bill Martin Jr.'s famous *Brown Bear, Brown Bear* (1967) lend themselves readily to the more specific strategies of making and changing predictions about words based on the patterns of the language, applying a phonics generalization, practicing a sight word, and any number of essential reading skills. Children love these stories, too; anyone who has used them knows the delight children experience in detecting the patterns and being able to "read" the book so quickly.

In the overall elementary curriculum, there is certainly room for a variety of reading materials for different purposes. So what purposes or benefits does one add with the intentional selection of multicultural literature? In the following chart, we borrow from Au (1993, pp. 177–178) to link purposes of using multicultural literature with the long-standing purposes of using any fine literature.

Linking Multiculturalism with Children's Literature

Long-Standing and Current Purposes for Using Children's Literature	Purposes and Benefits of Using Multicultural Children's Literature
■ To provide aesthetic experiences for children	To provide aesthetic experiences for children, particularly . . . ■ to develop pride in students of diverse backgrounds relative to their own identity and heritage
■ To provoke intellectual and emotional responses to the universal problems of humankind	To provoke intellectual and emotional responses to the universal problems of humankind, particularly . . . ■ to have both mainstream students and students of diverse backgrounds learn about diversity and the complexity of U.S. society ■ to help all students gain more complete and balanced views of the historical forces that have shaped U.S. society ■ to involve all students in exploring issues of social justice
■ To stimulate oral language development as well as reading and writing proficiency	To stimulate oral language development as well as reading and writing proficiency, particularly . . . ■ to engage students in reading, writing, and talking about issues of social importance to both mainstream and diverse individuals and groups

When deciding to use multicultural literature, teachers are seeking depth and universal themes related to the multicultural characters and problems of the world, not the immediate satisfaction of discovering a phonemic pattern or a predictable refrain. Another valuable way of thinking about the use of multicultural literature is to adapt Banks and Banks's (2001, pp. 20–26) model related to multicultural education, as follows:

Possibilities for Multicultural Literature within Multicultural Education

- Do your students know when, how, and why Muslims throughout the world celebrate Ramadan?

Content integration could use stories from a variety of cultures and groups to help teach key concepts and principles in a given subject area, such as social studies. The more students can identify with the content, the more relevant it becomes, and the more they learn.

- Do your students know about U.S. concentration camps for loyal Japanese Americans during World War II?

Knowledge construction could be stimulated through multicultural stories that help students understand how cultural assumptions and points of view influence how people perceive and report current and historical events. It is crucial to expand beyond one or two perspectives our knowledge of the world and its varied peoples.

- Do your students know and respect any of the values, beliefs, and hardships of other U.S. cultural groups?

Prejudice reduction could be promoted by using a variety of positive multicultural stories to help children develop more favorable attitudes toward different cultural groups. To prepare the future citizens of this complex world, emphasis must be placed on the common threads among all people and the unique positive qualities of culturally distinct groups.

- Do you have students who won't answer a question in front of their peers unless they are absolutely sure they are correct?
- Do you have students who will barely look at you when asked a question, but who interact easily with peers in a small student-led group discussion?

Equity pedagogy could be developed through the use of a variety of teaching strategies for evoking responses to the literature—strategies that respect the varied learning styles of cultural groups as well as individuals. Traditional education practices in the United States—such as teacher-led question and answer exchanges, oral reading of new material in front of peers, and an emphasis on right answers—can be traced to the early European American schools in New England established for a very limited population. Practices such as cooperative learning groups, private practice before public display, literature circles, and peer assistance bring more students into the classroom's success arena.

- Do the instructional materials in your school—posters, bulletin boards, book displays, decorations, and so on—reflect the diverse peoples of the United States and the world?

Empowering school culture could occur through organizing instructional groups, choosing staff members and volunteers, modeling cross-cultural interaction among adults and students so that students from diverse groups have equal access to the empowering experiences of achievement, successful participation in learning activities, and instructional materials containing positive images of themselves and others.

READINGS ABOUT MULTICULTURAL LITERACY AND LITERATURE

Au, K. (1993). *Literacy instruction in multicultural settings*. Fort Worth, TX: Harcourt Brace.

Banks, James, and Banks, Cherry (Eds.). (2001). *Multicultural education: Issues and perspectives* (4th ed.). New York: Wiley & Sons/Jossey Bass.

Combs, M. (1996). *Developing competent readers and writers in the primary grades*. Englewood Cliffs, NJ: Prentice-Hall.

Courts, Patrick. (1991). *Literacy and empowerment: The meaning makers*. New York: Bergin & Garvey.

Hancock, Marjorie. (2000). *A celebration of literature and response: Children, books, and teachers in K–8 classrooms*. Upper Saddle River, NJ: Prentice-Hall.

Heath, S., & Mangiola, L. (1991*). Children of promise: Literate activity in linguistically and culturally diverse classrooms*. Washington, DC: National Education Association.

Krashen, S. (1997/1998). Bridging inequity with books. *Educational Leadership, 55,* 18–22.

Langer, J. (1995). *Envisioning literature: Literary understanding and literature instruction*. New York: Teachers College Press.

Lehr, S. (Ed.). (1995). *Battling dragons: Issues and controversy in children's literature*. Portsmouth, NH: Heinemann.

May, F. (1998). *Reading as communication* (5th ed.). Upper Saddle River, NJ: Prentice-Hall.

McGee, L., & Richgels, D. (1996). *Literacy's beginnings: Supporting young readers and writers*. Boston: Allyn and Bacon.

McGowan, M. (1994). *Appreciating diversity through children's literature: Teaching activities for the primary grades*. Englewood, CO: Teachers Ideas Press.

Morrow, L. (1997). *Literacy development in the early years* (3rd ed.). Boston: Allyn and Bacon.

Morrow, L. (1996). *Motivating reading and writing in diverse classrooms: Social and physical contexts in a literature-based program*. Urbana, IL: National Council of Teachers of English.

Morrow, L. (Ed.). (1995). *Family literacy: Connections in schools and communities*. Newark, DE: International Reading Association.

Morrow, L., Tracey, D., & Maxwell, C. (Eds.). (1995). *A survey of family literacy in the United States*. Newark, DE: International Reading Association.

Paul, Dierdre. (2000). *Raising black children who love reading and writing: A guide from birth through grade six*. Palo Alto, CA: Bergin & Garvey.

Routman, R. (1996). *Literacy at the crossroads*. Portsmouth, NH: Heinemann.

Schmidt, P. (1998). The ABC's of cultural understanding and communication. *Equity & Excellence in Education, 31,* 28–38.

Temple, C., Martinez, M., Yokota, J., & Naylor, A. (1998). *Children's books in children's hands*. Boston: Allyn and Bacon.

Templeton, S. (1995). *Children's literacy: Contexts for meaningful learning*. Boston: Houghton Mifflin.

Tomlinson, C., & Lynch-Brown, C. (1996). *Essentials of children's literature* (2nd ed.). Boston: Allyn and Bacon.

Tompkins, G. (2001). *Literacy for the 21st century: A balanced approach*. Upper Saddle River, NJ: Prentice-Hall.

Wilkinson, P., & Kido, E. (1997). Literature and cultural awareness: Voices from the journey. *Language Arts, 74,* 255–265.

OTHER SOURCES CITED

Bunting, Eve. (1992). *How many days to America?* New York: Clarion Books.

Gardiner, John. (1980). *Stone Fox.* New York: Crowell.

Hoffman, Mary. (1991). *Amazing Grace.* New York: Dial Books for Young Readers.

Martin, Bill, Jr. (1967). *Brown bear, brown bear.* New York: Holt, Rinehart and Winston.

Martin, Bill, Jr. (1966–67). *Sounds of language readers.* New York: Holt, Rinehart and Winston.

Slobodkina, Esphyr. (1947). *Caps for sale.* New York: Scholastic.

Surat, M.M. (1983). *Angel child, dragon child.* New York: Scholastic.

Taylor, Mildred. (1987). *The gold Cadillac.* New York: Bantam Skylark.

Ward, Lynd. (1952). *The biggest bear.* Boston: Houghton Mifflin.

White, E. B. (1952). *Charlotte's web.* New York: Harper.

CHAPTER

5

Why should I choose different types of multicultural literature?

Multicultural literature can be identified by different criteria, ranging from the inclusion of only racial and ethnic minorities to the incorporation of categories of nationality, gender, age, exceptionalities, religion, and socioeconomic status, as well. What teachers consider to be multicultural literature is often tied to their concept of culture, their own racial or ethnic identity, and their experiences with people of other cultural groups. For a northern Minnesota upper-middle-class Caucasian teacher in a classroom with matching monocultural students in a matching monocultural community, Rylant's *The Relatives Came* (1986) may actually seem multicultural because the experiences and traditions of rural, lower-income southern Appalachian families, although Caucasian, are sharply different. For a teacher of Puerto Rican descent who lives and teaches in New York City in a school of predominantly Puerto Rican Americans, Mohr's *Felita* (1979) may not seem particularly multicultural, yet the African American teacher down the hall, recently transplanted from a southern or midwestern small town, may identify the book as clearly within the multicultural domain.

Regardless of the range of categories identifying groups under the heading of multicultural literature, if teachers are going to choose intellectually and emotionally stimulating multicultural literature, there are significant variations among the literature to be chosen. Au (1993) uses Banks and Banks's model to suggest four *levels* of multicultural education curriculum, which can be readily applied to the selection and use of multicultural literature.

1. The *contributions approach* focuses on heroes, holidays, and other components of various cultures, often in a rather superficial way. It may reinforce stereotypes and hinder deeper understandings. "Black History Month" or "Christmas around the World" are examples of curriculum content that match the contributions approach.
2. The *additive approach* adds concepts and content about other cultural groups to the core curriculum, as in studying different country's versions of the *Cinderella* and *Little Red Riding Hood* tales. However, the additions are still viewed from a mainstream perspective, and complex interrelationships between cultural groups are not examined.
3. The *transformation approach* involves studying concepts, events, and issues from various perspectives, including those of subordinate as well as dominant

cultural groups. For example, a unit on the westward expansion of the United States would include not just the European American viewpoint on problems of the pioneers but also the Native American perspective on the struggles of their peoples as well as the Chinese American views on their experiences.

4. The *decision-making and social action approach* challenges students to study issues from multiple perspectives, then to clarify their own values and take positive action. In a unit on democracy, for example, students might trace the history of voting practices and discrimination all the way to an examination of present-day local access to polling locations, then advocate for better transportation, lighting, or staffing of those places that discourage minority voters in their own community.

Banks and Banks (2001) believe that another dimension of multicultural education is "empowering school culture." They view five areas or dimensions that should be included within multicultural education: content integration, knowledge construction, equity pedagogy, prejudice reduction, and empowering school culture (pp. 22–23).

In our reading and study of multicultural literature, we realized that many books can be used at one or more of the dimensions of Banks and Banks's curriculum, depending on the teachers' and students' choices and interactions. Since we are working toward the integration of social studies and multicultural literature, we are naturally biased toward literature and instruction that is oriented toward promoting *greater understanding and acceptance of U.S. diversity*, and therefore *positive social action*. With Au's (1993) benefits of using multicultural literature in mind (see our discussion on page 25, coupled with Banks and Banks's dimensions of multicultural education just described, and considering Bishop's work (1997) as well, we suggest four very concrete ways of categorizing multicultural literature to be used for these various purposes.

Representations of U.S. Multicultural Diversity in Children's Literature

Egalitarian America

- Characters of more than one race, ethnicity, exceptionality, or nationality, but those differences are not an explicit focus of the story, *or*
- Characters of one cultural group, but characters from another cultural group could generally be substituted with little change in the plot
- *Could often be used in the Banks and Banks's transformation approach and the decision-making and social action approach*

Examples

A Chair for My Mother (Williams, 1982)
Flood (Calhoun, 1997)
Fly Away Home (Bunting, 1991)
A Freedom River (Rappaport, 2000)
Jamaica's Find (Havill, 1986)
Marven of the Great North Woods (Lasky, 1997)
Mending Peter's Heart (Wittbold, 1995)
On Call Back Mountain (Bunting, 1997)
Pearl Moscowitz's Last Stand (Levine, 1993)
Smoky Night (Bunting, 1994)
Staying Cool (Antle, 1997)
The Wall (Bunting, 1990)

This is the wall, my grandfather's wall. On it are the names of those killed in a war, long ago.

"Where is Grandpa's name?" I ask.

"We have to find it," Dad says.

He and I have come a long way for this and we walk slowly, searching. The wall is black and shiny as a mirror. In it I can see Dad and me. I can see the bare trees behind us and the dark, flying clouds.

A man in a wheelchair stares at the names. He doesn't have legs.

I'm looking, and he sees me looking and smiles.

—Excerpt from *The Wall* by Eve Bunting (1990, pp. 1–5)

Creative America

- A collection of poems, songs, fairy tales, folktales, myths, and legends often associated with specific cultural groups
  —based on country of origin, or
  —influenced by the history of a people in a particular geographic area
  —expressing American experiences
- *Commonly used with the contributions and additive approaches; some could and should be used with the transformation and decision-making and social action approaches instead*

Examples

The Ballad of Belle Dorcas (Hooks, 1990)
Death of the Iron Horse (Goble, 1993)
Freedom's Fruit (Hooks, 1996)
In Daddy's Arms I Am Tall (Steptoe, 1997)
The Legend of the Bluebonnet (de Paola, 1983)
The Legend of the White Doe (Hooks, 1988)
Papa Tells Chita a Story (Howard, 1995)
The Paper Crane (Bang, 1985)
The People Could Fly (Hamilton, 1985)
The Rough Face Girl (Martin, 1992)
The Talking Eggs (San Souci, 1989)
Work Song (Paulsen, 1997)

One day scouts galloped into camp, and told of something they called the Iron Horse: "It is huge! It breathes out smoke and has the voice of Thunder. It is coming this way. The white men are making an iron road for it to go on. Nothing can stop the Iron Horse!" They tried to describe it. People had terrifying images in their minds.

Was it an enormous snake, or even an underwater monster which had crawled out of the river? Was this what Sweet Medicine had spoken about? Then there was even greater fear. In the minds of the children fear grew that the Iron Horse would suddenly come over the hill, right into camp.

—Excerpt from *Death of the Iron Horse* by Paul Goble (1987, p. 5)

(continued)

Realistic America

- Problems of historical or current multi-cultural realities in the United States (or closely associated locales)
- Characters and situations representing their depicted race, religion, economic class, exceptionality, country of origin, and so on, for authenticity
- Historical events of injustice to a minority group and the support of family and other group members in surmounting those problems
- Problems and experiences more specific to one cultural group than another, even when there is no theme of overt injustice
- *Most can be used powerfully in the transformation approach and the decision-making and social action approach*

Examples

Amazing Grace (Hoffman, 1991)
Angel Child, Dragon Child (Surat, 1983)
Because of Winn Dixie (DiCamillo, 2000)
The Bracelet (Uchida, 1993)
The Butterfly (Polacco, 2000)
Charlie's House (Bulla, 1983)
Chicken Sunday (Polacco, 1992)
A Day's Work (Bunting, 1994)
The Friendship (Taylor, 1987)
Grandfather's Journey (Say, 1994)
How Many Days to America? (Bunting, 1988)
I Hate English (Levine, 1989)
Molly's Pilgrim (Cohen, 1983)
Pearl Moskowitz's Last Stand (Levine, 1993)
Peppe the Lamplighter (Bartone, 1993)
The Tangerine Tree (Hanson, 1995)
Tikvah Means Hope (Polacco, 1994)
Too Many Tamales (Soto, 1993)
Uncle Jed's Barbershop (Mitchell, 1993)

"Do you know a better hiding place?"

"No, but . . ." Charlie said slowly. "I don't always want to be hiding."

"You want to go where Master Greer will find you and take you back?"

"No, but in all this land there must be places where I can go—where Master Greer could never find me."

"You are not happy here?"

"Sometimes, but sometimes I feel the swamp around me like a prison!"

"Ah, yes . . ." Drogo looked away. His eyes had grown sad.

"Don't *you* ever think of going away and finding a place out in the world?" asked Charlie.

"You forget."

"What?"

"The color of my skin. Whoever saw me would know what I am—a slave who ran away. But if this is a prison to you, then you must go."

—Excerpt from *Charlie's House* by Clyde Robert Bulla (1983, pp. 89–90)

Informational America

- Multicultural characters and events in current society, history, government, politics, sports, ecology, scientific discovery, the arts, and so on
- *Potentially useful at all levels—contributions, additive, transformation and decision-making and social action approaches—but should be chosen and used with care in order to move beyond the contributions level*

Examples

Black Cowboys (Stewart, 1986)
The Brooklyn Bridge (Mann, 1996)
Cajun Home (Bial, 1998)
Dear Benjamin Banneker (Pinkney, 1994)
Kids at Work (Hine, 1994)
Learn Karate (Queen, 1998)
One April Morning: Children Remember the Oklahoma Bombing (Lamb, 1996)
A Migrant Family (Brimner, 1992)
River Ran Wild (Cherry, 1992)
Teammates (Golenbock, 1990)
Through My Eyes (Bridges, 1999)
When Justice Failed: The Fred Korematsu Story (Chin, 1993)

The general manager of the Brooklyn Dodgers baseball team was a man by the name of Branch Rickey. He was not afraid of change. He wanted to treat the Dodger fans to the best players he could find, regardless of the color of their skin. He thought segregation was unfair and wanted to give everyone, regardless of race or creed, an opportunity to compete equally on ballfields across America.

To do this, the Dodgers needed one special man.

Branch Rickey launched a search for him. He was looking for a star player in the Negro League who would be able to compete successfully despite threats on his life or attempts to injure him. He would have to possess the self-control not to fight back when opposing players tried to intimidate or hurt him. If this man disgraced himself on the field, Rickey knew, his opponents would use it as an excuse to keep blacks out of Major League baseball for many more years.

Rickey thought Jackie Robinson might be just the man.

—Excerpt from *Teammates* by Peter Golenbock (1990, pp. 7–9)

Note: All exemplar children's literature listed in this chart may be found in the annotated bibliography in Chapter 9.

Literature about celebrations and holidays has often been a part of the social studies curriculum. Such books are usually inviting, colorful, and entertaining; the multicultural titles about celebrations such as Kwanzaa, Ramadan, Christmas, Hanukkah, and the Chinese New Year are now abundant. However delightful, those books are not sufficient. Others, both fiction and nonfiction, realistic and artistic, painful and lyrical, provide a far more compelling kind of invitation to probe more deeply into the social fabric of our nation, past and present.

READINGS ABOUT FINDING AND USING MULTICULTURAL CHILDREN'S LITERATURE

Au, K. (1993). *Literacy instruction in multicultural settings.* Fort Worth, TX: Harcourt Brace.

Banks, James, & Banks, Cherry (Eds.). (2001). *Multicultural education: Issues and perspectives* (4th ed.). New York: Wiley/Jossey-Bass.

Barrera, Rosalinda, Thompson, Verlinda, & Dressman, M. (Eds.). (1997). *Kaleidoscope: A multicultural booklist for grades K–8.* Urbana, IL: National Council of Teachers of English.

Beckett, Sandra (Ed.). (1997). *Reflections of change: Children's literature since 1945.* Westport, CT: Greenwood Press.

Bishop, Rudine. (1997). Selecting literature for a multicultural curriculum. In V. Harris (Ed.), *Using multiethnic literature in the K–8 classroom* (pp. 1–19). Norwood, MA: Christopher-Gordon.

Bishop, Rudine. (Ed.). (1994). *Kaleidoscope: A multicultural booklist for grades K–8. NCTE Bibliography Series.* Urbana, IL: National Council of Teachers of English.

Clements, N., Gillespie, C., Powell, J., & Swearingen, R. (1994). A look at the Newbery Medal books from a multicultural perspective. *The Reading Teacher, 48,* 40–50.

Cox, Carole. (1997). *Crossroads: Literature and language in culturally and linguistically diverse classrooms.* Upper Saddle River, NJ: Merrill.

Danielson, Kathy, & LaBonty, Jan. (1994). *Integrating reading and writing through children's literature.* Boston: Allyn and Bacon.

Day, Frances. (1997). *Latina and Latino voices in literature for children and teenagers.* Portsmouth, NH: Heinemann.

Day, Frances. (1994). *Multicultural voices in contemporary literature: A resource for teachers.* Portsmouth, NH: Heinemann.

Diamond, B., & Moore, M. (1995). *Multicultural literacy: Mirroring the reality of the classroom.* White Plains, NY: Longman.

Finazzo, Denise. (1997). *All for the children: Multicultural essentials of literature.* Albany, NY: Delmar.

Harris, V. (Ed.). (1997). *Teaching multicultural literature in grades K–8.* Norwood, MA: Christopher-Gordon.

Helbig, A., & Perkins, A. (1994). *This land is our land: A guide to multicultural literature for children and young adults.* Westport, CT: Greenwood.

Lind, Beth. (1996). *Multicultural children's literature: An annotated bibliography.* Jefferson, NC: McFarland.

Muse, Daphne (Ed.). (1997). *The New Press guide to multicultural resources for young readers.* New York: New Press.

Ramirez, G., & Ramirez, J. (1994). *Multiethnic children's literature.* Albany, NY: Delmar.

Rogers, T., Soter, A., & Bishop, R. (1996). *Reading across cultures: Teaching literature in a diverse society.* New York: Teachers College Press.

Sage, C. (1993). One hundred notable picture books in the field of social studies. In M. Zarnowski & A. Gallagher (Eds.), *Children's literature and social studies: Selecting and using notable books in the classroom* (pp. 5–11). Washington, DC: National Council for the Social Studies.

Spann, M. (1992). *Literature-based multicultural activities: An integrated approach.* New York: Scholastic.

Temple, C., Martinez, M., Yokota, J., & Naylor, A. (1998). *Children's books in children's hands.* Boston: Allyn and Bacon.

Thomas, Rebecca. (1996). *Connecting cultures: A guide to multicultural literature for children.* New Providence, NJ: R. R. Bowker.

Valdez, Alora. (1999). *Learning in living color: Using literature to incorporate multicultural education into the primary classroom.* Boston: Allyn and Bacon.

INTERNET RESOURCES FOR FINDING AND USING MULTICULTURAL CHILDREN'S LITERATURE

African American images in children's books:
    http://www.scils.rutgers.edu/special/kay/afro.html
    http://www.scils.rutgers.edu/special/kay/afro1.html
Asian American images in children's books: http://www.scils.rutgers.edu/special/kay/asian.html
Asian American and Asian & Pacific Islands children's literature: http://falcon.jmu.edu/~ramseyil /mulasia.htm
Children's literature and language arts resources: http://falcon.jmu.edu/~ramseyil/childlit.htm
Children's literature resources: http://www.nwmissouri.edu/LIBRARY/courses/education2/ children.htm
Children's and young adult multicultural literature: http://www.lib.lsu.edu/lib/
Criteria for evaluating multicultural literature: http://members.aol.com/mcsing29/bookcrit.htm
Hispanic and Latin American images in children's books: http://www.scils.rutgers.edu/special/ kay/hispanic.html
Historical fiction: http://www.nypl.org/branch/kids/100/historical.html
Martin Luther King Jr. resources: http://www.lib.lsu.edu/hum/mlk/
Multicultural children's literature: http://www.ncrel.org/sdrs/areas/issues/educatrs/presrvce/ pe3lk28.htm
Multicultural children's literature in the elementary classroom: http://www.ed.gov/databases/ ERIC_Digests/ed423552.html
Multicultural children's literature resources (websites, books, journal articles): http://www.lib. msu.edu/corby/education/multicultural.htm
Multicultural resources for children: http://falcon.jmu.edu/~ramseyil/multipub.htm#B
Native American images in children's books: http://www.scils.rutgers.edu/special/kay/native. html

OTHER SOURCES CITED

Mohr, Nicholosa. (1979). *Felita.* New York: Dial Books.
Rylant, Cynthia. (1986). *The relatives came.* New York: Scholastic.

CHAPTER

6

Why should I blend social studies and multicultural literature?

> Mama wrapped me in a blanket while Daddy went outside and hitched the horse to the wagon. We had to travel about twenty miles into town to the hospital. It was midday when we got there. We had to go to the colored waiting room. In those days, they kept blacks and whites separate. There were separate public rest rooms, separate water fountains, separate schools. It was called segregation. So in the hospital, we had to go to the colored waiting room.
>
> Even though I was unconscious, the doctors wouldn't look at me until they had finished with all the white patients. When the doctors did examine me, they told my daddy that I needed an operation and that it would cost three hundred dollars.
>
> Three hundred dollars was a lot of money in those days. My daddy didn't have that kind of money. And the doctors wouldn't do the operation until they had the money.
>
> — Excerpt from *Uncle Jed's Barbershop*
> by Margaree King Mitchell (1993, pp. 12–13)

Whether you teach in a multicultural or monocultural setting, you already know the compelling power of a good story, regardless of the particular race, nationality, or culture of the characters in the story and the students in the classrooms. A story with strong characters and urgent problems, such as those in *Uncle Jed's Barbershop*, will evoke children's interest, emotions, compassion, and sometimes outrage. If a story "hooks" children strongly, you have opened the door to genuine involvement in social studies education. Children won't soon forget the plight of deathly ill Sarah Jean and her Uncle Jed, who sacrifices his dream to save her life when white doctors won't treat a poor black child. The contrast to standard textbook summaries, *Weekly Reader* snippets, or educational videotapes becomes obvious when you consider some of the major social studies concepts in this book: segregation, economics, business development, medical advancements, and changing modes of transportation.

We envision children leading lives as collaborative citizens in multicultural classrooms and communities. Therefore, our intention in promoting stories such as *Uncle Jed's Barbershop* is no surprise: We want children to become so caught up in compelling stories as part of their overall experience in studying social studies that they will become more compassionate and productive citizens in their multicultural world. Through experiences with literature, experiences where children feel and consider real human problems and solutions, we hope that children will develop greater understanding of the peoples of the world. We also hope that they will begin to see the importance of their own contributions to that world both now and in the future.

Compelling is the key in our thinking. A "cute" story or one simply contrived to teach a social studies concept, perhaps even inserted into a chapter in a social studies text, is unlikely to satisfy students or teachers. The lives of human beings today are complex, and children know that happily-ever-after endings occur in fairy tales, but often not in real life. Even very young children know the difference between stories that are powerful and those that are not. From television, children know that a princess can be miserable, get divorced, and die in a tragic accident; that an actor can go to jail for drug abuse; that a president may be charged with improper behavior. From their homes, they know there aren't always two happy parents. From the neighborhood, they may have learned to distrust police officers.

Does this mean that cute stories with happy endings are inappropriate choices? Not at all. We're not recommending a full diet of controversy, prejudice, and problems! But simplistic and idealistic stories shouldn't comprise the entire selection of literature either, and those characteristics aren't the main criteria for linking literature to meaningful social studies concepts. We recommend choosing from all four of our categories of multicultural literature—*egalitarian, creative, realistic,* and *informational* (see pages 30–33)—with an emphasis on the realistic selections in order to capture well-written, compelling human drama from different and authentic perspectives.

We aren't implying that realistic literature such as *Uncle Jed's Barbershop* (Mitchell, 1993) or *Molly's Pilgrim* (Cohen, 1983) should replace social studies textbooks, films, software, or maps and globes. However, they do offer opportunities far beyond the reach of traditional materials, especially opportunities for applying learning in daily life. Children's involvement with such stories leads to them taking an "emotional stake in understanding how and why people live as they do" (Temple, Martinez, Yokota, & Naylor, 1998, p. 83). Chosen well and treated with respect for the characters and their problems, stories invite children to examine information, concepts, values, and decision-making processes that may well lie outside their experiences, but not beyond their understanding.

You may teach in a monocultural or multicultural setting; you may have taught in one community or several markedly different places. You may have carefully read, quickly skimmed, or simply skipped other information in these introductory chapters. You may include some or all of the following aspects of diversity in your definition of *multicultural*: ethnicity, race, language, religion, economic status, gender, nationality, culture, and physical and mental abilities or disabilities.

Regardless of differences in experiences and concepts of multiculturalism, you know the world is changing. And you know the delight of children when they make connections between something in a book and their own lives. You also know the depth of your own satisfaction when you see children independently applying classroom lessons to their daily problems and interactions. The purpose of this book is to provide perspective, design, and effective strategies for your use of multicultural literature with social studies instruction, whether in a totally integrated, thematic curriculum design or as a separate-subject organization.

We're not going to be terribly radical in our pursuit of this purpose. If you have social studies textbooks, we don't suggest you throw them away. If you've never used literature with social studies, we don't recommend you redesign your whole instructional program immediately. Start because you are curious or dissatisfied. Start because you have the sense that something could be better, more meaningful. Start in a way you can handle with confidence. Start by reading some of the books we suggest—rich, complex, respectful, and satisfying stories about the diverse peoples of the United States.

READINGS ABOUT INTEGRATING SOCIAL STUDIES, LITERACY INSTRUCTION, AND MULTICULTURAL EDUCATION

Clegg, Luther, Miller, Etta, & Vanderhoof, Jr., William. (1995). *Celebrating diversity: A multicultural resource*. Albany, NY: Delmar.

Cordeiro, P. (Ed.). (1995). *Endless possibilities: Generating curriculum in social studies and literacy*. Portsmouth, NH: Heinemann.

Fredericks, Anthony. (1991). *Social studies through children's literature: An integrated approach*. Englewood, CO: Teachers Ideas Press.

Glandon, Shan. (2000). *Caldecott connections to social studies*. New York: Libraries Unlimited.

Guthrie, John, & Wigfield, Allan (Eds.). (1997). *Reading engagement: Motivating readers through integrated instruction*. Newark, DE: International Reading Association.

Paul, Dierdre. (2000). *Raising black children who love reading and writing: A guide from birth through grade six*. Palo Alto, CA: Bergin & Garvey.

Roberts, Patricia, Jarolimek, John, et al. (1996). *Integrating language arts and social studies for kindergarten and primary children*. Englewood Cliffs, NJ: Prentice-Hall.

Temple, Charles, Martinez, Miriam, Yokota, Junko, & Naylor, Alice. (1998). *Children's books in children's hands: An introduction to their literature*. Boston: Allyn and Bacon.

JOURNALS AND INTERNET RESOURCES FOR INTEGRATING SOCIAL STUDIES AND CHILDREN'S LITERATURE

Social Education (notable trade books summarized by NCSS strand each year)
   Lesson plans from *Social Education*: http://www.socialstudies.org/resources/lessons/home.html
Social Studies and the Young Child
   Teaching values: http://www.teachingvalues.com/childrensbooks.html

OTHER SOURCES CITED

Cohen, Barbara. (1983). *Molly's pilgrim*. New York: Lothrop, Lee & Shepard.
Mitchell, Margaree. (1993). *Uncle Jed's barbershop*. New York: Scholastic.

PART TWO

Organizing for Integrated Instruction

Well, you've read all or parts of Part One, and we have aroused your interest or rekindled your determination to move toward a more multicultural approach to education. Or you've turned directly to this Part Two because you're already somewhat of a multiculturalist and you're ready for more.

In this section, we provide specific and practical guidance in response to the following critical questions:

CHAPTER

7

How do I choose good multicultural literature to use with social studies?

Some of the concerns about choosing multicultural literature are no different from concerns and questions about choosing and using *any* literature:

- How do I find good literature?
- How do I know it's actually good?
- How do I know if a piece will work for the purpose I have in mind?
- Will my students (and their parents) respond well to this book?

A second set of questions pertain more specifically to using literature with *social studies:*

- How do I choose literature to correlate with social studies objectives?
- How do I blend instruction promoting aesthetic, intellectual, and emotional responses to literature with instruction focused on the content and processes of social studies?

Other questions are specific to *multicultural literature* and the sensitivity that teachers from all cultural backgrounds must employ when choosing and using this material:

- How do I make sure to include enough variety of cultural groups?
- How do I avoid perpetuating stereotypes?
- Which types of multicultural literature do I use for my students? How do I know if the literature is culturally authentic?
- If I choose a piece in which one cultural group is oppressed by another, and there's no immediate happy ending, how do I anticipate and respond to the negative reactions of children and parents from either cultural group?

The chapters in this section of the book and the exemplar units in the next section (Part Three) provide a measure of response to these questions, as well as strategies for you to begin your own processes of making choices. Our suggestions are:

- If you are relatively inexperienced with choosing multicultural literature for any purpose other than sharing holidays and celebrations, start with Phase 1 of this guide.
- If you are accustomed to making your own selections of literature, but have questions about multicultural literature, start with Phase 2.
- If you are ready to make decisions about using a book with social studies, then Phases 3, 4, and 5 are more relevant for you.

Guide to Selecting Multicultural Literature

Phase 1: Is This Book Appropriate for In-Depth Use as Literature?

If the answer to all four questions is yes, proceed to the next phase. If the answer to any question is no, you might not want to use the particular book in question, or you might want to use it in a lighter context.

1. Is this story a compelling narrative for *you*? Would *you* want to read it again? Would you want to treat it *seriously* with children?
2. Is this story well written, with style and language that will attract young readers? Would you enjoy reading it aloud? Would children enjoy hearing it again or rereading it themselves?
3. Is this text well formatted (size of print, type of font, amount of white space around print, quality of illustrations, size and clarity of maps and charts, etc.) so that it will be physically attractive to young readers?
4. Is the content of this story well matched to the intellectual and emotional maturity of your students? Will this story evoke feelings, strike a chord, or provoke your students to react with passion and/or critical thinking?

Phase 2: Is This Appropriate Multicultural Literature?

If the answer to all three questions is yes, proceed to Phase 3. If the answer to any question is no, or if you have other concerns about the book, talk with knowledgeable colleagues to gain additional perspectives before making a final decision.

5. Are there positively portrayed (in words and/or illustrations), well-developed minority and/or majority culture characters? If a child in your classroom is a member of this minority culture, would he or she be honored, satisfied, or pleased to encounter this character in classroom reading material? Would children of a majority culture recognize similarities and come to appreciate differences between themselves and the characters in the book?
6. If some culturally specific characters are depicted negatively, do they change and grow, or are there other characters of that culture who do have positive features? Will your students, of both majority and minority cultures, be able to discriminate between these negative and positive portrayals?

7. If there are characters or conditions that are stereotypical or inauthentic, does the quality of the story provide a powerful context for examining those problems?

Phase 3: Might This Book Be Useful with Social Studies Instruction?

If the answer to all for questions is yes, proceed to Phase 4. If the answer to any question is no, you might consider other uses outside social studies integration, or you might choose to focus young children on reading the book critically to uncover problems of prejudice or inauthenticity.

8. Does this story have one or more powerful literary components (plot, character, theme, setting, etc.) to integrate with essential ideas within one or more of the 10 NCSS themes?
9. Whether informational, fictional, poetic, mythic, or legendary, does the material contain problems and resolutions applicable to life in multicultural United States today?
10. Are there realistic and/or aesthetically pleasing portrayals of human relationships with each other, animals, technology, and/or nature?
11. Are there relevant, well-described, and/or illustrated elements of setting, such as time period and physical and social environment?

Phase 4: Will It Work for Your Grade Level, or Will You Recommend It to Someone Else?

If your answer to one of these questions is no, you may want to use this book earlier or later in the year or recommend it to someone at another grade level.

12. Does this story fit with any specific additional social studies expectations for your grade level? Do those expectations fall within an NCSS theme?
13. Does this story lend itself well to the literacy objectives of your grade level?

Phase 5: How Do You Decide What Thematic Unit to Build around This Book or Related Books?

14. Which NCSS themes seem to be the strongest match to this book? Can you choose two or three highly related themes to blend together in a cohesive unit? (Use the charts in Chapter 8 to note related themes already designated by the National Council for the Social Studies.)
15. Which performance expectations within these themes seem most appropriate to select as objectives for your unit?
16. Which literature-oriented objectives from your district's curriculum guide seem most appropriate to emphasize in this unit?

8 How do I match multicultural literature selections to NCSS themes?

This chapter displays all the specific objectives or "performance expectations" of each of the 10 themes or strands of the curriculum promoted by the National Council for the Social Studies. Each performance expectation is easily related to one or more of the other curriculum themes; therefore, we have noted those related strands. Following the chart of performance objectives and related themes, we present a second chart for each theme that shows exemplar titles of multicultural literature that are highly related to that theme. We include data about the cultural groups represented, the recommended grade level range, and other related themes.

We suggest that you use the charts in this chapter to begin adding books you might want to use with particular themes. They may be books you find in the annotated bibliography in Chapter 9 or books you find elsewhere that you want to remember. You certainly might note the title of a particularly compelling book under more than one theme to remind yourself of its potential impact regardless of how you might organize a social studies or other integrated unit.

I. Culture

Social studies programs should include experiences that provide for the study of *culture and cultural diversity*, so that the learner can:

Performance Expectations	Related Themes
a. Explore and describe similarities and differences in the ways groups, societies, and cultures address similar human needs and concerns.	II, III, IV
b. Give examples of how experiences may be interpreted differently by people from diverse cultural perspectives and frames of reference.	II, III, IV, V, IX
c. Describe ways in which language, stories, folktales, music, and artistic creations serve as expressions of culture and influence behavior of people living in a particular culture.	II, III, V, IX
d. Compare ways in which people from different cultures think about and deal with their physical environment and social conditions.	II, III, IV
e. Give examples and describe the importance of cultural unity and diversity within and across groups.	II, III, V, IX

Possible Books for Culture			
Title/Author/Year	*Cultural Group(s)*	*Grades*	*Performance Standards*
The Boy Who Sailed with Columbus (Michael Foreman, 1992)	Spanish American, Native American	3–4	a, b, d
Vejigante: Masquerader (Lulu Delacre, 1993)	Mexican American	K–2	a, c, d, e
Angel Child, Dragon Child (Michele Maria Surat, 1983)	Vietnamese American	1–4	b, c, d, e
The Last Princess (Fay Stanley, 1991)	Hawaiian	2–4	b, d, e

II. Time, Continuity, and Change

Social studies programs should include experiences that provide for the study of *the ways human beings view themselves in and over time*, so that the learner can:

Performance Expectations	Related Themes
a. Demonstrate an understanding that different people may describe the same event or situation in diverse ways, citing reasons for the differences in views.	I, II, III, IV
b. Demonstrate an ability to use correct vocabulary associated with time, such as past, present, future, and long ago; read and construct simple time lines; identify examples of change; and recognize examples of cause-and-effect relationships.	I, III, V, VIII
c. Compare and contrast different stories or accounts about past events, people, places, or situations, identifying how they contribute to one's understanding of the past.	I, III, X
d. Identify and use various sources for reconstructing the past, such as documents, letters, diaries, maps, textbooks, photos, and others.	I, III
e. Demonstrate an understanding that people in different times and places view the world differently.	I, III, IX
f. Use knowledge of facts and concepts drawn from history, along with elements of historical inquiry, to make informed decisions about and take actions on public issues.	I, III, V, VI, VII, VIII, IX, X

Possible Books for Time, Continuity, and Change			
Title/Author/Year	*Cultural Group(s)*	*Grades*	*Performance Standards*
The House on Maple Street (Bonnie Pryor, 1987)	Native American, European American	2–3	g, h, i
The Hundred Penny Box (Sharon Bell Mathis, 1975)	African American	2–4	a, b, d
Mrs. Katz and Tush (Patricia Polacco, 1992)	African American, Jewish	1–3	b, c, d, e

III. People, Places, and Environments

Social studies programs should include experiences that provide for the study of *people, places, and environments*, so that the learner can:

Performance Expectations	Related Themes
a. Construct and use mental maps of locales, regions, and the world that demonstrate understanding of relative location, direction, size, and shape.	IX
b. Interpret, use, and distinguish various representations of the earth, such as maps, globes, and photographs.	I
c. Use appropriate resources, data sources, and geographic tools such as atlases, databases, grid systems, charts, and maps to generate, manipulate, and interpret information.	
d. Estimate distance and calculate scale.	
e. Locate and distinguish among varying landforms and geographic features, such as mountains, plateaus, islands, and oceans.	IX
f. Describe and speculate about physical system changes, such as seasons, climate and weather, and the water cycle.	VIII, IX
g. Describe how people create places that reflect ideas, personality, culture, and wants and needs as they design homes, playgrounds, classrooms, and the like.	I, IV, V
h. Examine the interaction of human beings and their physical environment, the use of land, building of cities, and ecosystem changes in selected locales and regions.	VI, VIII
i. Explore ways that the earth's physical features have changed over time in the local region and beyond, and how these changes may be connected to one another.	II, IX
j. Observe and speculate about social and economic effects of environmental changes and crises resulting from phenomena such as floods, storms, and drought.	I, V, VII
k. Consider existing uses and propose and evaluate alternative uses of resources and land in home, school, community, the region, and beyond.	V, VII, VIII, IX, X

Possible Books for People, Places, and Environments			
Title/Author/Year	*Cultural Group(s)*	*Grades*	*Performance Standards*
Growing Up in Coal Country (Susan Bartoletti, 1996)	European American	4+	e, g, h, j
How Many Days to America? (Eve Bunting, 1988)	Caribbean	2–4	a, e, h
Grandfather's Journey (Allen Say, 1994)	Japanese American	K–3	a, b, c, d, e, g, h

IV. Individual Development and Identity

Social studies programs should include experiences that provide for the study of *individual development and identity*, so that the learner can:

Performance Expectations	Related Themes
a. Describe personal changes over time, such as those related to physical development and personal interests.	II
b. Describe personal connections to place—especially those associated with immediate surroundings.	III
c. Describe the unique features of one's nuclear and extended families.	I
d. Show how learning and physical development affect behavior.	
e. Identify and describe ways family, groups, and community influence the individual's daily life and personal choices.	I, V
f. Explore factors that contribute to one's personal identity, such as interests, capabilities, and perceptions.	
g. Analyze a particular event to identify reasons individuals might respond to it in different ways.	I, V
h. Work independently and cooperatively to accomplish goals.	X

Possible Books for Individual Development and Identity			
Title/Author/Year	*Cultural Group(s)*	*Grades*	*Performance Standards*
Peter's Chair (Ezra Jack Keats, 1967)	African American	K–1	a, b, c, d, e, g
Hawk I'm Your Brother (Byrd Baylor, 1976)	Native American	2–4	a, b, d, g
Amazing Grace (Mary Hoffman, 1991)	African American	K–3	a, b, c, d, e, f, g, h
Annie and the Old One (Miska Miles, 1971)	Navajo	2–4	a, b, c, d, e, f, g
Too Many Tamales (Gary Soto, 1993)	Mexican American	K–2	c, e, g, h
More than Anything Else (Marie Bradby, 1995)	African American	K–2	a, b, c, d, e, f, g, h

V. Individuals, Groups, and Institutions

Social studies programs should include experiences that provide for the study of *interactions among individuals, groups, and institutions,* so that the learner can:

Performance Expectations	Related Themes
a. Identify roles as learned behavior patterns in groups situations, such as student, family member, peer play group member, or club member.	I, IV
b. Give examples of and explain group and institutional influences—such as religious beliefs, laws, and peer pressure—on people, events, and elements of culture.	I, II, IV, VI, X
c. Identify examples of institutions and describe the interactions of people with institutions.	I, VI, X

(continued)

d. Identify examples of tensions between and among individuals, groups, or institutions, and how belonging to more than one group can cause internal conflicts.	I, II, IV, X
e. Identify and describe examples of tension between an individual's beliefs and a government's policies and laws.	II, IV, VI, X
f. Give examples of the role of institutions in furthering both continuity and change.	II, VI, VIII, X
g. Show how groups and institutions work to meet individual needs and promote the common good, and identify examples of where they fail to do so.	I, II, VI, X

Possible Books for Individuals, Groups, and Institutions

Title/Author/Year	Cultural Group(s)	Grades	Performance Standards
Follow the Drinking Gourd (Jeanette Winter, 1988)	African American	K–2	a, b, d, e, f, g
Smoky Night (Eve Bunting, 1994)	Korean American Mexican American African American	1–3	a, b, c, d, g
Off to School (Gwendolyn Battle-Lavert, 1995)	African American	1–3	a, c, d, f, g
I Hate English! (Ellen Levine, 1989)	Chinese American	K–2	a, c, d, f, g
One Night (Cristina Kessler, 1995)	Tuareg (Desert Islamic people)	K–3	a, b

VI. Power, Authority, and Governance

Social studies programs should include experiences that provide for the study of *how people create and change structures of power, authority, and governance*, so that the learner can:

Performance Expectations	Related Themes
a. Examine the rights and responsibilities of the individual in relation to his or her social groups, such as family, peer group, and school class.	V, X
b. Explain the purpose of government.	X
c. Give examples of how government does or does not provide for the needs and wants of people, establish order and security, and manage conflict.	I, V, IX
d. Recognize how groups and organizations encourage unity and deal with diversity to maintain order and security.	I, V
e. Distinguish among local, state, and national government and identify representative leaders at these levels, such as mayor, governor, and president.	X
f. Identify and describe factors that contribute to cooperation and cause disputes within and among groups and nations.	II, V, IX
g. Explore the role of technology in communications, transportation, information processing, weapons development, or other areas as it contributes to or helps resolve conflicts.	VII, VIII, IX
h. Recognize and give examples of the tensions between the wants and needs of individuals and groups, and concepts such as fairness, equity, and justice.	II, IX, X

Possible Books for Power, Authority, and Governance			
Title/Author/Year	*Cultural Group(s)*	*Grades*	*Performance Standards*
The Bracelet (Yoshiko Uchida, 1993)	Japanese American	1–3	a, c, d, f, h
Fly Away Home (Eve Bunting, 1991)	Homeless, European American	1–3	a, c, d, h

(continued)

The Gold Cadillac (Mildred Taylor, 1987)	African American	3–4	a, c, d, e, f, h
Cheyenne Again (Eve Bunting, 1995)	Native American	1–2	a, c, d, f, h

VII. Production, Distribution, and Consumption

Social studies programs should include experiences that provide for the study of *how people organize for the production, distribution, and consumption of goods and services*, so that the learner can:

Performance Expectations	Related Themes
a. Give examples that show how scarcity and choice govern economic decisions.	I, III
b. Distinguish between needs and wants.	IV
c. Identify examples of private and public goods and services.	V, VI
d. Give examples of the various institutions that make up economic systems, such as families, workers, banks, labor unions, government agencies, small businesses, and large corporations.	V
e. Describe how people depend on workers with specialized jobs and the ways in which they contribute to the production and exchange of goods and services.	V, VIII
f. Describe the influence of incentives, values, traditions, and habits on economic decisions.	I, II
g. Explain and demonstrate the role of money in everyday life.	I
h. Describe the relationship of price to supply and demand.	I, V
i. Use economic concepts—such as supply, demand, and price—to help explain events in the community and nation.	I, V, VI
j. Apply knowledge of economic concepts in developing a response to a current local economic issue, such as how to reduce the flow of trash into a rapidly filling landfill.	V, VI, VIII, X

Possible Books for Production, Distribution, and Consumption			
Title/Author/Year	Cultural Group(s)	Grades	Performance Standards
Chicken Sunday (Patrica Pollaco, 1992)	African American Russian American	K–2	a, c, f, g, h
A Day's Work (Eve Bunting, 1994)	Mexican American	2–4	d, e, f, g
Song of the Trees (Mildred Taylor, 1975)	African American	3–4	a, f, h, i
Uncle Jed's Barbershop (Margaree King Mitchell, 1993)	African American	K–3	a, b, d, e, f, g,
The Tangerine Tree (Regina Hanson, 1995)	Jamaican American	K–2	a, b, d, e, g, i

VIII. Science, Technology, and Society

Social studies programs should include experiences that provide for the study of *relationships among science, technology, and society,* so that the learner can:

Performance Expectations	Related Themes
a. Identify and describe examples in which science and technology have changed the lives of people, such as in homemaking, child care, work, transportation, and communication.	I, II, V, VII, IX
b. Identify and describe examples in which science and technology have led to changes in the physical environment, such as the building of dams and levees, offshore oil drilling, medicine from rain forests, and loss of rain forests due to extraction of resources and alternative uses.	III
c. Describe instances in which changes in values, beliefs, and attitudes have resulted from new scientific and technological knowledge, such as conservation of resources and awareness of chemicals harmful to life and the environment.	I, II, V, VI, VII, IX, X

(continued)

d. Identify examples of laws and policies that govern scientific and technological applications, such as the Endangered Species Act and environmental protection policies.	VI, X
e. Suggest ways to monitor science and technology in order to protect the physical environment, individual rights, and the common good.	VI, X

Possible Books for Science, Technology, and Society			
Title/Author/Year	*Cultural Group(s)*	*Grades*	*Performance Standards*
The Great Kapok Tree (Lynne Cherry, 1990)	South American	K–3	b, c, d, e
Death of the Iron Horse (Paul Goble, 1993)	Native American	3–4	a, b, c, d, e
The River Ran Wild (Lynne Cherry, 1992)	Native American European American	2–4	a, b, c, d, e
And Still the Turtle Watched (Sheila MacGill-Callahan, 1991)	Native American European American	K–3	c, d, e

IX. Global Connections

Social studies programs should include experiences that provide for the study of *global connections and interdependence*, so that the learner can:

Performance Expectations	**Related Themes**
a. Explore ways that language, art, music, belief systems, and other cultural elements may facilitate global understanding or lead to misunderstanding.	I, III
b. Give examples of conflict, cooperation, and interdependence among individuals, groups, and nations.	V, VI

c. Examine the effects of changing technologies on the global community.	VIII
d. Explore causes, consequences, and possible solutions to persistent, contemporary, and emerging global issues, such as pollution and endangered species.	III, VIII
e. Examine the relationships and tensions between personal wants and needs and various global concerns, such as the use of imported oil, land use, and environmental protection.	IV, VII, VIII
f. Investigate concerns, issues, standards, and conflicts related to universal human rights, such as the treatment of children, religious groups, and effects of war.	X

Possible Books for Global Connections

Title/Author/Year	Cultural Group(s)	Grades	Performance Standards
A Migrant Family (Larry Brimner, 1992)	Mexican American	3–4+	b, c, f
Coming to America: The Story of Immigration (Betsy Maestro, 1996)	Multicultural	K–2	b, e, f
This Is My House (Arthur Dorrow, 1992)	Multicultural	K–2	a, b, c
Boundless Grace (Mary Hoffman)	African American	K–2	a, b
The Bracelet (Yoshiko Uchida, 1993)	Japanese American	2–4	b, f

X. Civic Ideals and Practices

Social studies programs should include experiences that provide for the study of *the ideals, principles, and practices of citizenship in a democratic republic*, so that the learner can:

Performance Expectations	Related Themes
a. Identify key ideals of the U.S democratic republican form of government—such as individual human dignity, liberty, justice, equality—and the rule of law, and discuss their application in specific situations.	II, V, VI
b. Identify examples of rights and responsibilities of citizens.	II
c. Locate, access, organize, and apply information about an issue of public concern from multiple points of view.	I, II, V, IX
d. Identify and practice selected forms of civic discussion and participation consistent with the ideals of citizens in a democratic republic.	II, V, VI
e. Explain actions citizens can take to influence public policy decisions.	V, VI
f. Recognize that a variety of formal and informal actors influence and shape public policy.	V, VI
g. Examine the influence of public opinion on personal decision making and government policy on public issues.	V, VI
h. Explain how public policies and citizen behaviors may or may not reflect the stated ideals of a democratic republican form of government.	II, V, VI
i. Describe how public policies are used to address issues of public concern.	VI
j. Recognize and interpret how the "common good" can be strengthened through various forms of citizen action.	II, V, VI

Possible Books for Civic Ideals and Practices			
Title/Author/Year	*Cultural Group(s)*	*Grades*	*Performance Standards*
Pearl Moscowitz's Last Stand (Arthur Levine, 1993)	Multicultural	K–2	a, b, e, f
Felita (Nicholasa Mohr, 1979)	Puerto-Rican American	3–4	a, f, h, j
The Friendship (Mildred Taylor, 1987)	African American, European American	3–4	a, b, g, h, j
Harriet Tubman: The Road to Freedom (Rae Bains, 1982)	African American, European American	3–4	a, d, e, f, g, h, j
The Christmas Menorahs: How a Town Fought Hate (Janice Cohn, 1995)	Jewish, Christian	2–4	a, b, c, f, h, j

9

What are some recommended books already matched to NCSS themes?

This annotated bibliography can never be exhaustive; from the time the manuscript went to press and before it reached your hands, new powerful multicultural children's books were written and published. However, we've chosen well, and one or both of us have read every book included in this annotated bibliography. We included them because they meet our criteria of being compelling stories or highly interesting informational books. All books relate to one or more NCSS themes and represent major diverse groups of people in the United States. One shortcoming found in children's literature at this time is a paucity of books featuring Mideastern or Mideastern American people in settings and situations other than religious contexts.

Cultural Groupings

With very few exceptions, the books are set in the United States or contain a plot that directly connects the setting to the United States. Books are grouped by the identity of the major characters or the focus on one cultural group more than another. Cultural groups are defined by country of origin of characters or ancestors; there is a multicultural grouping and a religious cultures grouping. All groupings have economic, regional, and situational diversity. Many books contain major characters from one cultural group and minor characters from another. Some books are truly multicultural, with major characters from more than one cultural group. A brief synopsis of broad cultural characteristics and values is given at the beginning of each section, along with misleading and negative cultural stereotypes to avoid. These synopses should be interpreted as broad paintbrush strokes about the people in each group, and are not presented as comprehensive. We have, for the most part, chosen literature that does not continue to support negative images of people in minority groups; however, poverty and social problems are honestly depicted in many selections across all cultural groupings. We have chosen, and it is important for you to use, varied types of books within each broad cultural group so that children learn that diversity also exists within cultures.

Cultural Groups as Organizers of the Bibliography

African American	Characters are generally considered black, with specific African country of origin specified whenever given in the story	p. 63
Asian American	Characters have Chinese, Japanese, Korean, and Pacific Rim heritage, typically specified	p. 74
Caribbean and Caribbean American	Characters live in or have roots in areas of the Caribbean that are closely connected to the United States, such as Jamaica, the Virgin Islands, and the Bahamas	p. 78
European American	Characters are generally considered white, with country of origin specified whenever possible	p. 79
Hispanic/Latino American	Characters have Spanish, Mexican, South American, Central American, Puerto Rican, and Cuban heritage, specified whenever given in the story	p. 92
Mideastern and Mideastern American	Characters have Mideastern heritage, linked to countries such as Iraq, Iran, Turkey, and Israel, specified whenever given in the story	p. 94
Multicultural	Major characters represent more than one cultural group, as specified	p. 95
Native American	Characters are from different tribal nations and/or geographic regions, typically specified	p. 100
Religious cultures	Characters explicitly represent faith communities such as Christianity, Buddhism, Judaism, and Islam	p. 104

Type of Multicultural Literature

We have coded books using the social studies–oriented model of types of multicultural literature first shown on pages 30–33. The predominant choice of books is realistic (RE) multicultural literature, most of which could be used to promote the transformation or decision making and social action levels of Banks and Banks's multicultural curriculum. The second most frequent books were well-written informational (IN) and egalitarian (EG) books, selected because of the multicultural perspectives and quality of content, writing, and illustrations. Although many creative works (CR) are available, such as myths and legends, poetry and song, we included only a few with outstanding direct links to the reality of a people so that children could readily develop understanding of the NCSS themes through the use of these books. For integration with social studies, we intentionally omitted books whose characters were talking animals or machines, preferring to focus on children and adults in realistic situations as the most powerful vehicle for engagement and movement toward social action.

Codes and Characteristics of Books

RE (Realistic)
- Focuses on problems of historical or current multicultural realities in the United States
- Includes characters and situations representing their depicted race, religion, economic class, exceptionality, country of origin, and so on, for the story to be authentic
- Focuses on historical events of injustice to a minority group and the support of family and other group members in surmounting those problems
- Focuses on problems and experiences more specific to one cultural group than another, even when there is no theme of overt injustice

IN (Informational)
- Focuses on multicultural characters and events in current events, history, government, politics, sports, ecology, scientific discovery, the arts, and so on

EG (Egalitarian)
- Includes characters of more than one race, ethnicity, exceptionality, or nationality without making those differences an explicit focus of the story, or
- Focuses on characters of one cultural group, but characters from another cultural group could generally be substituted with little or no change in the plot

CR (Creative)
- Includes collections of poems, songs, fairy tales, folktales, myths, and legends associated with specific cultural groups based on country of origin, or influenced by the history of a people in a particular geographic area

Type of Book

The following codes denote the length and nature of the book:

PB: Picture book
NV: Novel or novella
SS: Compilation of short stories, legends, folktales, and so on
IT: Information book, predominantly text rather than pictures

Grade-Level Range

We have given the approximate level of interest and listening comprehension, not the readability level of the book. We know that you may have students whose abilities lie above or below our approximation; do not limit yourselves by the grade levels we suggest if you think another book is appropriate for your students!

NCSS Strands

Books can typically be used with more than one NCSS strand; we have indicated the Roman numerals of the strands with the strongest, most immediate relationships to the book's content. (See pages 00–00 for an introduction to these strands, and pages 00–00 for a listing of all the specific objectives or performance expectations associated with each strand as shown in Chapter 8.)

African American

Promote: Variety of occupations, physical features, settings; behaviors of leadership, problem solving, courage, pride, personal sacrifice; attitudes of faith, optimism, equality

Avoid: Exaggerated facial features and predominance of poverty, problems, single-parent homes, menial jobs, nonstandard English, overdependence on white benefactors

Adler, David. (1994). *A Picture Book of Sojourner Truth*. New York: Holiday House. Spellbinding account of the hardships of Sojourner Truth's childhood and young adulthood as a slave, followed by her ground-breaking successful lawsuits and years of travel to lecture about religion, slavery, and the rights of women. (IN/PB, grades 2–4, strands II, IV, V, VI)

Adler, David. (1993). *A Picture Book of Frederick Douglass*. New York: Holiday House. Fascinating history of the life and impact of the brilliant orator and writer, from birth in slavery to escape, marriage, and a life fighting against the evils of slavery. (IN/PB, grades 2–4, strands II, IV, VI)

Adler, David. (1992). *A Picture Book of Jesse Owens*. New York: Scholastic. Biography of the Olympic runner. (IN/PB, grades 2–4, strands II, IV, V, IX)

Adler, David. (1989). *A Picture Book of Martin Luther King, Jr.* New York: Holiday. Introduction to the life and contributions of this nonviolent man who contributed his entire life to the civil rights movement. (IN/PB, grades K–2, strands II, IV, V, VI)

Antle, Nancy. (1997). *Staying Cool.* New York: Dial Books for Young Children.
Young Curtis loves training at his grandfather's gym, but he must learn to control his temper and reactions when boxing. (EG/PB, grades K–3, strands IV, V)

Bains, Rae. (1982). *Harriet Tubman: The Road to Freedom.* Mahwah, NJ: Troll Associates.
Vivid biography of Harriet Tubman from childhood, through underground railroad activities, to post–Civil War civic accomplishments. (IN/IT, grades 3–4, strands IV, VI, X)

Barrett, Joyce. (1989). *Willie's Not the Hugging Kind.* New York: Harper & Row.
Because his friend says hugging is silly, Willie stops hugging his family. He tries hugging other things, like trees and stop signs, as he misses those hugs, then realizes he really wants family hugging and that hugs are not silly at all. (EG/PB, grades K–2, strands IV, V)

Battle-Lavert, Gwendolyn. (1995). *Off to School.* New York: Holiday House.
Wezielee, the youngest daughter in a sharecropping family, yearns to go to school, but must help her family by preparing and serving the noon meal each day. Her cooking grows worse each day until Papa and the family support her in going to school. (RE/PB, grades K–2, strands IV, V, VII)

Belton, Sandra. (1994). *May'naise Sandwiches & Sunshine Tea.* New York: Four Winds Press.
Little Miss enjoys sharing Big Mama's scrapbook of memories, especially those about her childhood friendship with a wealthier child and the lessons she learned about honor in dreams, goals, and determination. (EG/PB, grades 1–3, strands II, IV, V)

Bradby, Marie. (1995). *More Than Anything Else.* New York: Orchard Books.
Stunningly illustrated narrative account of the young Booker T. Washington's drive to learn to read and write amidst the long hours of labor in the salt mines of West Virginia. (IN/PB, grades K–3, strands II, IV, V, VII)

Brady, April. (1995). *Kwanzaa Karamu: Cooking and Crafts for a Kwanzaa Feast.* Minneapolis: Carolrhoda Books.
Information about Kwanzaa, followed by many recipes and craft designs. (IN/PB, grades 2–4, strands I, IV)

Bridges, Ruby. (1999). *Through My Eyes.* New York: Scholastic Press.
First-person account of a small girl's courage when integrating an elementary school in New Orleans. Powerful photographs and text inserts by others involved in the historic event, including Ruby's teacher, a child psychiatrist, and newspaper reports. (IN/IT, grades 3–4, strands V, VI, IV)

Burns, Khephra, and Miles, William. (1995). *Black Stars in Orbit: NASA's African American Astronauts.* San Diego: Gulliver Books.
Fascinating account of the struggles and successes of African American scientists and pilots in their quest to fully participate in the space program. Many valuable photographs. (IN/IT, grades 3–4+, strands II, V, VI, VIII)

Clifton, Lucille. (1973). *All Us Come Cross the Water.* New York: Holt, Rinehart and Winston.

A young boy experiences conflict with his teacher in a social studies lesson about geographic origins of class members, then turns to family and friends to explore his African heritage. He resolves his discomfort about the uncertainty of his ancestors' country in Africa when he realizes all African American people had come across the water. (RE/PB, grades 1–3, strands IV, II, IX)

Coleman, Evelyn. (1996*). White Socks Only*. Morton Grove, IL: Albert Whitman & Company.

A little girl sneaks away to go to town by herself years ago in Mississippi. Seeing a sign, "Whites Only," on a drinking fountain, she removes her shoes to step up in only her clean white socks. She and other blacks are beaten by an enraged white man until one old man intercedes in a mysterious way. (RE/PB, grades 1–3, strands II, IV, V, VI, X)

Curtis, Christopher. (1999). *Bud, Not Buddy*. New York: Delacorte Press.

The story of a 10-year-old motherless boy who escapes the perils of foster homes during the 1930s to search for his father with hopes of becoming a jazz musician. (RE/NV, grades 4+, strands I, IV, V)

Curtis, Gavin. (1998). *The Bat Boy and His Violin*. New York: Simon & Schuster.

The son of a coach in the Negro baseball league is in conflict with his father who wants him to work as a bat boy instead of playing his "fiddle." When the father realizes the beauty of the boy's violin playing is inspirational to the team and others, he learns new appreciation for his son's commitment. (RE/PB, grades K–3, strands IV, V)

English, Karen. (1996). *Neeny Coming, Neeny Going*. New York: Bridgewater Books.

A young girl on Daufuskie Island near South Carolina is thrilled that her favorite cousin is coming home for a visit. She is disappointed to find the cousin has changed and no longer enjoys the delights and customs of the island. (RE/PB, grades K–3, strands II, IV)

Ferris, Jeri. (1988). *Walking the Road to Freedom: A Story about Sojourner Truth*. Minneapolis: Carolrhoda Books.

A moving biography of Sojourner Truth, her pain and her passion, and the long-lasting effects she had on America. (IN/IT, grades 3–4+, strands I, II, III, V, VI, X)

Ferris, Jeri. (1988). *Go Free or Die*. Minneapolis: Carolrhoda Books.

A well-written chapter book about Harriet Tubman's childhood and first escape. Additional descriptions of her subsequent trips to free other slaves. Rich details and gripping accounts of danger. (IN/IT, grades 2–4, strands II, V, VI)

Flournoy, Valerie. (1995). *Tanya's Reunion*. New York: Dial Books for Young Readers.

Tanya visits the old farm with Grandma as they prepare for a family reunion. Homesick and disappointed in the farm at first, Tanya learns to appreciate the farm, its memories, and her place in the family. (RE/PB, grades K–2, strands II, IV, V)

Flournoy, Valerie. (1985). *The Patchwork Quilt*. New York: Dial Books for Young Readers.

Tanya and her family pick up the work on the family quilt when Grandma becomes too sick to continue. A story of love and memories through three generations of a family. (RE/PB, grades K–2, strands II, V)

Fox, Mem. (1994). *Sophie*. San Diego: Harcourt Brace & Company.
Vividly illustrated story of the love shared by Sophie and her grandfather from her birth to adulthood, then to his decline and death, then the birth of her baby. (EG/PB, grades K–1, strands IV, V)

Golenbock, Peter. (1990). *Teammates*. San Diego: Harcourt Brace Jovanovich.
Historical account of Jackie Robinson's courageous struggle as the first black player for a major league baseball team and Pee Wee Reese's also courageous stand to support and recognize him as a teammate against the opposition of his white friends, neighbors, and other team members. (IN/PB, grades 2–4, strands II, IV, X)

Greenfield, Eloise. (1977). *Mary McLeod Bethune*. New York: HarperCollins.
Very well-written biography of this incredible early educator who made her dreams come true for her own education and the education of many African American students who came along later. (IN/IT, grades 3–4, strands II, IV, X)

Greenfield, Eloise. (1974). *She Come Bringing Me That Little Baby Girl*. Philadelphia: Lippincott.
A little boy adjusts to the addition of a baby sister with the help of his understanding parents and a wise uncle. Tender award-winner. (RE/PB, grades K–2, strands IV, V)

Greenfield, Eloise. (1973). *Rosa Parks*. New York: HarperCollins.
Award-winning biography of this feisty woman known as the "Mother of the Civil Rights Movement." (IN/IT, grades 1–4, strands II, IV, VI, X)

Hamanaka, Sheila. (1995). *Peace Crane*. New York: Morrow Junior Books.
Lyrical plea to Sadako's peace crane from a young girl who is frightened by the violence in her city and hopes for peace throughout the world. (EG/PB, grades K–2, strands II, V, IX)

Hamilton, Virginia. (1985). *The People Could Fly*. New York: Alfred A. Knopf.
Compilation of tales told by slaves, typically with a second layer of meaning unrecognized by slave owners and focused on the theme of escape to freedom. Told in the Gullah dialect, with explanations, pronunciation guides, and glossary. (CR/SS, grades 3–4+, strands I, II, V, VI)

Havill, Juanita. (1995). *Jamaica's Blue Marker*. Boston: Houghton Mifflin.
Russell is annoying, and Jamaica is glad he's going to move away until she realizes the pain he's feeling. (EG/PB, grades K–2, strands IV, V)

Havill, Juanita. (1993). *Jamaica and Brianna*. Boston: Houghton Mifflin.
Jamaica and a classmate discover they both resent wearing hand-me-down boots when they trade insults and later apologize. (EG/PB, grades K–1, strands IV, V)

Havill, Juanita. (1989). *Jamaica Tag-Along*. Boston: Houghton Mifflin.
Jamaica discovers how older kids feel about the intrusion of younger ones, then learns the satisfaction of being gracious. (EG/PB, grades K–1, strands IV, V)

Havill, Juanita. (1986). *Jamaica's Find.* Boston: Houghton Mifflin.
When Jamaica brings home a stuffed animal she found in the park, her mother helps her realize the problems of her actions. After she takes the toy to the lost-and-found counter, she finds the girl hunting for it and happily takes *her* to the lost and found department. (EG/PB, grades K–2, strands IV, V, X)

Hill, Elizabeth. (1967). *Evan's Corner.* New York: Holt, Rinehart and Winston.
Evan longs for an area of his own in his family's small fourth-floor apartment in the busy city. Decorating and organizing his own corner seems to be the perfect solution until he realizes he wants to help his younger brother create his own special corner, too. (EG/PB, grades K–2, strands IV, V, VII)

Hoffman, Mary. (1996). *Boundless Grace.* New York: Dial Books for Young Readers.
Grace visits her father and his second family in Africa and adjusts to a stepmother and stepsiblings as well as a very different culture. (RE/PB, grades K–2, strands I, III, IV, V)

Hoffman, Mary. (1991). *Amazing Grace.* New York: Dial Books for Young Readers.
Bolstered by her mother's outrage and her grandmother's encouragement, Grace overcomes her classmates' resistance to a black child playing Peter Pan in the class play. Grace wins both the part and everyone's admiration. (RE/PB, grades K–2, strands IV, V)

Hooks, William. (1996). *Freedom's Fruit.* New York: Alfred A. Knopf.
A conjure tale of the Carolinas "low country" that is both haunting and hopeful. By casting a spell on the grapes, Mama Marina brought slaves Sheba and Joe Nathan to the point of death after eating the grapes, enabling her to buy them cheaply from the master, then lifted the spell as she sent them away to freedom. (CR/PB, grades 2–4, strands I, II, V, VI)

Hooks, William. (1990). *The Ballad of Belle Dorcas.* New York: Alfred A. Knopf.
A conjure tale of the Gullah people along the Carolina coastline and offshore islands. The story chronicles the life of a "free issue" girl and the slave she married. When the master sells him and forbids Belle Dorcas to go along, she has a cunger woman cast a spell to keep her husband with her forever. (CR/PB, grades 3–4, strands I, II, V, VI)

Hopkinson, Deborah. (1993). *Sweet Clara and the Freedom Quilt.* New York: Alfred A. Knopf.
After years of careful listening and stitching the map to freedom into a quilt, Clara and Young Jack escape slavery via the Underground Railroad to Canada, leaving behind the quilt for others to follow. (RE/PB, grades 2–4, strands II, III, IV, VI)

Howard, Elizabeth. (1995). *Papa Tells Chita a Story.* New York: Simon & Schuster Books for Young Readers.
A partly true, partly exaggerated story of a brave soldier's adventures during the Spanish-American War as told to his little girl. (CR/PB, grades K–2, strands II, IV, IX)

Johnson, Dolores. (1994). *Seminole Diary: Remembrances of a Slave.* New York: Macmillan.

Story of the relationship of black slaves and Seminole Indians in Florida who protected them from slave catchers. Conflict occurs when the youngest daughter is adopted by a Seminole family moving to the Everglades, and the rest of the tribe is forcibly shifted to a reservation in Oklahoma. (RE/PB, grades 2–4, strands I, II, III, V, VI)

Johnston, Tony. (1996). *The Wagon*. New York: Tambourine Books.

Seen through the eyes of a young slave boy, life and the land are both beautiful and hateful because he is not free to fully enjoy either one. The wagon he and his father built for the master finally carry them to freedom. (RE/PB, grades 2–4, strands IV, V, VI)

Keats, Ezra Jack. (1967). *Peter's Chair*. New York: Harper & Row.

Peter must adjust to the use of his outgrown things for a new baby sister. (EG/PB, grades K–2, strands IV, V).

Kelso, Richard. (1993). *Walking for Freedom: The Montgomery Bus Boycott*. New York: Stech-Vaughn Company.

Compelling account of the events and prejudicial treatment leading up to Rosa Parks's famous refusal to give up her seat on the bus to a white man and the subsequent 13-month black citizens' boycott of the bus system in Montgomery, Alabama, until laws and civic practices were changed. (IN/IT, grades 1–4, strands II, V, VI, VII, X)

Kent, Deborah. (1996). *African-Americans in the Thirteen Colonies*. New York: Children's Press.

Detailed account of Africans in early America who were free men, explorers, soldiers, indentured servants, and slaves. Shows how and why slavery of Africans became the norm in some areas when enslavement of Native Americans was unsuccessful, and the long-lasting problems resulting from that situation. (IN/IT, grades 3–4+, strands I, II, V, VI, IX)

King, Sarah. (1994). *Maya Angelou*. Brookfield, CT: The Millbrook Press.

Fascinating biography of this nation's great poet, from childhood separations and difficulties to the stresses of adulthood, from a variety of short-term jobs to singing in world tours, to singing in nightclubs, to writing and publishing poetry, and finally to writing and reading her poem for the 1993 presidential inauguration. (IN/IT, grades 3–4+, strands II, IV, VI)

Lester, Julius. (1998). *From Slave Ship to Freedom Road*. New York: Dial Books.

Arresting and sometimes brutally honest description and examination of the human and economic questions regarding slavery and human weaknesses. Powerful self-reflection activities for readers. (IN/PB, grades 4+, strands II, V, VII)

Livingston, Myra. (1994). *Keep on Singing: A Ballad of Marian Anderson*. New York: Holiday House.

A poetic and moving biography of the ground-breaking singer. Beautifully illustrated. (IN/PB, grades K–4, strands II, III, IV, V)

Mathis, Sharon. (1975). *The Hundred Penny Box*. New York: Viking Press.

A three-generation family experiences tension when the elderly grandmother's health is failing, and her highly stressed daughter-in-law wants to get rid of her old dirty box when cleaning up. The young child in the family understands her grandmother, respects the old box of memories, and mediates between them, revealing the uncanny love and acceptance of young and old. (RE/NV, grades 3–4, strands II, IV, V)

Mathis, Sharon. (1971). *Sidewalk Story*. New York: Viking Press.

Lilly Etta fights the eviction of her best friend's family from their apartment, seemingly to no avail. When an apparently disinterested reporter finds her asleep in the rain on the top of that family's belongings piled on the sidewalk, his news story about her commitment moves the community into action. (RE/NV, grades 3–4+, strands IV, V, VI, X)

McGovern, Ann. (1965). *"Wanted Dead or Alive." The True Story of Harriet Tubman*. New York: Scholastic.

A spell-binding account of Harriet Tubman's life and bravery from childhood to old age. (IN/PB, grades 2–4, strands II, III, IV, V, VI, X)

McKissack, Patricia, and McKissack, Fredrick. (1994). *African-American Inventors*. Brookfield, CT: The Millbrook Press.

Detailed and fascinating history of many amazing inventions and the African Americans who created them. (IN/IT, grades 4+, strands II, V, VI, VII, VIII)

McKissack, Patricia, and McKissack, Fredrick. (1989). *A Long Hard Journey: The Story of the Pullman Porter*. New York: Walker & Company.

Award-winning, powerful account of an early union fight against unfair labor practices, with the first African American union of Pullman porters making years of courageous sacrifices to eventually battle the corporate giant successfully. (IN/IT, grades 4+ strands II, V, VI, VII)

McKissack, Patricia, and McKissack, Fredrick. (1992). *Madam C. J. Walker*. Hillside, NJ: Enslow Publishers.

Easy-to-read biography of America's first self-made female millionaire. Creativity, economics, racial tensions, and philanthropy are all part of her story. (IN/IT, grades 1–3, strand VII)

Mead, Alice. (1995). *Junebug*. New York: Farrar Straus Giroux.

Provocative novel of a young boy in the inner city who must confront the dangers of drug dealers and gangs, protect his little sister, and somehow find and define himself with a powerful sense of integrity and hope. (RE/NV, grades 4+, strands IV, V)

Medearis, Angela. (1997). *Rum-A-Tum-Tum*. New York: Holiday House.

Brightly illustrated, poetic story of the street vendors, their wares, and their songs in turn-of-the-century New Orleans, as seen through the eyes of a young girl who loves the sights and sounds, but especially the parade. (EG/PB, grades K–2, strands III, VII)

Medearis, Angela. (1995). *Poppa's New Pants*. New York: Holiday House.

Sent to the general store to buy last-minute supplies before company arrives, Poppa and his son George also choose a new pair of pants for Poppa even though they need to be hemmed. Three different women refuse to hem the pants that night because of fatigue, then each in turn secretly hems them during the night. The resultant pants fit George instead. (EG/PB, grades K–2, strands II, V, VII)

Medearis, Angela. (1994). *Annie's Gifts*. Orange, NJ: Just Us Books.
Although everyone in her family is musically talented, Annie is simply not. With her father's help, Annie overcomes her feelings of failure by recognizing that her gifts lie in writing poetry and painting pictures instead. (EG/PB, grades K–2, strands IV, V)

Medearis, Angela. (1994). *Dare to Dream: Coretta Scott King and the Civil Rights Movement*. New York: Lodestar Books.
Fascinating biography of Coretta Scott King from childhood through widowhood, her dreams and ambitions, her support of Martin Luther King and his commitments, and her contributions to the civil rights movement. (IN/IT, grades 3–4, strands II, IV, V, VI)

Mendez, Phil. (1989). *The Black Snowman*. New York: Scholastic.
Jacob resents being poor and black until powerful magic occurs through a snowman he and his brother built from the grimy, sooty, black snow. Shown the pride and power of African warriors, Jacob gains the courage to save his brother from a fire and gains a clearer vision of who he is. (CR/PB, grades 3–4, strands IV, IX)

Miller, Robert. (1995). *Buffalo Soldiers: The Story of Emanuel Stance*. Morristown, NJ: Silver Press.
Exciting story of the first African American soldier to win a Congressional Medal of Honor, awarded for his exceptional bravery against Comanche warriors. Fascinating history of the Old West and the highly respected Buffalo Soldiers. (IN/PB, grades K–3, strands II, IV, V)

Miller, Robert. (1995). *The Story of Nat Love*. Morristown, NJ: Silver Press.
Brightly illustrated biography of the famous cowboy, Nat Love (AKA Deadwood Dick) from a childhood of slavery on a Tennessee plantation to his adventures in the West. (IN/PB, grades K–3, strands II, IV)

Mitchell, Margaree King. (1993). *Uncle Jed's Barbershop*. New York: Scholastic.
Sarah Jean's favorite uncle cuts hair and dreams of owning his own barbershop. He sacrifices that dream and his life savings to pay for an operation to save her life, then begins saving again. When the bank fails and his money is lost, he starts again. He helps others survive during the depression and starts saving yet again. Eventually his dream comes true. (RE/PB, grades K–2, strands II, V, VII)

Mitchell, Rhonda. (1997). *The Talking Cloth*. New York: Orchard Books.
Amber is fascinated with her aunt's collection of things from her travels, especially her *adinkra*, or "talking cloth" from Ghana. Amber learns about the symbols and their rich meanings as she imagines herself to be an Ashanti princess among her akinkra-wearing family. (RE/PB, grades K–2, strands I, IV, V)

Myers, Walter Dean. (1993). *Young Martin's Promise*. New York: Dialogue Systems.
The first puzzling experiences with segregation laws and customs formed the basis for Martin Luther King Jr.'s later efforts to champion the civil rights of African Americans. (IN/PB, grades K–1, strands II, V, VI)

Paulsen, Gary. (1993). *Nightjohn*. New York: Delacorte Press.

Story of the fear, courage, and mistreatment of slaves who risked their lives to learn to read and write and the escaped slave who secretly taught them. (RE/NV, grades 4+, strands II, IV, V, VI)

Pilkey, Dav. (1996). *The Paperboy*. New York: Orchard Books.
Early-morning activities of a young boy delivering newspapers with pride. (EG/PB, grades K–1, strands IV, VII)

Pinkney, Andrea. (1998). *Duke Ellington*. New York: Hyperion Books for Children.
Bright and stylish illustrations accompany a lively text about the Duke and his powerful contributions to music. (IN/PB, grades 2–4, strands I, IV, V)

Pinkney, Andrea. (1994). *Dear Benjamin Banneker*. San Diego: Harcourt Brace & Company.
An account of the phase of Benjamin Banneker's life when he developed the first almanac published by a black man and corresponded with Thomas Jefferson about racism and the need for changes in the lives of black people. (IN/PB, grades 3–4, strands V, VI, VII, VIII)

Ringgold, Faith. (1992). *Aunt Harriet's Underground Railroad in the Sky*. New York: Crown Publishers.
Mixing young Cassie's present-day fantasy with a sojourn into history, this dramatic picture book traces Harriet Tubman's route used to help slaves escape. (CR+IN/PB, grades K–4, strands II, III, V, VI)

Ringgold, Faith. (1991). *Tar Beach*. New York: Crown Publishers.
Picnicking on the tar-paper roof of their tenement apartment in Harlem, Cassie imagines flying over the city and helping her family. Her father has been excluded from the union of construction workers because of racial discrimination. Multiple award-winning book. (CR+RE/PB, grades K–4, strands V, VII)

Ritter, Lawrence. (1995*). Leagues Apart: The Men and Times of the Negro Baseball Leagues*. New York: Morrow Junior Books.
Fast-paced lively material about great baseball players and their prejudicial treatment that much of the world never knew about. (IN/PB, grades 2–4, strands II, V, VI)

Rosen, Michael. (1995). *A School for Pompey Walker*. San Diego: Harcourt Brace & Company.
Based on many true stories, an old man tells his life story to young schoolchildren—a story of slavery and so-called freedom. He tells of raising money through incredible and courageous trickery to build a school for young "Negro" children who have escaped to Ohio, and how a new school, named for him, eventually replaced that first four-room school, "Sweet Freedom." (RE/NV, grades 3–4, strands II, IV)

Schlissel, Lillian. (1995*). Black Frontiers: A History of African American Heroes in the Old West*. New York: Simon & Schuster Books for Young Readers.
Many fascinating histories of African Americans' participation in and contributions to the development of the west after the Civil War. (IN/SS, grades 3–4+, strands II, III, V)

Schroeder, Alan. (1996). *Minty: A Story of Young Harriet Tubman*. New York: Dial Books for Young Readers.

Based on actual events during Harriet Tubman's childhood of slavery and mistreatment, the fictionalized narrative shows her rebellious spirit and drive for freedom that led to her courageous adult life. (RE/PB, grades K–3, strands II, III, V, VI)

Schroeder, Alan. (1995). *Carolina Shout!* New York: Dial Books for Young Readers.

Set in Charleston, South Carolina, before World War II, the story shows a young girl walking through town, enjoying hearing music in every sound pattern, but especially in the short songs, or "shouts" of the street vendors. (RE/PB, grades 1–3, strands I, II, VII)

Steptoe, Javaka (Illustrator). (1997). *In Daddy's Arms I Am Tall*. New York: Lee and Low Books.

Exceptional poems honoring African American fathers. Striking collages celebrate each poem. (CR/PB, grades K–4, strands I, IV)

Stolz, Mary. (1988). *Storm in the Night*. New York: Harper & Row.

Thomas seeks the company of his grandfather during a frightening thunderstorm. His grandfather understands his feelings, tells a story of being frightened by a storm when he was a child, and sensitively convinces Thomas that such fear is quite natural. (EG/PB, grades K–2, strands II, IV)

Taylor, Mildred. (1995). *The Well*. New York: Dial Books for Young Readers.

In another story of the Logan family, David and his brother, Hammer, are young boys wrestling with their anger about racial injustices and their awareness of what behavior was necessary for survival in Mississippi in the early 1900s. Their young white tormentors are eventually caught for their misdeeds, and the Logan family's dignity is maintained. (RE/NV, grades 3–4+, strands II, III, IV, V, VI)

Taylor, Mildred. (1987). *The Friendship*. New York: Bantam Skylark.

A poignant novella of an era when friendships between blacks and whites were uncommon, viewed with suspicion by blacks and denied by whites. When Tom Bee brings his lifelong friendship with John Wallace into public view by calling his white "friend" by his first name in front of other whites, John shoots Tom Bee in the leg to preserve his social status in the white community. (RE/NV, grades 4+, strands I, II, IV, V, X)

Taylor, Mildred. (1987). *The Gold Cadillac*. New York: Bantam Skylark.

An arresting novella focusing on family conflicts about the use of money to buy a new car instead of saving to buy a house, then subsequent conflict with the law when the family drives their new car through the South and are suspected of stealing it simply because they are black. Family unity and strength prevail. (RE/NV, grades 3–4+, strands II, V, VI)

Taylor, Mildred. (1975). *Song of the Trees*. New York: Dial Books.

The Logan children, known to older readers in *Roll of Thunder, Hear My Cry*, work to save their precious trees from a cheating businessman who was not going to pay for their true value. (RE/NV, grades 3–4+, strands III, V, VI, VII)

Thomas, Joyce. (1998). *I Have Heard of a Land*. New York: Joanna Cotler Books.

Breathtaking illustrations and poetry tell the story of newly freed African Americans settling the West during the homesteading period of the Oklahoma Territory. (IN/PB, grades 2–4, strands II, III, V, VII)

Thomassie, Tynia. (1996). *Mimi's Tutu*. New York: Scholastic.

Richly surrounded with family and family traditions, Mimi attends African dance classes with her mother. Suddenly and surprisingly jealous of another child's tutu and dancing ability, Mimi grows quiet and thoughtful. Her grandmother gives her the gift of a magnificent African *lapa* to wear instead of a typical tutu. Mimi wears it to the next dance class and proudly celebrates her ancestry. (RE/PB, grades K–2, strands I, IV, V)

Walker, Alice. (1991). *Finding the Green Stone*. New York: Harcourt Brace Jovanovich.

Beautifully illustrated story of a community in which everyone has a metaphorically special green stone. When Johnny loses his stone, everyone helps him search, but he realizes that only he can find his stone, and he can do so only when he rejects envy and reclaims the love in his heart. (CR+EG/PB, grades 2–4, strands IV, V, X)

Walter, Mildred Pitts. (1990). *Two and Too Much*. New York: Bradbury Press.

Humorous story of a boy helping his mother by babysitting his 2-year-old sister and constantly cleaning up the havoc she created. (EG/PB, grades K–1, strands IV, V)

Walter, Mildred Pitts. (1989). *Have a Happy . . . .* New York: Lothrop, Lee & Shepard.

Chris is miserable when his father is out of work at Christmas, money is short, and his birthday falls on Christmas Day with no prospect of the bicycle he wants so badly. The story is interwoven with information about the celebration of Kwanzaa, and the principles of Kwanzaa are realized in very tangible ways. (RE/NV, grades 3–4+, strands I, IV, V, VII)

Walter, Mildred Pitts. (1986). *Justin and the Best Biscuits in the World*. New York: Lothrop, Lee & Shepard.

Justin leaves the teasing and scolding of his sisters and mother behind in the city as he visits with his grandfather on his ranch. There he learns to cook and clean, to enjoy the variety of work a man can do. Winning ribbons at a rodeo festival tops off his visit. He cooks supper for his family the first night back home and amazes all of them. (RE/NV, grades 3–4+, strands III, IV, V)

Walter, Mildred Pitts. (1983). *My Mama Needs Me*. New York: Lothrop, Lee & Shepard.

Jason overreacts to the possibility that his mother might need him because of the new baby. He cuts himself off from friends and neighbors because his "mama might need" him. Frustrated over the baby sleeping and his mother resting so much, Jason realizes being needed doesn't mean all the time. (RE/PB, grades K–2, strands IV, V)

Williams, Sherley. (1992). *Working Cotton*. Orlando: Harcourt Brace Jovanovich.

Story of a workday as seen through the eyes of Shelan, the young daughter of migrant workers. With powerful illustrations, the story chronicles the pre-dawn bus ride, the cold, the labor, the family's closeness, and the long hours, using authentic dialect. (RE/PB, grades K–1, strands V, VII)

Winter, Jeanette. (1988). *Follow the Drinking Gourd*. New York: Alfred A. Knopf.
Powerfully illustrated and narrated story of the terrors and triumphs of the Underground Railroad movement, told from the perspective of escaping slaves, with additional historical information provided about the song and people who guided them to freedom. (IN/PB, grades K–3, strands II, III, V, VI)

Yarbrough, Camille. (1979). *Cornrows*. New York: Coward, McCann and Geoghegan.
Beautifully illustrated book showing how different styles of braided hair symbolize many qualities of human beings, such as courage, honor, and wisdom. References to many historically significant African Americans are woven into the story. (RE/PB, grades 1–4, strands I, II)

Asian American

Promote: Variety of physical features and settings; value and honor associated with family, education, obedience, culture, religion, resilience, and independence

Avoid: Exaggerated facial features; predominance of nonstandard English, passivity or subservience, model behavior of children; stereotypical jobs as launderers, gardeners, waiters, and house servants

Balgassi, Haemi. (1996). *Peacebound Trains*. New York: Clarion Books.
After her father's death, young Sumi lives with her grandmother while her mother spends time in the Army with the promise of a financed college education and a teaching career. Sumi is lonely, and sits gazing at a train, wishing it would bring her mother home. Her grandmother tells of riding such a train away from her beloved husband at his urging in order to escape the ravages of war in Korea and to save their two small children. Her husband died in that war, but they affirm together that Sumi's mother will come home one day. (RE/NV, grades 3–4, strands II, V, IX)

Bang, Molly. (1985). *The Paper Crane*. New York: Greenwillow Books.
A restaurant struggling to survive economically is visited one evening by a stranger who, after being generously fed by the poor owner and his helper, folds a paper napkin into the shape of a crane and gives it to them in payment for the meal. For many months, the paper crane would come alive at the clap of their hands, and the restaurant thrived with new business. Such success continued even after the stranger returned and flew away on the back of his crane. (CR/PB, grades K–4, strand VII)

Bunting, Eve. (1982). *The Happy Funeral*. New York: Harper & Row.
A young child's sadness, understanding, and acceptance of her grandfather's

death as the family pays respects in a mixture of Chinese and American traditions. (RE/NV, grades 2–4, strands I, IV, V)

Cha, Dia. (1996). *Dia's Story Cloth*. New York: Lee and Low Books.

Using photographs of sections her hand-embroidered Hmong story cloth, the author tells of her family's journey over the years through various Asian countries, in refugee camps, and finally to America. (IN/PB, grades 2–4+, strands II, III, V, VI)

Chang, Heidi. (1988). *Elaine, Mary Lewis, and the Frogs*. New York: Crown Publishers.

When Elaine moves from San Francisco to Iowa, she is lonely and feels out of place. For a school project, she and classmate Mary Lewis build a frog kite together with the help of Elaine's father, learn interesting history of Chinese kites, and greatly impress the class. (RE/NV, grades 3–4, strands I, II, IV, V))

Chin, Steven. (1993). *When Justice Failed: The Fred Korematsu Story*. New York: Steck-Vaughn Company.

Biography of a Japanese American man imprisoned in U.S. Army internment campus during World War II and his 40-year battle to win from the U.S. government an apology and compensation for all those so imprisoned. (IN/IT, grades 3–4+, strands V, VI, IX, X)

Coerr, Eleanor. (1988). *Chang's Paper Pony*. New York: Harper & Row.

A lonely Chinese immigrant working with his grandfather in a rough gold mining camp, Chang longs for his own pony. He pans unsuccessfully for gold, then sweeps gold dust from a miner's cabin floor and receives a pony as a reward from the grateful miner. (RE/NV, grades K–2, strands II, V, VII)

Friedman, Ina. (1984). *How My Parents Learned to Eat*. Boston: Houghton Mifflin.

Humorous account of her parents' courtship told by a young girl. Her American sailor-father tries to eat with chopsticks while her Japanese mother tries to handle silverware so that they can learn each other's way of eating. They marry, and their daughter is pleased to eat both ways. (RE/PB, grades K–2, strands I, IV, V)

Garland, Sherry. (1993). *The Lotus Seed*. San Diego: Harcourt Brace & Company.

Touching story of Vietnamese American grandchildren glimpsing the painful history of their grandmother's war-torn past. Powerful focus on her pride and hope for the future. (RE/PB, grades K–2, strands II, V)

Gogol, Sara. (1996). *A Mien Family*. Minneapolis: Lerner Publications Company.

A blending of American and traditional Mien customs for this family who has emigrated to the United States. (IN/IT, grades 4+, strands I, II, V, IX)

Hamanaka, Sheila. (1990). *The Journey: Japanese Americans, Racism, and Renewal*. New York: Orchard Books.

Inspired by her own 25-foot mural depicting the horrors of the Japanese American concentration camps, the author/artist tells the story of her family and others by using parts of the mural interwoven with bold text. (IN/PB, grades 3–4+, strands I, II, III, V, VI, IX)

Heo, Yumi. (1995*). Father's Rubber Shoes*. New York: Orchard Books.
   A young Korean American boy is homesick for his friends in Korea and has not yet made friends in the Unites States. His father comforts him with a story about the rubber shoes he loved as a child and how he wants to give Yungsu something of permanent value as the reason for being in their new country. (RE/PB, grades K–2, strands III, IV)

Hoyt-Goldsmith, Diane. (1992). *Hoang Anh: A Vietnamese-American Boy*. New York: Holiday House.
   The first of his family to be born in America, Hoang Anh mixes ordinary American activities like school and football with traditional Vietnamese celebrations, food, and gifts. Rich photographs. (IN/IT, grades 3–4+, strands I, II, III, V, IX)

Kidd, Diana. (1989). *Onion Tears*. New York: Orchard Books.
   Moving story of a young refugee from Vietnam who feels so much pain and loss that she can neither speak nor cry during a long difficult period of adjustment to the United States. (RE/NV, grades 3–4, strands III, IV, V, IX)

Kraus, Joanna. (1992). *Tall Boy's Journey*. Minneapolis: Carolrhoda Books
   Fictionalized, compelling story based on the experiences of the author and her adopted son who came from Korea at age 8½. Startling and painful insights into the many adjustments and initial misunderstandings of such a cross-cultural adoption. (RE/NV, grades 3–4+, strands I, IV, V)

Lee, Milly. (1997). *Nim and the War Effort*. New York: Farrar, Straus and Giroux.
   Nim is gathering newspapers in Chinatown for the paper drive during World War II. Her conflicts with a cheating boy who doesn't consider her an American and with an austere grandfather are resolved with an unusual kind of help from the police. (RE/PB, grades 2–4, strands I, IV, V)

Levine, Ellen. (1989). *I Hate English!* New York: Scholastic.
   Mei Mei resists learning English when she moves from China to New York and must attend school. Although she quickly understands most of what she hears, Mei Mei worries about losing her identity and refuses to speak English until tricked in the most delightful way by an understanding teacher. (RE/PB, grades 1–3, strands I, III, IV, V)

Little, Mimi. (1996). *Yoshiko and the Foreigner*. New York: Frances Foster Books.
   In telling some of her family history, the author shares the story of a young couple in love and how they first bridged the two different cultures of Japan and America. (RE/PB, grades 1–4, strands I, V)

Namioka, Lensey. (1995). *Yang the Third and Her Impossible Family*. Boston: Little, Brown.
   Rolicking story of a Chinese American immigrant family and their mishaps in adjusting to American customs. Centers on Yingmei, or "Mary," and her drive for the acceptance of her peers as she comes to realize the universal value of honesty in friendship. (RE/NV, grades 3–4+, strands I, IV, V)

Nunes, Susan. (1995). *The Last Dragon*. New York: Clarion Books.
   Peter discovers a dirty, torn dragon in a shop while staying with his aunt in Chinatown. He helps various shopkeepers all summer in exchange for their

repairs of parts of the dragon until it is fully mended and magnificent. (RE/PB, grades 2–3, strands I, IV, V, VII)

O'Connor, Karen. (1992). *Dan Thuy's New Life in America*. Minneapolis: Lerner Publications.

Account of a Vietnamese's family's transition from Vietnam, through a refugee camp in Thailand, to settlement in southern California. Sensitive depiction of the mixture of feelings toward both countries and cultures, and the determination to overcome adversity. (IN/IT, grades 4+, strands I, II, IV, V, IX)

Paek, Min. (1978). *Aekyung's Dream*. San Francisco: Children's Book Press.

A recent immigrant from Korea, Aekyung struggles with ethnic identity, fitting in, and adjusting to a sometimes hostile classroom. She dreams of an earlier age of royalty in Korea and finds strength to be herself, then subsequently becomes accepted by her classmates. (RE/PB, grades 1–3, strands I, IV, V)

Rattigan, Jama. (1993). *Dumpling Soup*. Boston: Little, Brown.

Delightful story of an extended family living in Hawaii, a family so blended with Korean, Japanese, Chinese, Native Hawaiian, and white that one grandmother calls them "chop suey" (all mixed up). For the New Year's Eve gathering, young Marisa makes dumplings that don't look quite right, but they taste great and earn her much praise. (RE/PB, grades K–2, strands I, IV, V)

Sakai, Kimiko. (1990). *Sachiko Means Happiness*. San Francisco: Children's Book Press.

Young Japanese American Sachiko is distressed and resentful about the changes in her grandmother. When she begins to understand the effects of her grandmother's Alzheimer's disease, she becomes a protective caregiver. (EG/PB, grades K–2, strands IV, V)

Say, Allen. (1999). *Tea with Milk*. Boston: Houghton Mifflin.

After her high school graduation in San Francisco, May's parents decide to return to their homeland of Japan. May is miserable until she strikes a balance between her American culture and the possibilities in Japan. She eventually meets and marries a young man, and the author is their first child. (RE/PB, grades 2–4, strands I, IV, V).

Say, Allen. (1996). *Emma's Rug*. Boston: Houghton Mifflin.

Attached to the rug given her as a baby, Emma amazes everyone with her prolonged gazing at the rug and her early ability to draw and paint. When the rug is ruined in the washer, Emma weeps, throws away her artwork and prizes, and stops drawing altogether. One day, she again sees the visions of her own creative imagination and realizes she can still draw without the rug. (EG/PB, grades K–2, strand IV)

Say, Allen. (1993). *Grandfather's Journey*. Boston: Houghton Mifflin.

Poignant story of the author's grandfather and himself, focused on their love for both Japan and California and their joy in each setting coupled with longing for the other. (IN/PB, grades K–4, strands I, II, III, IV, V)

Say, Allen. (1990). *El Chino*. Boston: Houghton Mifflin.

True story of Bong Way "Billy" Wong, a Chinese American whose immigrant father taught him that growing up in America meant he could be anything he wanted to be. An aspiring and excellent basketball player, Billy was too short to become the professional player of his dreams. He turned to engineering, but was restless. On his first vacation, he went to Spain and discovered the lure of bullfighting. Billy set a new goal and reached it—to become a famous matador. (IN/PB, grades K–3, strands I, III, IV, V, IX)

Stanley, Fay. (1991). *The Last Princess: The Story of Princess Ka'iulani of Hawai'i*. New York: Four Winds Press.

Biographical account of the last princess of Hawaii, who did not become its queen because the United States annexed Hawaii. (IN/IT, grades 4+, strands II, III, V, VI)

Surat, Michele Maria. (1983). *Angel Child, Dragon Child*. New York: Scholastic.

Homesick for Vietnam and her mother, Ut wrestles with cross-cultural teasing and lack of understanding from classmates in New York City. Her conflicts with one child mount until the principal forces the two children to create a solution. Their ideas draw many diverse people closer together and bring Ut's mother to New York. (RE/PB, grades 1–3, strands I, IV, V, VII)

Tunnell, Michael, and Chilcoat, George. (1996). *The Children of Topaz: The Story of a Japanese-American Internment Camp*. New York: Holiday House.

The book is created around the daily diaries kept by Japanese American third-graders while they were "relocated" to the internment camp in Topaz, Utah, during World War II. Although facing hardships and injustices, the children wrote of normal events, such as playing with animals, having class parties, and worry about illnesses. They also wrote of war-related problems, such as bombers flying overhead, making blankets for the Red Cross, and relatives joining the army. (IN/IT, grades 4+, strands II, III, V, VI, IX)

Uchida, Yoshiko. (1993). *The Bracelet*. New York: Philomel.

Forced from her home in California during World War II, Emi wears a bracelet given to her by her best friend as she and her family enter a U.S. concentration camp for Japanese Americans. She adjusts to the loss of her home, her best friend, and then the bracelet. (RE/PB, grades 2–4, strands II, III, IV, V, VI, IX, X)

Waters, Kate, and Slovenz-Low, Madeline. (1990). *Lion Dancer: Ernie Wan's Chinese New Year*. New York: Scholastic.

An exceptionally beautiful photographic study and fascinating description of a family in New York City as they prepare for and celebrate the Chinese New Year. (IN/PB, grades K–2, strands I, V)

Whelan, Gloria. (1992). *Goodbye, Vietnam*. New York: Random House.

Unforgettable story of a family's escape from Vietnam, including the difficult conditions on the overcrowded boat and at the refugee camp in Hong Kong as they awaited clearance to emigrate to America. (RE/NV, grades 4+, strands III, IV, V, VI, IX)

Wong, Janet. (2000). *The Trip Back Home*. San Diego: Harcourt.

A little girl and her mother travel back to Korea to spend time with her grandparents and aunt. Fascinating accounts of their arrival, gift giving, activities, and departure. (RE/PB, grades K–1, strands I, III, V)

Caribbean and Caribbean American

Promote: Variety of appearances and occupations; attitudes of problem solving, family closeness

Avoid: Attitudes of laziness; predominance of poverty, lack of education, and nonstandard English

Binch, Caroline. (1994). *Gregory Cool*. New York: Dial Books for Young Readers.
  Gregory, a "cool" American youngster, has come to visit his grandparents in Tobago. Adjusting to their tiny house, unfamiliar food, the heat, and no TV was not easy. Gradually, he comes to enjoy his cousin, the beach, coconut milk, and the possibilities of an enjoyable four weeks. (RE/PB, grades 1–2, strands II, III, IV, V)

Bunting, Eve. (1988). *How Many Days to America?* New York: Clarion Books.
  A family and other community members flee an oppressive government, relinquishing all their money and valuable possessions for passage on a decrepit boat. The journey is extremely perilous, but they maintain hope and courage, then are welcomed upon arrival in the United States. (RE/PB, grades 1–4, strands III, V, VI)

Dorris, Michael. (1992). *Morning Girl*. New York: Hyperion Books for Children.
  Set in the Bahamas at the time of Christopher Columbus's discovery of these islands, Morning Girl and her brother, Star Boy, tell the story of their lives and their community through times of trouble and celebration. (RE/NV, grades 3–4, strands I, III, V)

Gordon, Ginger. (1993). *My Two Worlds*. New York: Clarion Books.
  Young Kirsy Rodriguez shares in photographs and narrative her two worlds of New York City and Puerto Plata in the Dominican Republic. She enjoys family, friends, activities, and the environment in each world. (RE/PB, grades K–2, strands I, III, IV, V)

Hanson, Regina. (1995). *The Tangerine Tree*. New York: Clarion Books.
  Ida struggles to understand the economic necessity of her father leaving their beloved island of Jamaica to find work in New York and how to adjust to his absence. (RE/PB, grades K–2, strands III, IV, VII)

Picó, Fernando. (1991). *The Red Comb*. Mahwah, NJ: BridgeWater Books.
  Set in nineteenth-century Puerto Rico, the story is an outgrowth of the local folklore and stories of runaway slaves. Despite the common expectations that black families would help slavecatchers in exchange for badly needed cash, one young girl and an old widow conspire to save the life of a young woman

and outwit the slavecatcher in clever ways that frighten him away. (RE/PB, grades K–3, strands I, II, V, VI)

Pomerantz, Charlotte. (1989). *The Chalk Doll*. Philadelphia: Lippincott.

One day at naptime, Rose asks for stories about her mother's childhood in Jamaica, including those about a birthday party, porcelain "chalk" dolls in stores being preferred over homemade rag dolls, and high-heeled shoes made from mango pits. Instead of napping, she gets up to make a rag doll with her mother. (RE/PB, grades K–2, strands I, II, IV)

European American

Promote: Variety of physical appearances, settings, social classes, and occupations; values of independence, generosity, justice, family, education; skills of problem solving and making choices

Avoid: Predominance of prejudicial treatment of others, especially minorities; extreme independence or freedom from social norms; extreme competitiveness; predominance of wealth and success in all endeavors

Adler, David. (1990). *A Picture Book of Helen Keller*. New York: Holiday House.

The difficulties and triumphs of Helen Keller after an illness left her both blind and deaf. (IN/PB, grades K–3, strands IV, V)

Alexander, Sally. (1992). *Maggie's Whopper*. New York: Macmillan.

Although intent on catching a fish larger than her brother's, Maggie doesn't hesitate to throw her large trout to a marauding bear in order to save her elderly uncle's life. (EG/PB, grades 1–3, strands IV, V)

Ancona, George. (1990). *Riverkeeper*. New York: Macmillan.

One man's passionate effort to keep the Hudson River clean despite various problems of pollution. Outstanding photographs. (IN/PB, grades 2–4+, strands III, VI, VIII, X)

Anderson, Joan. (1986). *Pioneer Children of Appalachia*. New York: Clarion Books.

Photographed at a living history museum, the book provides rich, realistic details of pioneer life in the Appalachian Mountains. Emphasis on the self-sufficiency of the pioneer families. (IN/PB, grades 2–4, strands V, III, VII)

Andrews, Jan. (1991). *The Auction*. New York: Macmillan.

While preparing to auction off the farm, Todd and his grandfather share memories with sadness and humor, then begin to adjust to the change through a most delightful creative activity begun by his deceased grandmother as a child. (EG/PB, grades 1–3, strands II, V)

Ballard, Robert. (1993). *Finding the Titanic*. New York: Scholastic.

A fascinating and respectful account of the first sighting of the sunken *Titanic*, with historical references to its tragedy. (RE/PB, grades 1–3, strands II, III, VIII)

Bartoletti, Susan. (1996). *Growing Up in Coal Country*. Boston: Houghton Mifflin.
Gripping account of the horrendous treatment of coal miners and their families, including the widespread abuse of child labor, in earlier years of the United States. Depicts pride and unity of coal-mining families in the face of extreme hardships. (IN/IT, grades 4+, strands II, III, IV, V, VI, VII, VIII)

Bartone, Elisa. (1996). *American Too*. New York: Lothrop, Lee & Shepard.
As a recent immigrant from Italy, Rosie experiences conflict between her family maintaining Italian traditions and her desire to fit in with Americans, to be "modern." As queen of a parade in her community, Rosie breaks tradition in a way that suits everyone by dressing as the Statue of Liberty. (RE/PB, grades 2–3, strands I, II, IV, V)

Bartone, Elisa. (1993). *Peppe the Lamplighter*. New York: Lothrop, Lee & Shepard.
Against his father's wishes, young Peppe finds temporary work as a lamplighter in the pre-electricity days of Little Italy in New York City. He works with pride and hopes for the future despite his father's displeasure until his father realizes the importance of his son's contribution. (RE/PB, grades 2–3, strands II, V, VII, VIII, IX)

Baylor, Byrd. (1982). *The Best Town in the World*. New York: Charles Scribner's Sons.
A father's recollection of the amazing perfection of his childhood town are enjoyed and questioned by his family. (EG/PB, grades 1–3, strands II, V)

Beard, Darleen. (1995). *The Pumpkin Man from Piney Creek*. New York: Simon & Schuster Books for Young Readers.
Young Hattie sees a jack-o-lantern and longs to make one, but their pumpkin harvest must be sold for family income. The kindly buyer returns to her the one he cut to test, since he can't sell it, and she makes her first jack-o-lantern. (EG/PB, grades K–3, strands VII)

Bethel, Jean. (1980). *Three Cheers for Mother Jones*. New York: Holt, Rinehart and Winston.
Fictionalized account of one instance of Mother Jones's undying efforts to rid the country of its child labor practices and the barriers she encountered. (RE/IT, grades 1–3, strands II, IV, V, VI, VII)

Bial, Raymond. (1998). *Cajun Home*. Boston: Houghton Mifflin.
Fascinating account of the history of the Cajun people, from France to Canada, through persecution and dispersement, and eventually to the bayous of Louisiana. With vivid photographs, the author shares the life and culture of this close-knit, complex people. (IN/IT, grades 3–4+, strands I, II, V)

Boulton, Jane. (1994). *Only Opal: The Diary of a Young Girl*. New York: Philomel Books.
Based on the diary of Opal Whiteley, a young orphan girl in the early 1900s who expressed both her loneliness and inner strength as she lived with and worked for a family in the lumber camps of Oregon. (RE/PB, grades 2–3, strands IV, V, VII)

Bunting, Eve. (1997). *On Call Back Mountain*. New York: The Blue Sky Press.
Stunning, nearly mystical story of the relationship of two young boys, a tall old man who serves as the lookout in the fire tower each summer, and the

long-awaited return of a wolf the night after the old man dies. (EG/PB, grades 1–3, strands III, V)

Bunting, Eve. (1996). *Train to Somewhere*. New York: Clarion Books.

One of 13 orphans sent by train from New York to the midwest, Marianne hopes a family will adopt her. Passed over by prospective parents at every stop, she is the last one on the train until, after mutual disappointment, she finds an accepting family. (EG/PB, grades 3–4, strands II, III, IV, VI, X)

Bunting, Eve. (1995). *Dandelions*. San Diego: Harcourt Brace & Company.

In moving by covered wagon from Illinois to a homestead in the plains of Nebraska, Zoe and her family face many challenges. There are no trees nor close neighbors, and Zoe's pregnant mother is sad and unsure of the wisdom of their move. Zoe brightens her mother's birthday by planting dandelions on top of their sod house. (RE/PB, grades 1–2, strands II, III, V)

Bunting, Eve. (1991). *Fly Away Home*. New York: Clarion Books.

Courageous story of a homeless young boy and his father who stay in an airport, perfecting the art of not being noticeable. The boy maintains his sense of hope by remembering the bird he watched for days when it was trapped, frightened and struggling, until a door opened and it escaped. (EG/PB, grades 3–4, strands V, VI, VII, X)

Bushnell, Jack. (1996). *Sky Dancer*. New York: Lothrop, Lee & Shepard.

A young girl and a redtail hawk form a special bond that is threatened when neighboring farmers complain of missing chickens and set out to shoot a marauding hawk. (EG/PB, grades 1–4, strands IV, VII)

Byars, Betsy. (1972). *The House of Wings*. New York: Viking Press.

Free-spirited Sammy is left with his eccentric grandfather while his parents seek jobs and housing in the city. Sammy reacts with disbelief and rage until his grandfather enlists his help in caring for an injured, blind crane. Sammy learns to accept his situation and to appreciate life with his grandfather and the variety of wild birds who share his farmhouse. (EG/NV, grades 3–4+, strands III, IV, V)

Cahn, Rhoda, and Cahn, William. (1972). *No Time for School, No Time for Play: The Story of Child Labor in America*. New York: Julian Messner.

Chilling story with haunting photographs of the widespread abuse of children through unfair labor practices in the United States, including slavery, apprenticeships, migrant farm work, and employment in unsafe coal mines and factories. (IN/IT, grades 4+, strands II, IV, V, VII)

Calhoun, Mary. (1997). *Flood*. New York: Morrow Junior Books.

A family works together to protect their home and community during the Midwest floods of 1993. Despite having to evacuate, they recognize how fortunate they are to have each other. (EG/PB, grades 1–3, strands III, V)

Carlson, Laurie. (1998). *Boss of the Plains: The Hat That Won the West*. New York: DK Publishing.

Fascinating account of how the Stetson cowboy hat was invented, marketed, and distributed, as well as why it became so popular. (IN/PB, grades 2–4, strands III, VII)

Cleary, Beverly. (1983). *Dear Mr. Henshaw*. New York: Morrow.
> A young boy writes to his favorite author about his struggles in adjusting to his parents' divorce, life in a new place, and his father's absence. (RE/NV, grades 3–4, strands IV, V)

Coerr, Eleanor. (1986). *The Josefina Story Quilt*. New York: Harper & Row.
> A family moves westward in a wagon train with a pet hen who is mostly trouble, but saves their belongings from thieves one night. Young Faith works on a quilt to tell the story of their journey and her beloved hen's death. (EG/NV, grades 1–2, strands II, III, V)

Cohen, Barbara. (1982). *Gooseberries to Oranges*. New York: Lothrop, Lee & Shepard.
> Story of the difficult journey of a young girl emigrating from Russia to the United States during the early twentieth century. When she earns her first dime, she spends half of it on two oranges, and knows she is finally home when the first one tastes like "heaven." An ALA Notable Book. (RE/PB, grades 2–4, strands II, IV, V, IX)

Cooney, Barbara. (1996). *Eleanor*. New York: Viking.
> Beautifully told and illustrated, but sad biography of Eleanor Roosevelt's childhood until a teacher befriends and inspires her. (IN/PB, grades 3–4, strands II, IV)

Cooney, Barbara. (1982). *Miss Rumphius*. New York: Puffin Books.
> Alice Rumphius grows up to accomplish three purposes in her life, including the hardest one of all: making the world more beautiful. (EG/PB, grades 2–3, strands II, III, IV, IX)

DeFelice, Cynthia. (1990). *Weasel*. New York: Macmillan.
> Alone in the Ohio frontier of 1839, and face to face with a deranged, evil man called Weasel, Nathan must wrestle with anger and pain unknown to an 11-year-old. With the help of a white man who identified with the Shawnees and who was hated and feared by other whites, and with the guidance of his father, Nathan learns not to hate Weasel, who injured them both and killed so many others. (RE/NV, grades 4+, strands II, III, IV, V)

DiCamillo, Kate. (2000). *Because of Winn Dixie*. New York: Scholastic.
> Opal Buloni befriends a homeless dog she names Winn Dixie. Along with her father, the "preacher," she learns valuable lessons about love and care for all creatures. (EG/NV, grades 3–4, strands I, III, VI, X)

Denslow, Sharon. (1995). *Radio Boy*. New York: Simon & Schuster Books for Young Readers.
> Fictionalized account of the boyhood of Nathan Stubblefield, who fascinated his rural neighbors with many inventions, including electric batteries and a type of radio he called "the wireless telephone." (RE/PB, grades 1–3, strands IV, VII, VIII)

dePaola, Tomi. (1981). *Now One Foot, Now the Other*. New York: G. P. Putnam's Sons.
> Tender story of a child helping his grandfather recover from a stroke and learn to walk again, just as his grandfather had first taught him to walk. (EG/PB, grades K–2, strands II, IV)

Dionetti, Michelle. (1991). *Coal Mine Peaches*. New York: Orchard Books.
    Three generations of an Italian immigrant family work to make their living,
    love each other, and center on the grandfather who tells stories through the
    years from his childhood to old age, stories both based in truth and greatly
    exaggerated for the pleasure of his listeners. (RE/PB, grades K–2, strands II,
    IV, V, IX)

Fisher, Leonard. (1990). *The Oregon Trail*. New York: Holiday House.
    Accompanied with powerful photographs and illustration, the book chroni-
    cles the people and places of the Oregon Trail westward. (IN/IT, grades 4+,
    strands II, II, V)

Fox, Mem. (1985). *Wilfrid Gordon McDonald Partridge*. New York: Kane/Miller Book
    Publishers.
    In a delightfully fresh manner, a very young boy helps a very old woman
    recover her memories. A real tribute to the special relationship of young and
    old. (EG/PB, grades K–4, strands II, IV, V)

Friedrich, Elizabeth. (1996). *Leah's Pony*. Honesdale, PA: Boyds Mills Press.
    Story of the beginning of the depression in the drought-ridden Dust Bowl of
    the Great Plains. When her family, like so many others, is forced to auction
    off all their possessions, Leah quietly sells her beloved pony before the auc-
    tion, then uses that dollar to bid on her father's tractor. No one bids against
    her, and the tractor is saved. Neighbors all follow suit and offer single low
    bids, then give each item back to the family. Leah discovers her pony similarly
    returned the next morning. (RE/PB, grades 1–3, strands III, V, VII)

Fritz, Jean. (1980). *Where Do You Think You're Going, Christopher Columbus?* New
    York: G. P. Putnam's Sons.
    A biography that reads like a novel. Fascinating details of Columbus's three
    trips to the islands in the Caribbean and his unfailing, but mistaken, beliefs
    about what he'd found. (IN/IT, Grade 4+, strands II, III, V)

Gardiner, John. (1980). *Stone Fox*. New York: Crowell.
    Faced with the possible loss of his home because of his grandfather's illness
    and inability to work on the farm, a young boy enters a dogsled race with his
    beloved pet. He hopes to win the cash prize to save the farm. When his dog
    dies within feet of the finish line, his greatest rival provides surprising help.
    (EG/NV, grades 3–4, strands VII, III, IV)

George, Jean Craighead. (1995). *There's an Owl in the Shower*. New York: Harper-
    Collins.
    Amidst the struggle between the ecologists and the logging industry in the
    Northwest, a logging family cares for an orphaned owlet and surprises them-
    selves by learning more about the complex interrelationships of nature,
    humans, and the industries so many depended on for livelihood. (EG/NV,
    grades 3–4+, strands III, V, VI, VII, VIII)

Giblin, James. (1994). *Thomas Jefferson: A Picture Book Biography*. New York: Scho-
    lastic.
    Exceptionally well-illustrated biography of Thomas Jefferson, including his
    contradictory beliefs and practices regarding slavery. (IN/PB, grades 2–4,
    strands II, VI, VII)

Gilbert, Suzie. (1996). *Hawk Hill*. San Francisco: Chronicle Books.
Lonely in a new town, Pete discovers a barn filled with wild birds being treated for injuries and rehabilitated for release back into the wild. Drawn to the birds and the woman caring for them, Pete learns to help in their care and to accept his loss when they return to freedom. (EG/PB, grades 2–4, strands III, IV, VIII)

Harshman, Marc. (1990). *Snow Company*. New York: Cobblehill Books.
Teddy's family takes in a surprising amount of company when the blizzard causes people to become stranded and desperate for shelter. (EG/PB, grades 1–3, strands III, V)

Hartford, John. (1986). *Steamboat in a Cornfield*. New York: Crown Publishers.
Fascinating account of a series of mishaps for the steamboat *Virginia* as the rivers she traveled rose and fell with flooding and drought before the days of controlling rivers with locks and dams. A most interesting account of the steamer running aground, then being stranded in a cornfield when the flood waters receded. (IN/PB, grades K–4, strands II, III, VII, VIII)

Harvey, Brett. (1988). *Cassie's Journey: Going West in the 1860's*. New York: Holiday House.
Based on true events, this compelling story is told through the eyes of a young girl who shares the adventures and suffering of a wagon train. (RE/PB, grades 2–4, strands II, III, V)

Hathorn, Libby. (1994). *Grandma's Shoes*. Boston: Little, Brown.
Grieving after her beloved grandmother dies, a young girl tries on her grandmother's shoes every night and is transported to beautiful places in search of her grandmother, perhaps through her dreams. When she finds her, the child understands and accepts her loss, then assumes a new mentoring role for her little sister. (EG/PB, grades 2–3, strands IV, V)

Hooks, William. (1988). *The Legend of the White Doe*. New York: Macmillan.
Tale of the birth and disappearance of the first English child in America, Virginia Dare, told as a fascinating blend of factual history and legend. (RE/NV, grades 3–4+, strands II, IV, V)

Jacobs, William. (1990). *Ellis Island: New Hope in a New Land*. New York: Charles Scribner's Sons Books for Young Readers.
Compelling history with many photographs of early European immigration. Broadens to include earlier, alternative, or later arrivals of other immigrants. Discuss difficulties of each group, such as the frequent nonacceptance by those already settled into the country and the challenges of finding work, housing, education, and learning a new language. (IN/PB, grades 3–4, strands I, II, III, V, VI)

Jam, Teddy. (1993). *The Year of Fire*. New York: Margaret K. McElderry Books.
While watching the fire cook sap into maple syrup, a young girl asks her grandfather about the biggest fire he'd ever seen. The old man tells of a major forest fire when he was little, its probable cause, the damage it caused, and the changes in the land during the many years afterwards. (EG/NV, grades 2–4, strands II, III)

Johnson, Paul. (1997). *Farmer's Market*. New York: Orchard Books.
> Laura leaves the farm on Saturday morning to work with her family as they sell their produce at the farmer's market in town. After a morning of hard work, Laura is allowed to play with a friend in the afternoon until time to drive back home. (EG/PB, grades K–1, strands V, VII)

Johnston, Tony. (1994). *Amber on the Mountain*. New York: Dial Books for Young Children.
> Happy in her isolated mountain home, Amber makes friends with the road-builder's daughter, who teaches her to read. After her friend moves away, Amber teaches herself to write so she can answer her friend's letters. Beautifully illustrated, told in rich mountain dialect. (EG/PB, grades K–2, strands IV, V)

Joosse, Barbara. (1998). *Lewis & Papa: Adventure on the Santa Fe Trail*. San Francisco: Chronicle Books.
> Touching account of a father and son's struggles and triumphs as they travel west with a wagon train. (RE/PB, grades 2–4, strands II, III, VII)

Krensky, Stephen. (1987). *Who Really Discovered America?* New York: Hastings House Publishers.
> A look at the multiple ways early humans walked to the Americas in search of game, and the later travels of explorers who sailed to the various islands and shores of North and South America. Raises fascinating questions about the ancestry of various "native" groups. (IN/IT, grades 4+, strands I, II, III, IX)

Kroll, Steven. (1996). *Pony Express!* New York: Scholastic.
> Beautifully illustrated account of the Pony Express and the young men who risked their lives to deliver the mail from the East to the West in the days of the California Gold Rush. (IN/IT, grades 3–4+, strands II, VIII)

Kroll, Steven. (1994). *By the Dawn's Early Light*. New York: Scholastic.
> Well-told and illustrated story of the events leading up to Francis Scott Key writing the poem that became the national anthem of the United States. (IN/IT, grades 3–4+, strands II, VI, IX)

Lasky, Kathryn. (1997). *Marven of the Great North Woods*. San Diego: Harcourt Brace.
> To escape the flu epidemic, Marven is sent out of the city to live in a logging camp. Only 10 years old, he is frightened, but adjusts and develops an accounting system to help with the business. Based on experiences of the author's father. (EG/PB, grades 3–4, strands III, V, VII)

Lasky, Kathryn. (1995). *She's Wearing a Dead Bird on Her Head!* New York: Hyperion Books for Children.
> Fictionalized account of the founding of a branch of the Audubon Society in Massachusetts. Strong message about the wasting of precious animal life for human decoration. (RE/PB, grades 2–4, strands I, II, III, V)

Lasky, Kathryn. (1983). *Sugaring Time*. New York: Macmillan.
> Sharp black-and-white photographs and well-written text tell the story of a family as they tap maple trees in late winter and spend the next four weeks making maple syrup. (IN/PB, grades 3–4, strands III, V, VII)

Lasky, Kathryn. (1980). *The Weaver's Gift*. New York: Frederick Warne.

Engaging chronicle of a family who raises sheep, from the early birth of a lamb in life-threatening winter weather, through the shearing of the flock, to the eventual weaving of a soft wool blanket for a neighbor's toddler. Vibrant black-and-white photographs. (IN/PB, grades 3–4, strands III, VII, VIII)

Locker, Thomas. (1988). *Family Farm*. New York: Dial Books.

A year of struggle and success on a family farm where everyone's contribution makes a difference. (EG/PB, grades K–3, strands III, V, VII)

Lyon, George. (1994). *Mama is a Miner*. New York: Orchard Books.

Poetic and plaintive story of a mother who works as a coal miner. (EG/PB, grades K–2, strands III, VII, VIII)

Lyon, George. (1990). *Come a Tide*. New York: Orchard Books.

Lighthearted story of flooding in the mountains and how the community responds to such adversity. (EG/PB, grades K–2, strands III, V)

MacLachlan, Patricia. (1994). *All the Places to Love*. New York: HarperCollins.

A baby boy is born into a family of parents and grandparents on a farm. Each share with him their special places in their world during the next few years— the brook, the barn, the earth of the field—and when his sister is born, he plans to show her all the places he loves. (EG/PB, grades K–2, strands III, IV, V)

MacLachlan, Patricia. (1994). *Skylark*. New York: HarperCollins.

In the sequel to *Sarah, Plain and Tall*, a widespread drought in the plains causes families to give up and leave their homes. After struggling with fire and the lack of water, Sarah takes the children back to Maine for a few months, leaving Jacob to protect their farm. The joyful reunion a few months later includes the announcement of her pregnancy. (RE/PB, grades 3–4, strands III, V, VII)

MacLachlan, Patricia. (1991). *Journey*. New York: Dell Publishing.

Left by his mother for his grandparents to raise, Journey reacts with more anger and resentment than his older sister. Gradually, he comes to appreciate his grandfather's love and to realize how similar they are. (EG/NV, grades 3–4+, strands II, IV, V)

MacLachlan, Patricia. (1985). *Sarah, Plain and Tall*. New York: HarperCollins.

Sarah comes west in response to Pap's newspaper ad to find a wife and mother for his children. Papa, the two children, and Sarah cautiously begin to love each other, but Sarah is homesick for the sea until she realizes she would miss her new family more than her former home. (RE/PB, grades 3–4, strands III, V)

Mann, Elizabeth. (1996). *The Brooklyn Bridge*. New York: Miyaka Press.

Stunningly illustrated account of the building of the Brooklyn Bridge and the people who designed and carried out the work. (IN/PB, grades 2–4, strands II, III, V, VI, VII, VIII)

Martin, Jr., Bill, and Archambault, John. (1985). *The Ghost Eye Tree*. New York: Henry Holt and Company.

A young boy, with his condescending older sister, must conquer his fear of a frightening tree on the way to get milk from the farmer at the other end of town. (EG/PB, grades K–3, strands II, VII)

McCully, Emily. (1996). *The Ballot Box Battle*. New York: Alfred A. Knopf.
Based on the efforts of Elizabeth Cady Stanton to secure voting rights for women, this book focuses on her effect on one fictitious young girl. Cordelia is amazed at Mrs. Stanton's courage and begins to reexamine her own ideas about gender-limiting roles and her identity. (RE/PB, grades 2–4, strands II, III, VI, X)

Mills, Lauren. (1991). *The Rag Coat*. Boston: Little, Brown.
Surrounded by a loving but poor Appalachian family, Minna delays going to school after the death of her father because she doesn't have a coat. Friends and neighbors, the "Quilting Mothers," donate scraps of fabric and piece together a coat that Minna loves until the children tease her. Minna stands up for herself and her coat when she shows them how her coat is made of *their* rags and their memories. (RE/PB, grades K–3, strands IV, V, VII)

Moss, Marissa. (1994). *In America*. New York: Dutton Children's Books.
With alternating types of illustrations, past and present are shown while Walter learns why his grandfather left Lithuania to come to America. (RE/PB, grades K–2, strands II, III, IV, V)

Munsch, Robert. (1986). *Love You Forever*. Willowdale, Ontario, Canada: Firefly Books Ltd.
The touching, loving relationship of a mother and her baby boy as he grows up and older, cares for her in her old age, and begins the family cycle again with his own baby daughter. (EG/PB, grades K–3, strands IV, V)

Peck, Richard. (2000). *A Year Down Yonder*. New York: Dial Books for Young Readers.
A Newbery Medal Book, which is a sequel to Peck's *A Long Way from Chicago*. A young girl learns to adjust to a life with her unpredictable grandmother in a strange environment. (RE/NV, grades 4+, strands II, IV)

Provensen, Alice, and Provensen, Martin. (1987). *Shaker Lane*. New York: Viking Kestrel.
Changes in the occupants and use of land over time from farmland, to a mutually supportive poor community, to a reservoir and middle-class neighborhood. (EG/PB, grades 1–3, strands II, III)

Pryor, Bonnie. (1996). *The Dream Jar*. New York: Morrow Junior Books.
Young Russian immigrant Valentina wants to work to earn money to help her papa realize his dream of owning a store in America. But no one will hire a little girl, until she realizes she can teach others to read and write in the language she's learning at school. She happily contributes her earnings to the "dream jar" until the day comes to see papa's store. (RE/PB, grades K–3, strands IV, V, VII)

Pulver, Robin. (1990). *Mrs. Toggle's Zipper*. New York: Scholastic.
When the teacher's zipper is stuck in her coat, the children try to help her themselves, then enlist the help of the nurse, the principal, and finally the

custodian. The custodian, with his tools and technical knowledge, solves the problem. (EG/PB, grades K–1, strands V, VII)

Rabin, Staton. (1994). *Casey Over There*. San Diego: Harcourt Brace & Company.

A strikingly illustrated story of a family with one son in France, fighting in World War II, and one son at home missing his brother terribly. The younger brother, Aubrey, writes "Uncle Sam" about his brother. President Wilson responds with a respectful letter hoping for peace. The war ends; Casey returns; Aubrey writes Uncle Sam and the president a thank-you note. (EG/PB, grades 1–3, strands V, VI, IX)

Rand, Ted. (Illustrator) (1990). *Paul Revere's Ride*. New York: Dutton Children's Books.

A beautifully illustrated version of Longfellow's famous poem about Paul Revere's midnight ride during the Revolutionary War. (IN+CR/PB, grades 2–4, strands II, VI, IX)

Ransom, Candice. (1995). *When the Whippoorwill Calls*. New York: Tambourine Books.

Although extremely poor, a little girl and her family love their home in the Blue Ridge Mountains. When the land is sold to turn the area into Shenandoah National Park, they must move to the valley. On a later visit to their decaying homeplace, Papa and his daughter resolve their lingering sadness and accept the change. (RE/PB, grades K–4, strands II, III, VI)

Rappaport, Doreen. (1987*). Trouble at the Mines*. New York: Thomas Y. Crowell.

Exciting story of an 1989–89 miner's strike in Pennsylvania, and the successful efforts of Mary Harris Jones (Mother Jones) and the women and girls who led the battle against the unfair owners for eight difficult months. (RE/NV, grades 2–4, strands II, III, V, VI, VII, X)

Ray, Deborah. (1990). *My Daddy Was a Soldier: A World War II Story*. New York: Holiday House.

Fears and experiences of a young girl while her father is away fighting a war. (EG/PB, grades 1–3, strands II, IV, VII, IX)

Roop, Peter, and Roop, Connie. (1986). *Buttons for General Washington*. Minneapolis: Carolrhoda Books.

Story of a youthful spy for the American army and how he smuggles an important message to General Washington hidden in his coat buttons. (RE/NV, grades 1–2, strands II, V, VI, IX)

Roop, Peter, and Roop, Connie. (Eds.). (1990). *I, Columbus: My Journal—1492–3*. New York: Walker and Company.

Well-chosen and edited excerpts from Columbus's diary tell the story of his first trip across the ocean, discoveries on "San Salvador" and other Caribbean islands, and his journey back to Portugal. (IN/IT, grades 4+, strands II, III, V)

Ryder, Joanne. (1991). *When the Woods Hum*. New York: Morrow Junior Books.

A family's three-generation fascination with cicadas that emerge from the ground every 17 years. (EG/PB, grades 2–3, strands II, III)

Rylant, Cynthia. (1991). *Appalachia: The Voices of Sleeping Birds*. San Diego: Harcourt Brace Jovanovich.

With striking photographs and nearly reverent respect, Rylant describes the people of the southern Appalachian mountains. (IN/PB, grades 2–4, strands I, III)

Rylant, Cynthia. (1989). *Mr. Griggs' Work*. New York: Orchard Books.

Mr. Griggs passionately loves his work at the post office and is happier than ever when he returns to work after being sick at home for a day. (EG/PB, grades K–2, strands IV, VII)

Rylant, Cynthia. (1985). *The Relatives Came*. New York: Scholastic.

The house of one family becomes delightfully crowded and busy when the Appalachian relatives come to visit. The extended family spends time cooking, eating, playing, and telling stories in ways of the mountains and rural South. (RE/PB, grades K–2, strands I, V, VII)

Rylant, Cynthia. (1982). *When I Was Young in the Mountains*. New York: E. P. Dutton.

Gentle memories of simpler times long ago in the mountains, including nighttime trips to the outhouse, baptisms in a muddy swimming hole, and baths in round tin tubs in front of an old black stove. (EG/PB, grades K–2, strands II, III)

San Souci, Robert. (1995). *Kate Shelley: Bound for Legend*. New York: Dial Books for Young Readers.

Powerfully illustrated story of incredible courage of a 15-year-old girl who braved a fierce gale and raging floodwaters to warn trains to stop before reaching the site of a train crash at a washed-out bridge. After reaching the train station with her message, she led rescuers to the two survivors caught in the swollen creek. (IN/IT, grades 2–4, strands II, III, IV, V)

Sanders, Scott. (1989). *Aurora Means Dawn*. New York: Bradbury Press.

A young family travels west to Ohio to homestead, but must find help from others to clear away the trees downed by a storm and free their wagon from the mud. (RE/PB, grades K–2, strands II, III, V)

Sandler, Martin. (1995). *Immigrants*. New York: HarperCollins.

Pages of black-and-white or color photographs interspersed with illustrations and combined with supportive text tell the story of early European immigrants, their hardships, and their success in overcoming obstacles through hard work and the education of children. Moves to current immigrants and the rich mosaic of America. (IN/PB, grades 3–4, strands I, II, III, V, VI)

Saul, Carol. (1995). *Someplace Else*. New York: Simon & Schuster Books for Young Readers.

In her later years, Mrs. Tillby grows restless and decides to visit other places to see if she might like to live there instead of her apple farm. She enjoys each place, but is still restless, and finally solves her dilemma by buying a small travel trailer. (EG/PB, grades K–2, strands III, IV, VII)

Shannon, George. (1993). *Climbing Kansas Mountains*. New York: Bradbury Press.

A father lovingly provides his bored little boy a creative lesson in geography from a high point in Kansas—an eight-story grain elevator. (EG/PB, grades K–2, strand III)

Shelby, Anne. (1995). *Homeplace*. New York: Orchard Books.
> Remarkable evolution of a house and ways of living through seven generations of a family. Wonderful, detailed illustrations. (EG/PB, grades K–2, strands II, III, V)

Smith, Robert. (1984). *The War with Grandpa*. New York: Dell Publishing.
> Both Peter and his grandfather must adapt when Grandpa comes to live with Peter's family after the death of his wife. Peter resents giving up his room, and two-way teasing with Grandpa turns into hurtful actions toward the old man. Grandpa designs the solution. (EG/NV, grades 3–4, strands IV, V)

Spinelli, Jerry. (1997). *Wringer*. New York: HarperTrophy.
> Palmer is dreading his tenth birthday. Everyone approaching age 10 wants to be a wringer so they can participate in the annual pigeon day—everyone except Palmer, who must find courage to oppose the event. (EG/NV, grades 4+, strands III, IV, VI)

Stewart, Sarah. (1997). *The Gardener*. New York: Farrar, Straus and Giroux.
> Lydia Grace moves in with her Uncle Jim in the city because her parents are out of work. She brings her country-bred love of gardening and transforms the drab city into blooming colors in windowboxes and on the rooftop of her uncle's building. (EG/PB, grades 1–3, strands III, VII)

Tunnell, Michael. (1997). *Mailing May*. New York: Greenwillow Books.
> Creative problem solving among many conspirators helps a young girl visit her grandmother. When her family can't afford a ticket to ride the train, May is mailed for 53 cents, and delivered from the train to her grandmother by the postman. Based on a true story! (EG/PB, grades 1–3, strands V, VII)

Turner, Ann. (1987). *Nettie's Trip South*. New York: Macmillan.
> An unusual perspective on pre–Civil War slavery practices in the South, movingly told through the voice of a young northern girl on her first trip to the South. Based on the diary of the author's great-grandmother. (RE/NV, grades 3–4, strands II, V, VI, VII)

Van Leeuwen, Jean. (1995). *Across the Wide Dark Sea: The Mayflower Journey*. New York: Dial Books for Young Readers.
> A fresh telling of this frightening and difficult experience through the eyes of a young boy. (RE/PB, grades K–2, strands II, V, VII)

Ward, Lynd. (1952). *The Biggest Bear*. Boston: Houghton Mifflin.
> A boy brings home a bear cub that quickly outgrows his status as a pet and becomes a major nuisance to the boy's family and neighboring farmers. The boy attempts to take the bear away to distant locales, but he always comes back home. The boy leaves one last time with his shotgun and a promise to take care of the problem himself. A surprise trap and relocation to a zoo provide a delightful solution. (EG/PB, grades K–2, strands IV, VII)

Warren, Andrea. (1996). *Orphan Train Rider: One Boy's True Story*. Boston: Houghton Mifflin.
> A sometimes painful, sometimes uplifting account of the children taken from orphanages in the East, placed in groups on trains, and placed with families

in the Midwest. Analysis of why this adoption practice began and how it was viewed at the time. (IN/IT, grades 4+, strands II, III, IV, V, VI)

Wells, Rosemary. (1996). *The Language of Doves*. New York: Dial Books for Young Readers.

A moving account of a young girl, her grandfather, and their shared love of doves. Recalling his Italian boyhood of caring for doves, including time as a 9-year-old "soldier" in World War II, her grandfather promises Julietta that her dove will fly home when Julietta has learned "the language of doves." After his death, Isabella is sold, but flies home with a poignant message from her grandfather in the aluminum capsule. (RE/PB, grades 2–4, strands II, IV, V, IX)

Williams, David. (1993). *Grandma Essie's Covered Wagon*. New York: Alfred A. Knopf.

Biographical recollections of the author's grandmother as he shares her stories of moving with the westward expansion. (IN/PB, grades 2–3, strands II, III, V)

Wright-Frierson, Virginia. (1999). *A North American Rain Forest Scrapbook*. New York: Walker and Company.

A woman shares her notes, photographs, paintings, and awesome wonder about her discoveries in the temperate rain forest of Washington's Olympic Peninsula. (IN/PB, grades 3–4+, strands III, VIII)

Yolen, Jane. (1992). *Letting Swift River Go*. Boston: Little, Brown.

Told through the eyes of a young girl living in one of the Swift River towns in western Massachusetts, a story of the purchase of such towns by the government before drowning them to create the Quabbin Reservoir. (EG/PB, grades 1–4, strands II, III, VI)

Hispanic/Latino American

Promote: Variety of physical features, settings, and occupations; family love, closeness, and mutual support; qualities of pride, honesty, dignity, hard work, and loyalty; respect for the elderly, authority figures, tradition, education, religion

Avoid: Exaggerated clothing and physical features; riding donkeys in modern cities; predominance of poverty, nonstandard English, unemployment or migrant work only; stereotypical behaviors of male oppression, female subservience, laziness, disrespect for time

Ada, Alma Flor. (1993). *My Name Is María Isabel*. New York: Macmillan.

In her new school there are already two girls named María, so the teacher decides to call María Isabel Salazar López by a different name from the one that means so much to her—just Mary López. Many misunderstandings follow, and María Isabel is very unhappy until a writing assignment called "My Greatest Wish." (RE/NV, grades 3–4, strands I, III, V)

Anaya, Rudolfo. (1980). *Farolitos of Christmas*. New York: Hyperion Books for Children.

With her grandfather too ill to chop wood to hold the outdoor candles on Christmas Eve, and her father away at war, Luz worries that the holiday will not be celebrated properly. Her solution and resultant support of family and friends in her small village in New Mexico is heartwarming, as is her father's homecoming. (RE/PB, grades 2–4, strands I, IV, V)

Brimner, Larry. (1992). *A Migrant Family*. Minneapolis: Lerner Publications.

With crisp photographs and honest descriptions, the author shows the difficulties and mutual support of Mexican migrant workers in California. (IN/IT, grades 3–4+, strands III, VII, X)

Bunting, Eve. (1996). *Going Home*. New York: Joanna Cotler Books.

A family of migrant workers goes home to Mexico for Christmas, with the U.S.-born children wondering why it's so special to their parents to go home. Gradually they come to realize the importance of "home" to their parents and what a sacrifice they've made to provide opportunities for their children. (RE/PB, grades K–2, strands I, V, VII)

Bunting, Eve. (1994). *A Day's Work*. New York: Clarion Books.

To help his grandfather who just immigrated from Mexico, Francisco lies about his gardening ability to the man who hires them for a day's work. They weed the wrong plants and must face the employer's anger. Overcoming the language barrier, the grandfather maintains his intense dignity and honor, and Francisco learns a valuable lesson about honesty and restitution. (RE/PB, grades K–2, strands IV, V, VII)

Bunting, Eve. (1990). *The Wall*. New York: Clarion Books.

A father takes his young son to the Vietnam Veterans Memorial in Washington, D.C., to find his own father's name. As others come to the wall for their own purposes, the two reflect on the mixture of sadness and pride they feel. (EG/PB, grades 2–3, strands II, IV, IX)

Cherry, Lynne. (1990). *The Great Kapok Tree*. San Diego: Harcourt Brace & Company.

Animals and a child of the South American rain forest plead for the preservation of their home to a sleeping woodcutter. When he awakes, he sees the wonder of his environment and leaves without his ax. (CR+RE/PB, grades K–4, strands III, IX)

Cowley, Joy. (1996). *Gracias the Thanksgiving Turkey*. New York: Scholastic.

A delightful story of a turkey who became a beloved pet while being fattened up for Thanksgiving dinner. (EG/PB, grades K–2, strands I, V)

Delacre, Lulu. (1993). *Vejigante/Masquerader*. New York: Scholastic.

Ramón plans secretly and successfully to be a vejigante (masquerader) in the month-long February festival in Puerto Rico, but his costume is torn to shreds the first day by a mean goat. Cheered by older boys for his bravery, and helped by his mother, Ramón prepares to return to the festival with a mended outfit. Dual English/Spanish text. (RE/PB, grades K–2, strands I, IV, V)

Dorros, Arthur. (1993). *Radio Man*. New York: HarperCollins Children's Books.
    Diego, a child in a family of Mexican American migrant workers, keeps his radio with him at all times, listening for Spanish language channels whenever possible. He finally utilizes a call-in station to find his best friend at an apple orchard. English and Spanish text. (RE/PB, grades 1–3, strands III, IV, VII)

Dorros, Arthur. (1991). *Abuela*. New York: Dutton Children's Books.
    A walk in the park with grandma becomes an imaginary flight over the city to see the sights and visit the places important to both of them. Text mixes Spanish with English. (CR/PB, grades K–1, strands I, V)

Hoyt-Goldsmith, Diane. (1994). *Day of the Dead: A Mexican-American Celebration*. New York: Holiday House.
    Delightful California twins tell the story of their lives and their family's celebration of the Day of the Dead. Outstanding color photographs. (IN/IT, grades 3–4+, strands I, V)

Johnston, Tony. (1997). *Day of the Dead*. San Diego: Harcourt Brace & Company.
    The story shows preparations for and community observance of the Mexican and Mexican American celebration, Day of the Dead. (RE/PB, grades K–2, strands I, V)

Kleven, Elisa. (1996). *Hooray, A Piñata!* New York: Dutton Children's Books.
    Clara chooses a dog-shaped piñata for her birthday party, then pretends it's a real pet and doesn't want to break it. Despite his teasing about her "pet," Clara's friend Samson brings her a monster piñata to break at the party. (RE/PB, grades K–2, strands I, IV, V)

Mohr, Nicholosa. (1979). *Felita*. New York: Dial Books.
    A Puerto Rican family in New York City saves their money to move to a "better" neighborhood, but are not accepted by the new neighbors because of racial prejudice. (RE/NV, grades 4+, strands V, VI, X)

Roe, Eileen. (1991). *Con Mi Hermano/With My Brother*. New York: Bradbury Press.
    In English and Spanish, the story of a little boy's adoration of his older brother and their activities together. (EG/PB, grades K–1, strands IV, V)

Soto, Gary. (1995). *Boys at Work*. New York: Delacorte Press.
    When Rudy accidentally breaks a young gang member's Discman, he worries about his safety while he and a friend try to earn money to pay for it. With much humor and a touch of real fear, the boys take on an amazing variety of odd jobs to solve the problem. (RE/NV, grades 3–4, strands V, VII)

Soto, Gary. (1993). *Too Many Tamales*. New York: G. P. Putnam's Sons.
    Maria secretly borrows her mother's diamond ring, then forgets she's wearing it as she buries her hands in the dough to help make tamales. Remembering later, she enlists all her young cousins' help in eating the tamales to find the ring, only to find nothing. When Maria confesses to her mother, who is wearing the missing ring, all the relatives are forgiving as they make a second batch of tamales. (RE/PB, grades K–2, strands I, V)

Thomas, Jane. (1994). *Lights on the River*. New York: Hyperion Books for Children.
    Story of a Mexican American family of migrant workers—their labor, love, and living conditions, and how they keep hope and dignity alive. (RE/PB, grades 2–4, strands I, III, V, VII)

Torres, Leyla. (1995). *Saturday Sancocho*. New York: Farrar, Straus and Giroux.
  Maria Lili looks forward to chicken stew every Saturday, but once there was
  no money and no food except for a dozen eggs. Maria Lili and her grandmother walk to the market and shrewdly barter with the merchants until
  they have all the necessary ingredients for a delicious sancocho. (RE/PB,
  grades K–2, strands V, VII)
Williams, Vera. (1982). *A Chair for My Mother*. New York: Greenwillow Books.
  Story of a family saving coins in a big glass jar every day. They had lost everything in a fire, and the little girl is determined to buy a big comfortable chair
  for her working mother. When the jar is full, they go shopping. (EG/PB,
  grades K–2, strands V, VII)

Mideastern and Mideastern American

Promote: Variety of physical appearances, settings, occupations; family closeness
and respect; values of faith, individual responsibility, honesty, generosity

Avoid: Exaggerated features; predominance of nomadic, desert-dwelling characters; stereotypes of angry males linked to terrorism and subservient females as
often shown on television

Heide, Florence. (1990). *The Day of Ahmed's Secret*. New York: Lothrop, Lee & Shepard.
  A young boy is thrilled with his work in the streets of Cairo because he is
  strong and because he is helping his family. He finally can share his secret in
  the evening, when work is over—he can write his name. (RE/PB, grades
  K–3, strands III, IV, V, VII)
Kessler, Cristina. (1995). *One Night*. New York: Philomel Books.
  Muhammed, a young Tuareg boy in Niger, cares responsibly for his goats in
  the desert and spends the night alone with the herd as one of his goats gives
  birth for the first time. (RE/PB, grades K–3, strands I, III, IV)
Nye, Naomi. (1994). *Sitti's Secrets*. New York: Four Winds Press.
  An American child visits her grandmother, Sitti, far away and is enchanted
  with sounds of the Arabic language, food preparation, games with her cous-
  ins, and ancient customs still practiced because the people don't want to forget. When Mona goes home, she writes to the president about her beloved
  grandmother coupled with her concern from watching the news. She asserts
  that if the people of the United States could meet Sitti, they'd like her, then
  wishes the president good luck in his hard job and votes for peace, saying,
  "My grandmother votes with me." (RE/PB, grades K–3, strands II, III, V, VI,
  IX)

Multicultural (Major Characters Representing More Than One Cultural Group)

Adams, Barbara. (1992). *The Go-Around Dollar*. New York: Four Winds Press.
Story of the multiple transferences of a dollar bill during a day, interspersed with factual information about the dollar. (IN/PB, grades K–2, strands V, VII)

Ancona, George. (1983). *Team Work*. New York: Thomas Y. Crowell.
Vivid photographs and clear text show how people depend on each other to accomplish their work. Many unexpected, nontraditional work activities shown, such as mountain climbing. (IN/IT, grades 3–4, strands V, VIII)

Bang, Molly. (1997). *Common Ground: The Water, Earth, and Air We Share*. New York: The Blue Sky Press.
A parable of human use and misuse of the environment, and the consequences for everyone. (IN/PB, grades K–4, strands III, VII, VIII)

Blake, Robert. (1977). *Akiak*. New York: Philomel Books.
Intriguing story of cooperation between humans and dogs as the rule-governed Iditarod race is run in Alaska. (EG/PB, grades 1–3, strands   III, V)

Bunting, Eve. (1996). *The Blue and the Gray*. New York: Scholastic Press.
Workmen are building houses on a former Civil War battleground. Two young friends, one black and one white, rejoice in becoming neighbors and learn of the horrors of the war from one boy's father. They vow never to fight each other as friends and brothers once did. (RE/PB, grades 1–2, strands II, III, V, IX)

Bunting, Eve. (1994). *Smoky Night*. San Diego, CA: Harcourt Brace & Company.
Against the backdrop of strained race relations within an Oakland, California, neighborhood, residents overcome their differences when saving each other and themselves from the fires caused by the riots. Their determination to rebuild their lives and community crosses racial barriers in a powerful message. (EG/PB, grades 1–3, strands III, V, VII, X)

Cherry, Lynne. (1992). *The River Ran Wild*. San Diego: Harcourt Brace Jovanovich.
True account of the ruin and then restoration of the Nashua River through the centuries. (IN/PB, grades 2–4, strands II, III, VII, VIII, X)

Cohen, Barbara. (1974). *Thank You, Jackie Robinson*. New York: Scholastic.
Sam, a young Jewish boy, becomes best friends with Davy, an older Christian black man who is the chef in his mother's inn. They share a fanatic interest in the Brooklyn Dodgers, and manage to attend many games together until Davy has a heart attack. Denied hospital visitation privileges, Sam goes to a game alone, gets Jackie Robinson and his teammates to autograph a baseball for his friend, and sneaks into the hospital with the help of Davy's son-in-law. Devastated when his friend dies, Davy begins to come to terms with his loss when he listens to another Dodger's game. (RE/NV, grades 3–4+, strands IV, V, VI)

Dorros, Arthur. (1992). *This Is My House*. New York: Scholastic.
Colorful pictures and descriptions of different kinds of houses all over the

world. The language of each place accompanies the English text. (IN/PB, grades K–2, strand III)

Fleming, Denise. (1996). *Where Once There Was a Wood*. New York: Henry Holt and Company.

Brilliant illustrations contrast the once-thriving woods with the neighborhood of homes that replaced it. Information also provided about providing backyard habitats for wildlife displaced by humans' buildings. (IN/PB, grades K–1, strands III, VIII)

Foreman, Michael. (1992). *The Boy Who Sailed with Columbus*. New York: Arcade Publishing.

A retelling, from a cabin boy's perspective, of the famous voyage and first encounters with native people in the New World. Conflicts among cultures are sharply portrayed, with very plausible changes in the boy who remains behind when Columbus sails back to Spain. (RE/NV, grades 3–4, strands I, II, III)

Hamanaka, Sheila. (1995). *Be Bop-A-Do-Walk!* New York: Simon & Schuster Books for Young Readers.

Young friends take a long walk with Emi's father to Central Park in New York City, enjoying the many people and sights along the way. A minor conflict with another child at the park is resolved in a peaceful way. (EG/PB, grades K–2, strands III, V)

Hine, Lewis. (1994). *Kids at Work*. New York: Clarion Books.

A detailed and pictoral account of the misuse and abuse of children working in cotton, steel, and glass factories, coal mines, canneries, and on the streets prior to the enactment of child labor laws. (IN/IT, grades 3–4+, strands II, III, VI, VII)

Houk, Randy. (1995). *Wolves in Yellowstone*. Fairfield, CT: The Benefactory, Inc.

In narrative verse, the history of wolves in Yellowstone National Park, their dwindling numbers and endangered species status, and their reentry in the park engineered by the humans who had previously threatened their existence. (IN/PB, grades 2–3, strands III, X)

Jackson, Donna. (1996). *The Bone Detectives*. Boston: Little, Brown.

For students fascinated with detective work coupling history and science, this book presents amazing findings from investigating human bones. (IN/IT, grades 4+, strands II, III, VIII)

Keeler, Patricia. (1995). *Unraveling Fibers*. New York: Atheneum Books for Young Readers.

Extremely well-illustrated and organized book of the development of natural fibers from plants and animals as well as the synthetic fibers. (IN/PB, grades 3–4+, strands VII, VIII, IX)

Kuklin, Susan. (1992). *How My Family Lives in America*. New York: Bradbury Press.

An introduction to three children and their families, wherein at least one parent grew up in another country: Senegal, Puerto Rico, or Taiwan. Delightful depiction of traditions and teasing from both cultures in each family and how much the children enjoy their dual heritage. (RE/PB, grades K–3, strands I, IV, V, IX)

Lamb, Nancy. (1996). *One April Morning: Children Remember the Oklahoma City Bombing*. New York: Lothrop, Lee & Shepard.

Told with many of the children in Oklahoma City, a moving account of the bombing of the Murrah Federal Building and its aftermath, including the healing and hope. Powerful illustrations. (IN/PB, grades 3–4+, strands V, VI, X)

Lauber, Patricia. (1991). *Summer of Fire*. New York: Orchard Books.
Breathtaking photographs and energetic text bring to life the problems and advantages of the fires that raged in Yellowstone National Park in the summer of 1988. (IN/IT, grades 3–4+, strands II, III)

Levine, Arthur. (1993). *Pearl Moscowitz's Last Stand*. New York: Tambourine Books.
From childhood to old age, Pearl Moscowitz has seen many changes on Gingko Street—trees planted, trees dying, families moving in and out, and urban renewal. When the city workers come to cut down the one remaining tree, Pearl and the other grandmothers halt such "progress" in delightfully effective ways. (EG/PB, grades K–3, strands II, III, VI, X)

Levine, Ellen. (1995). *The Tree That Would Not Die*. New York: Scholastic.
Story of the evolution, attempted destruction, and efforts to save a 500-year-old oak tree in Austin, Texas. (IN/PB, grades K–4, strands II, III, VI, VIII, X)

Lewin, Ted. (1996). *Market!* New York: Lothrop, Lee & Shepard.
A colorful depiction of goods and market customs in a variety of communities around the world, including New York City. (EG/PB, grades 1–3, strands III, VII, IX)

Littlesugar, Amy. (1997). *Jonkonnu*. New York: Philomel Books.
Based on the true story behind Winslow Homer's controversial painting, *Dressing for the Carnival*, this version is told through the eyes of a little white southern girl watching the Yankee artist confront white prejudice as he draws and interacts with the black community "down the red clay road." Stunning illustrations of black people preparing for and celebrating Jonkonnu, a freedom holiday, while whites celebrate the Fourth of July separately. (RE/PB, grades 1–3, strands I, II, V, VI)

London, Jonathan. (1996). *Red Wolf Country*. New York: Dutton Children's Books.
Hauntingly illustrated story of red wolves working to survive in the wild, and conflict with man that still brings danger. An afterword provides additional information about the endangerment of this species and successful programs of protection and release. (IN/PB, grades K–4, strands II, III, VIII)

MacGill, Sheila. (1991). *And Still the Turtle Watched*. New York: Dial Books for Young Readers.
An elderly Delaware carves a turtle in a large stone overlooking a river. Over the years of change, the turtle watches the Delaware leave, strangers chop down the forest, the river turn brown, and loud teenagers spray paint his eyes. In the darkness, he finally feels hands caring for him, transporting him to a botanical garden, and removing the graffiti. There, children come to see him again. (CR+RE/PB, grades 2–3, strands I, II, III, VIII, X)

Maestro, Betsy. (1996). *Coming to America: The Story of Immigration*. New York: Scholastic.
High spirited, but accurate account of the varied people who have immigrated

to America, how and why they did so, the initial difficulties of adjustment, and the richness of American diversity. (IN/PB, grades K–2, strands I, II, III, V, VI)

Morris, Ann. (1990). *Loving*. New York: Lothrop, Lee & Shepard.
Glorious color photographs of families all over the world and how they care for and love their children. (RE/PB, grades K–1, strands V, IX)

Nichols, Joan. (1989). *New Orleans*. New York: Macmillan.
Colorful photographs and description of the life and people in this unusual and exciting city. (IN/PB, grades 3–4+, strands III, V)

Paulsen, Gary. (1997). *Work Song*. San Diego: Harcourt Brace & Company.
With beautiful oil color illustrations, a poetic depiction of the varieties of work accomplished across America on any given day. (EG/PB, grades K–1, strands III, V, VII)

Peterson, Cris. (1996). *Harvest Year*. Honesdale, PA: Boyds Mills Press.
Eye-catching photographs and clearly written text show harvests in every month of the year throughout the United States. (IN/PB, grades K–2, strands III, VII)

Polacco, Patricia. (1992). *Chicken Sunday*. New York: Scholastic.
Three children work to earn money to buy an Easter hat for an especially beloved grandmother. In so doing, they gain the respect of a merchant who previously distrusted and disliked them. (RE/PB, grades 1–3, strands I, V, VII)

Pryor, Bonnie. (1987). *The House on Maple Street*. New York: William Morrow and Company.
Transformation of the use of a plot of land over 300 years from a pre–Native American settlement through a settler's homestead to a modern home. The various pasts and present are linked through the discovery of an arrowhead inside a china cup in the yard. (RE/PB, grades K–3, strands II, III, VIII)

Queen, J. Allen. (1998). *Learn Karate*. New York: Sterling.
First karate text with color photographs published for children. Includes active instruction in a print and photo format with demonstrations from boys and girls from various ethnic groups. Detailed focus on developing responsible behavior. (IN/IT, grades 2–3, strands IV, X)

Raschka, Chris. (1993). *Yo! Yes?* New York: Orchard Books.
Two young boys who are strangers meet, and with minimal conversation, overcome their hesitations and become friends. (EG/PB, grades K–1, strands IV, V)

Rylant, Cynthia. (1992). *An Angel for Solomon Singer*. New York: Orchard Books.
Living in a hotel for men, Solomon Singer is lonely and longs for his boyhood home in Indiana. Wandering the streets at night as he used to roam the fields, he enters the Westway Café and is greeted warmly by a waiter named Angel. He eats there every night for a year, and gradually comes to enjoy the city and realize some of his modest dreams. (EG/PB, grades 1–3, strands III, IV, VII)

Say, Allen. (1997). *Allison*. Boston: Houghton Mifflin.
A Japanese American child realizes she doesn't look like her white parents and agonizes over the uncertainties of adoption from another country. She envies her classmates' families whose members look like each other. When

her parents welcome her request to take in a stray cat, she realizes how happy her own family is. (RE/PB, grades K–2, strands IV, V)

Tamar, Erika. (1996). *The Garden of Happiness*. San Diego: Harcourt Brace & Company.

Delightful story of the transformation of a trash-filled empty lot in New York City into a neighborhood garden of food-plants from the various parts of the world the residents once claimed as home. One tiny spot becomes the place for Marisol's seed, which grows into a sunflower to delight the whole block. Marisol is devastated when the season ends and the sunflower dies, but teenagers paint brilliant sunflowers on a bare wall of a building across the street. (RE/PB, grades K–3, strands III, V, IX)

Native American

Promote: Variety of physical features, occupations, dwellings, and settings; values of family love, generosity, harmony with nature and neighbors; respect for nature, spirituality, personal honor and courage; pride in cultural heritage and traditions

Avoid: Exaggerated physical features and stereotypical clothing, such as feathers and loincloths; predominance of "TV" behavior, such as always grunting or gesturing to communicate, shooting bows and arrows and attacking white settlers; predominance of poverty and lack of education; use of derogatory terms such as *brutal, savage, primitive, redskin, backward, uncivilized,* and so on

Ancona, George. (1995). *Earth Daughter: Alicia of Ácoma Pueblo*. New York: Simon & Schuster Books for Young Readers.

With excellent photographs, the book focuses on Alicia's family and their tradition of making beautiful pottery. (IN/IT, grades 3–4, strands I, II, VII)

Andrews, Jan. (1986). *Very Last First Time*. New York: Macmillan.

Eva is initiated into Inuit culture by walking alone on the bottom of the sea, under the ice at low tide, to collect mussels, as the women do in her home in northern Canada. (RE/PB, grades K–2, strands I, IV, VII)

Arnold, Caroline. (1992). *The Ancient Cliff Dwellers of Mesa Verde*. New York: Clarion.

Fascinating history of the early Anasazi Indians in Colorado, constructed from discoveries of their pottery, tools, and buildings. Excellent color photographs. (IN/IT, grades 4+, strands I, II, III, V)

Baylor, Byrd. (1976). *Hawk, I'm Your Brother*. New York: Charles Scribner's Sons.

A young boy Rudy wants to fly and thinks of nothing else. Caught up in his dreams of flying, Rudy steals a young redtail hawk from its nest and raises it until he realizes that only by releasing the hawk to fly in freedom can he, too, become part of the wind and sky and fly like the hawk who calls to him. (RE/PB, grades 2–4, strands III, IV)

Baylor, Byrd. (1975). *The Desert Is Theirs.* New York: Charles Scribner's Sons.
>A story of the Desert People (Papago Indians) and how they understand and respect the desert and its inhabitants. (RE/PB, grades K–4, strands I, III)

Bruchac, Joseph. (1996). *Children of the Longhouse.* New York: Dial Books for Young Readers.
>A novel of the conflict between those who want peace and those who want war, set in a fifteenth-century Mohawk village. Ohkwa'ri and his twin sister, Otsi:stia, must confront the danger posed by a group of older boys who are eager to raid another village. (RE/NV, grades 4+, strands I, IV, V, VI, IX)

Bruchac, Joseph. (1997). *Eagle Song.* New York: Dial Books for Young Readers.
>Danny Bigtree and his family have moved from the Akwesasne Reservation to Brooklyn, where the Mohawk boy encounters open prejudice and ridicule for the first time in his life. After a series of difficult events, Danny finds inner strength and determination to follow the path of peace toward eventual friendship. (RE/NV, grades 3–4+, strands I, IV, V)

Bruchac, Joseph. (1994). *A Boy Called Slow.* New York: Philomel Books.
>Story of the birth, early life, and first courageous battle fought by Sitting Bull, whose childhood name was Slow. (RE/PB, grades 3–4+, strands I, IV)

Bruchac, Joseph. (1993). *Fox Song.* New York: Philomel Books.
>Jamie's beloved great-grandmother has died, and Jamie comes to terms with her death by remembering their walks together in the woods and all that her Grama Bowman taught her. Jamie goes to the woods alone and sings a special greeting song, which draws a fox close to her. Jamie realizes she will really never be alone. (RE/PB, grades 2–3, strands I, II, III, IV)

Bulla, Clyde. (1978). *Conquista!* New York: Thomas Y. Crowell.
>Alone in the southwestern desert on his journey to find his man-name, Little Wolf discovers a horse left behind by Coronado's explorers. Frightened by the unfamiliar animal, he gradually comes to know it, ride it, respect it, then leaves his sojourn as a young brave with a new name, bringing to his people the animal that will change their lifestyle forever. (RE/NV, grades 3–4, strands I, III, IV)

Bunting, Eve. (1997). *Moonstick: The Seasons of the Sioux.* New York: HarperTrophy.
>Poetic and poignant description of the seasons associated with each of the 13 moons of the year. Changes seen over time in the earth from the grandfather to narrator to his grandson. (RE/PB, grades 1–4, strands I, VIII)

Bunting, Eve. (1995). *Cheyenne Again.* New York: Clarion Books.
>Painful historical account of a 10-year-old Cheyenne boy taken from his reservation and placed in a boarding school for Indians. Headmasters and teachers attempt to rob him of his heritage and make him like them. (RE/PB, grades 1–2, strands I, II, IV, V, VI)

Dorris, Michael. (1996). *Sees through Trees.* New York: Hyperion Books for Children.
>Based on the lives of the Powhatan Indians of Virginia, a story of a sight-impaired young boy who must learn to adjust to his disability and unique gifts, while still fulfilling expectations for young men in his tribe. (RE/NV, grades 4+, strands II, III, IV, V)

Dorris, Michael. (1994). *Guests*. New York: Hyperion Books for Children.
  In that awkward phase between being a little boy and a young man, Moss is grouchy, argumentative, and angry about the guests (Pilgrims) coming to his village's annual feast. He leaves home for his "away time" in the forest, spends time with a young girl from his tribe who is wrestling with her own difficulties, and deepens in understanding of himself and others. He returns to participate in preparing for and caring for the guests, despite not really wanting them there. (RE/NV, grades 3–4, strands I, IV, V, X)

Goble, Paul. (1993). *Death of the Iron Horse*. New York: Aladdin Books.
  Having seen the ravages of the white man and fearing the effects of the "iron horse" and its "iron bands" constricting the earth, the Cheyenne successfully attack the train. But it is only a matter of time until more trains and more white men come, changing their world forever. (CR+RE/PB, grades 2–4, strands I, II, III, V, VI, VIII)

Griese, Arnold. (1995). *Anna's Athabaskan Summer*. Honesdale, PA: Boyds Mills Press.
  Once the long Alaskan winter is over, Anna enjoys returning to the fish camp on the river during the summer. Through helping her family interact with the environment in the traditional ways of Athabaskan Indians, she learns more of her heritage. (IN/PB, grades K–2, strands I, III, V)

Hillerman, Tony. (1972). *The Boy Who Made Dragonfly*. Albuquerque: University of New Mexico Press.
  Gentle retelling of a Zuni myth emphasizing the need for humans to respect their environment and to care for each other. (CR/NV, grades 4+, strands I, III, V)

Hoyt-Goldsmith, Diane. (1993). *Cherokee Summer*. New York: Holiday House.
  With many vivid color photographs, Bridget tells the story of her modern life and the proud heritage of her Cherokee Nation in Oklahoma. (IN/IT, grades 3–4+, strands I, II, V, VIII)

Hoyt-Goldsmith, Diane. (1991). *Pueblo Storyteller*. New York: Holiday House.
  Ten-year-old April tells the story of many Pueblo traditions, with emphasis on the creation of pottery, clay sculptures, and drums as well as participation in rituals and celebrations. (IN/IT, grades 3–4, strands I, III, V, VII)

Hoyt-Goldsmith, Diane. (1990). *Totem Pole*. New York: Holiday House.
  A child in Washington State, whose father is from the Tsimshian tribe and whose European American mother has been adopted into the Eagle Clan of the tribe, tells the story of his father's carving of a totem pole and the celebration accompanying its raising. Vivid photographs. (IN/IT, grades 3–4+, strands I, V)

Jeffers, Susan. (1991). *Brother Eagle, Sister Sky*. New York: Dial Books.
  A lavishly illustrated poetic message from Chief Seattle of the Suquamish and Duwamish Indians, given at treaty negotiations in the 1850s. Strong, reverent plea to care for the earth. (CR+RE/PB, grades K–4, strands II, III)

Keegan, Marcia. (1991). *Pueblo Boy: Growing Up in Two Worlds*. New York: Cobblehill Books.

The life of Timmy Roybal, a Pueblo Indian living on a reservation in New Mexico, who lives a modern life in many ways while maintaining strong connections to the heritage of his people. Vivid photographs. (IN/IT, grades 3–4, strands I, III, V)

Kendall, Russ. (1992). *Eskimo Boy: Life in an Inupiaq Eskimo Village*. New York: Scholastic.

Life for the Inupiaq Eskimos on the small island of Shismaref off the coast of Alaska maintains much of the traditional customs of the tribe, with little interference from the Western world. Some modern conveniences have been adopted, but much has not changed for generations. (IN/PB, grades 3–4, strands I, III, VII)

Littlechild, George. (1993). *This Land Is My Land*. San Francisco: Children's Book Press.

Built around his own paintings, the author gives brief explanations of various aspects of the history of the Plains Cree Indians in Canada from the time of meeting Europeans to modern difficulties in city life. Poignant and humorous. (IN/PB, grades 3–4+, strands I, II, III, V)

Locker, Thomas. (1991). *The Land of Gray Wolf*. New York: Dial Books.

Transformation of the land, its use, and its animals from the time of the Native Americans to the intrusion of white settlers to their departure and the gradual return of the land back to the animals. (RE/PB, grades 1–3, strands II, III, V, VIII)

Martin, Jr., Bill. (1987). *Knots on a Counting Rope*. New York: Henry Holt and Company.

Grandfather and grandson jointly tell the story of the child's birth and boyhood triumphs over blindness. Breathtaking illustrations and language. (RE/PB, grades 1–4, strands I, IV, V)

Miles, Miska. (1971). *Annie and the Old One*. Boston: Little, Brown.

A young girl must come to terms with her grandmother's impending death and learn the Navajo ways of accepting and celebrating the cycle of life. (RE/NV, grades 3–4, strands I, II, IV, V)

Peters, Russell. (1992). *Clambake: A Wampanoag Tradition*. Minneapolis: Lerner Publications.

Narrative of the traditional ceremonial celebration of the clambake among the Wampanoag people of Massachusetts. Excellent color photographs. (IN/IT, grades 3–4+, strands I, V)

Rendon, Marcie. (1996). *Powwow Summer: A Family Celebrates the Circle of Life*. Minneapolis: Carolrhoda Books.

Interweaving of the Anishinabe (also called Ojibway or Chippewa) people's belief in the endless circle of life and extended family care for children with the example of the Downwind family at home in Minnesota and on their summer trips to various powwows. Excellent color photographs. (IN/PB, grades 2–4, strands I, IV, V)

Regguinti, Gordon. (1992). *The Sacred Harvest: Ojibway Wild Rice Gathering*. Minneapolis: Lerner Publications.

Narrative of a Minnesota family and the celebration of the wild rice harvest on their reservation. Outstanding color photographs and warmly written text. (IN/IT, grades 3–4+, strands I, III, V, VII)

Scott, Ann. (1996). *Brave as a Mountain Lion*. New York: Clarion Books.
Set in a Shoshone reservation, the story of a boy warmly supported by his family to conquer his fears of being on stage in the school's spelling bee. (EG/PB, grades K–3, strands IV, V)

Sewall, Marcia. (1990). *People of the Breaking Day*. New York: Atheneum.
How the Wampanoags, a tribe living in southeastern Massachusetts when the Pilgrims landed, lived throughout the seasons of the year at that time. (IN/PB, grades 3–4, strands I, III, VII)

Shaw-MacKinnon, Margaret. (1996). *Tiktala*. Toronto, Canada: Stoddart Publishing.
A young Eskimo girl, Tiktala, yearns to be a carver, but must first prove herself on a three-day journey by herself to search for a spirit helper. She is transformed into a harp seal, the very animal she wishes to carve, and travels with another harp seal, who speaks angrily toward her about human mistreatment of seals. Tiktala rises up to protect the other seal's baby against a hunter preparing to club it and immediately regains her human form with new understanding of how seals have been mistreated. (CR/PB, grades 1–4, strands I, III, VII)

Sneve, Virginia Driving Hawk. (1993–1997). *The First Americans Series*. New York: Holiday House.
A series of books focused on individual Native American tribes, including the Apaches, Cherokees, Iroquois, Navajos, Nez Perce, Seminoles, and Sioux. Each provides an overview of the tribe's history, culture, and present life, then describes particular struggles and accomplishments. (IN/IT, grades 3–4+, strands I, II, III, V, VI)

Yolen, Jane. (1992). *Encounter*. San Diego: Harcourt Brace Jovanovich.
A provocative, chilling Taino Indian child's perspective of the arrival of Columbus and the permanent impact on his people. (RE/PB, grades 2–4, strands I, II, III, V)

Religious Cultures

Adler, David. (1993). *A Picture Book of Anne Frank*. New York: Holiday House.
Powerfully illustrated and narrated story of Anne Frank from her happy childhood to the time of hiding in the attic to the concentration camp and her eventual death. (IN/PB, grades 2–4, strands III, V, VI, IX)

Bial, Raymond. (1994). *Shaker Home*. Boston: Houghton Mifflin.
With photographs as stunning in their simplicity as the Shaker lifestyle and

their crafted furniture, buildings, and other products, the author tells the history of this religious group. (IN/IT, grades 3–4+, strands I, II, V, VIII)

Bial, Raymond. (1993). *Amish Home*. Boston: Houghton Mifflin.

With photographs respectfully absent of the Amish people themselves, the author tells their fascinating story. (IN/IT, grades 3–4+, strands I, II, III, V, VIII)

Bloom, Lloyd. (1995). *One Yellow Daffodil: A Hanukkah Story*. San Diego: Gulliver Books.

Years after the Holocaust, florist Morris Kaplan still avoids the memories of childhood, including holiday celebrations. Thanks to a loving family, Morris remembers the one lone daffodil in the concentration camp, which brings back a flood of other memories, including the location of a long-forgotten menorah which he brings to the family to share Hanukkah with them. (RE/PB, grades 3–4, strands I, II, III, IV, IX)

Cohen, Barbara. (1987). *The Christmas Revolution*. New York: Lothrop, Lee & Shepard.

Jewish twins face another round of Christmas activities at their school; Emily feels uncomfortable, which puzzles Sally. A new Orthodox Jewish child escalates peer pressure and hostility between Jewish and Christian children until deceit is uncovered, a Hanukkah celebration is shared, and friendships are restored. (RE/NV, grades 4+, strands I, IV, V)

Cohen, Barbara. (1983). *Molly's Pilgrim*. New York: Lothrop, Lee & Shepard.

As a Jewish immigrant from Russia, Molly was unhappy in school with American children who teased her all the time. Her mother helped Molly make a pilgrim doll for homework, but the children again teased her about its Russian appearance until Molly defined her mother as a pilgrim, and the teacher firmly taught the Jewish origins of Thanksgiving and the real meaning of being a pilgrim. (RE/PB, grades 2–4, strands I, V, VI, IX)

Cohen, Barbara. (1981). *Yussel's Prayer: A Yom Kippur Story*. New York: Lothrop, Lee & Shepard.

A story of contrasts between a poor, uneducated orphan boy with a true understanding of God and those villagers who attend the Yom Kippur service with the outward appearance of piety but inner lack of concentration, interest, and conviction. (RE/PB, grades 2–4, strands I, V)

Cohn, Janice. (1995). *The Christmas Menorahs: How a Town Fought Hate*. Morton Grove, IL: Albert Whitman & Company.

Based on real events in Billings, Montana, during Hanukkah in 1993. Several race-based hate crimes had occurred, with specific attacks against Jewish families displaying menorahs in their windows. Non-Jewish families fought back by placing menorahs in their windows, too, and the attacks stopped. (RE/PB, grades 2–4, strands I, V, X)

Ehrlich, Amy. (1989). *The Story of Hanukkah*. New York: Puffin Pied Piper Books.

Illustrated with vibrant colors, a simple and straightforward account of the history behind the eight-day Jewish celebration of Hanukkah. (IN/PB, grades K–2, strands I, II, V)

Ghazi, Suhaib Hamid. (1996). *Ramadan*. New York: Holiday House.
Appearing to be set in the United States, the book follows Hakeem and his family through the days and evenings in the Muslim holy month of Ramadan. Explanation of customs and beliefs is presented in an engaging style. (IN/PB, grades 3–4+, strands I, II, V, IX)

Grimes, Nikki. (1996). *Come Sunday*. Grand Rapids, MI: William B. Eerdmans Publishing.
Poetic description provides rich details of an African American child's Sunday centered around church. (CR/PB, grades K–2, strands I, V)

Harvey, Brett. (1987). *Immigrant Girl: Becky of Eldridge Street*. New York: Holiday House.
Becky tells the story of her adjustment to the hustle and bustle of New York City after emigrating from Russia, and how the family maintains the Jewish faith and customs. (RE/PB, grades 3–4, strands I, II, V)

Joseph, Lynn. (1992). *An Island Christmas*. New York: Clarion Books.
Family and community preparations for Christmas on a Caribbean island. Loving story written in rhyme, using local dialect. (CR/PB, grades 1–3, strands I, III, V)

Kenna, Kathleen. (1995). *A People Apart*. Boston: Houghton Mifflin.
With great care and respect, the author shows the lives and customs of Old Order Mennonites through text and rare photographs. (IN/IT, grades 4+, strands I, III, V, VIII, X)

Leighton, Maxinne. (1992). *An Ellis Island Christmas*. New York: Viking.
Story of the difficult boat trip to America of a Polish immigrant family, the hope engendered by the sight of the Statue of Liberty, the frightening passage through customs on Ellis Island, a Christmas surprise for little Krysia, and the reunion with her papa. (RE/PB, grades 1–3, strands IV, V, VI, IX)

Livingston, Myra. (1986). *Poems for Jewish Holidays*. New York: Holiday House.
Beautiful brief poems to be appreciated across all cultures. (CR/PB, grades K–4, strands I, V).

Manushkin, Fran. (1995). *The Matzah That Papa Brought Home*. New York: Scholastic.
Predictable pattern book focused on the Jewish celebration of Passover. Additional information given at the end of the story. (CR+RE/PB, grades K–2, strands I, II)

Matthews, Mary. (1996). *Magid Fasts for Ramadan*. New York: Clarion Books.
Set in Egypt, an engaging and informative story of a boy too young to fast for Ramadan and how he learns to observe the Islamic holy month in a way his young body and spirit can handle. (RE/NV, grades 4+, strands I, IV)

McKissack, Patricia, and McKissack, Fredrick. (1994). *Christmas in the Big House, Christmas in the Quarters*. New York: Scholastic.
Celebrating Christmas in the master's house and in the slave quarters is shown with the joy of the faith, the interrelationships of the lives of both groups of people, and the stark contrast of those lives. Powerful illustrations. (IN/IT, grades 3–4+, strands I, II, V, VI)

Mitchell, Barbara. (1993). *Down Buttermilk Lane*. New York: Lothrop, Lee & Shepard.

Except for a questionable car in one illustration, an authentic and delightful portrayal of Amish family life and language variety. Excellent companion book to *Amish Home* by Raymond Bial. (RE/PB, grades K–3, strands II, V)

Moss, Marissa. (1996). *The Ugly Menorah*. New York: Farrar, Straus and Giroux.

Rachel spends Hanukkah with her widowed grandmother and is appalled at her ugly wood and tin menorah. When she hears how her grandfather made it, Rachel sees its beauty and finds new meaning in celebrating Hanukkah. (RE/PB, grades K–2, strands I, II, V)

Oberman, Sheldon. (1994). *The Always Prayer Shawl*. Honesdale, PA: Boyds Mills Press.

When young Adam must leave Russia with his parents, his grandfather Adam stays behind, but gives him his own prayer shawl that belonged to his grandfather Adam and his grandfather Adam before him. As Adam matures and grows old, he mends the prayer shawl many times and wears it every Saturday. When his grandson Adam is old enough, he explains the history of their name and the Always Prayer Shawl. (RE/PB, grades 2–4, strands I, II)

Oppenheim, Shulamith. (1992). *The Lily Cupboard*. New York: HarperTrophy.

Miriam's parents hide her with a non-Jewish family in Holland during World War II. Miriam must adjust to being without her parents and learn to hide quickly in the secret cupboard in the wall. (RE/PB, grades 1–3, strands II, V, VI, IX)

Polacco, Patricia. (2000). *The Butterfly*. New York: Philomel Books.

Set in Europe during World War II, this true story of a family hiding Jews from the Nazis is written for younger readers. Emphasis on courage, cunning, and risk taking to protect others being unjustly persecuted. Poignant, powerful. (RE/PB, grades 2–4, strands I, V, VI)

Polacco, Patricia. (1994). *Tikvah Means Hope*. New York: Delacorte Press.

Jewish neighbors invite two non-Jewish children to celebrate the Jewish thanksgiving, Sukkoth, with them. They build a Sukkah together, and the children sleep in the open-air structure that night. The next day the Oakland fires come too close, and they must flee to safety. Upon later return, everyone finds their homes destroyed, but the Sukkah still stands. Neighbors give thanks together for their lives, and the tiny cat, Tikvah, miraculously emerges to join them. (RE/PB, grades 1–3, strands I, III)

Polacco, Patricia. (1992). *Mrs. Katz and Tush*. New York: Dell Publishing.

An elderly Jewish lady, a small black boy, and the kitten he gives her become close friends after her husband dies. Over the years, their friendship is interwoven with her memories of mistreatment in Poland and comparisons to mistreatment of blacks, participation in Jewish celebrations and customs, his family and their descendants, and eventually a kaddish for Mrs. Katz. (RE/PB, grades K–2, strands I, II, V, IX)

Polacco, Patricia. (1990). *Just Plain Fancy*. New York: A Bantam Little Rooster Book.

Surrounded by the value of plain dress and behavior, an Amish girl longs for something fancy as she raises chickens. When she learns that her community shuns those who are too fancy, she worries about her unusual chick who is not plain. But the community considers her beautiful peacock to be a gift from God. (RE/PB, grades 1–3, strands I, V)

Presilla, Maricel. (1994). *Feliz Nochebuena, Feliz Navidad: Christmas Feasts of the Hispanic Caribbean.* New York: Henry Holt and Company.

With frequent contrasts to Latino Christmas celebrations in Miami, the author describes the Christmas feasts and traditions in her native Cuba and in her relatives' home in Puerto Rico. History, recipes, and songs in English and Spanish. (IN/IT, grades 3–4+, strands I, II, V)

Rael, Elsa. (1996). *What Zeesie Saw on Delancey Street.* New York: Simon & Schuster Books for Young Readers.

On her birthday, at a special party, Zeesie witnesses her father's friend doing a good deed in the "money room"—where taking or donating cash were both considered appropriate and were never to be discussed. Moved to tears by the experience, Zeesie quietly donates her birthday dollar and proudly realizes she will never tell. (RE/PB, grades 3–4, strands I, IV, V, X)

Ray, Mary Lyn. (1994). *Shaker Boy.* San Diego: Browndeer Press.

Life with the Shakers was always busy and productive for the orphans they adopted. Some left, but Caleb and many others stayed throughout their lives, satisfied with the Shaker life and culture and fulfilled by the roles they played. (RE/PB, grades 1–3, strands II, IV, V)

Rylant, Cynthia. (1987). *Children of Christmas: Stories for the Season.* New York: Orchard Books.

Moving nontraditional stories of unexpected happiness on Christmas Eve. (EG/SS, grades 3–4+, strands I, IV, V)

Schnur, Steven. (1995). *The Tie Man's Miracle: A Chanukah Tale.* New York: Morrow Junior Books.

A touching, but unresolved story of a loving family who welcomes a lonely old man one year at Hanukkah, hears of his life and dreams, then never sees him again. (RE/PB, grades 2–3, strands I, II, V)

Schotter, Roni. (1995). *Passover Magic.* Boston: Little, Brown.

An extended family celebrates Passover in the traditional way, except for a delightful uncle who is also a magician. (RE/PB, grades 1–2, strands I, II, V)

Silverman, Maida. (1992). *The Glass Menorah and Other Stories for Jewish Holidays.* New York: Four Winds Press.

Eight contemporary short stories centered on one family and their celebration of Jewish holidays. (RE/SS, grades 2–4, strands I, IV, V)

Turner, Ann. (1997). *Shaker Hearts.* New York: HarperCollins.

Information and poetry reveal the life and values of the Shaker communities of previous centuries. (CR/PB, grades 3–4, strands I, II, V)

10 How do I plan for thematic instruction of social studies and literature?

There are a variety of ways to design integrated units. Some teachers are comfortable with the model of starting with a very broad theme, such as Boyer's (1995) "Living with Purpose," and developing a graphic organizer, or web, to lay out the components of the unit. Each strand on the web includes content objectives and activities related to that theme, focused on each individual area of the curriculum. Other teachers use a model that focuses on one area—for example, a science concept or a theme such as "Changes"—and then choose objectives and activities from other areas of the curriculum to be subsumed under the narrower focus of the unit. Still others develop entire units around a single novel, bringing in related objectives and activities for other curricular areas, but keeping the major focus on the communication objectives associated with studying the novel.

Allen and Piersma (1995, p. 38) suggest three models for thematic units that use literature as a major component:

1. *Literature Supplement Model:* Literature selections are used to enhance the study of a specific topic (e.g., space, transportation, state history), but the books serve more as resources to the students than as the central focus of any teacher-directed lessons.
2. *Literature-Centered Model:* Instruction focuses on the study of story elements in a specific piece of literature and the promotion of students' responses to the literature; teachers help students make connections to other curriculum areas through additional activities.
3. *Literature-Infused Model:* Unit design and instruction strive for a balance between the study of children's literature and the concepts/objectives selected from all other areas of the curriculum. Literature is actually used as the vehicle for teaching the concepts, skills, attitudes, and values from those content areas.

Our unit designs come closest to Allen and Piersma's literature-infused model, except that we suggest integrating only social studies and literature rather than all areas of the curriculum. Literature will be used as the vehicle for teaching the social studies concepts, with other nonliterature-based instructional activities to be expected. Although it is certainly possible to fully implement the literature-infused model—that is, to integrate all areas of the curriculum through the NCSS themes and literature—we have chosen not to recommend that level of complexity at this time. Rather, we have selected two models, both of which are closely aligned with literature infusion, but focus most heavily on balancing social studies and literature. Quite simply, they are the single-book model and the multiple-book model.

The Single-Book Model

One book is used as the focal text of the thematic unit; the content of the book is the major source for teaching the concepts/skills of social studies and literacy. Instructional activities focus almost exclusively on the content of the book as the vehicle for developing understanding of the NCSS theme and achieving the specific objectives or performance expectations related to that theme. Literacy objectives are held as equal to social studies objectives, and neither type of objective is taught in isolation. Other social studies materials—such as textbooks, maps, newspapers, and magazine articles—are considered supplementary to the central piece of literature under study.

The Multiple-Book Model

Although there is still a balance between teaching social studies and literacy, the central focus of the unit is the NCSS theme. Several pieces of literature are used to develop understanding of that theme, but none of the pieces would receive the amount of in-depth focus promoted by the single-book model. A wide variety of instructional activities and materials focus on the NCSS theme as the unifying element of the unit and serve as multiple vehicles for helping students achieve the specific objectives or performance expectations related to that theme. Literacy objectives are held as equal to social studies objectives, and neither type of objective is taught in isolation.

We suggest the following steps for designing a unit using either the single-book or the multiple-book model:

1. Select a *theme* for the unit of study.
   - You might choose one of the 10 NCSS themes.
   - You might choose a broader theme that encompasses more than one NCSS theme.
   - You might study your state or local curriculum guide in social studies and choose an area or a cluster of objectives and concepts that could be closely aligned with an NCSS theme.
   - You might rethink a favorite piece of literature required or recommended for a book study at your grade level in terms of what NCSS theme(s) it strongly matches.

- Consider your rationale for the theme. Will this thematic study help propel you and your students toward the *transformation* or *decision-making and social action approaches* of multicultural education?

2. Examine several books that are specifically relevant to the chosen theme, then select one or more best suited to your students and community.
   - You might start with our worksheets for linking social studies and multicultural literature in Chapter 8.
   - You might also use the steps for evaluating the worth of the literature for in-depth study in Chapter 7.
   - You might use our annotated bibliography in Chapter 9 to consider stories that represent different cultural groups in the United States.
   - You might use sources we mention for finding multicultural literature at the end of Chapter 5, especially the annual volume of *Social Education*, which reviews and links new publications to various areas of the social studies, including the NCSS strands.

3. Align specific objectives that are common to both the theme and the book(s).
   - You might visualize this alignment by marking cells in the chart seen on the next page. Where do the major elements of the literature align with NCSS themes in the book you're considering?
   - You might choose performance standards related to the NCSS themes (see Chapter 8) and add in state or local objectives for literacy that could be taught through the book(s).
   - You might examine your state or local social studies objectives, link them to the theme you've chosen, and add in state or local objectives for literacy.
   - You might choose your literacy objectives first, perhaps because you are more familiar with teaching literature, then add in the appropriate social studies objectives or NCSS performance expectations.

4. Plan lessons/activities that will promote students' achievement of the unit's objectives.
   - You might use or modify some of the activities in our exemplar units (Part Three).
   - You might modify previously successful lessons/activities in social studies and literature to blend the content of the two areas.
   - You might want to try one of our units in its totality if this is your first thematic unit. You don't have to start something new from ground zero!
   - You might check the Internet sources we listed at the end of Chapter 5 for lesson plans and ideas.

5. Decide on a logical sequence of objectives and activities.
   - Think about an initiating activity that provides a powerful introduction to the unit.
   - Plan lessons/activities for the "chunks" of a book to be read in one sitting.
   - Consider whether there is a sense of sequence to the unit's objectives and whether some objectives are likely to need reteaching in later lessons.
   - For the multiple-book model, consider whether there is a desired sequence for your use of the different books.

Potential Integration Points for Social Studies and Children's Literature

NCSS Themes	Four Major Elements of Fine Children's Literature			
	Character-ization	Plot/Problem	Setting	Theme
I. Culture				
II. Time, Continuity, and Change				
III. People, Places, and Environments				
IV. Individual Development and Identity				
V. Individuals, Groups, and Institutions				
VI. Power, Authority, and Governance				
VII. Production, Distribution, and Consumption				
VIII. Science, Technology, and Society				
IX. Global Connections				
X. Civic Ideals and Practices				

- Decide how long each lesson should last, considering the length of related text material and the time needed to complete the activities of the lesson.
- Decide whether you wish to integrate any other areas of the curriculum in order to enhance students' mastery of the social studies and literacy objectives of the unit.
- Think about a culminating activity that promotes the demonstration of major understandings developed by students during the unit.

6. Develop at least two evaluation strategies for assessing students' achievement of objectives in each lesson and in the entire unit. (You might not use two strategies in each lesson, but you'll have the flexibility if you need it for assessing the achievement of diverse learners.)

- You might want to use ideas in the next chapter to plan for evaluating your unit, your lessons, and your students' learning.
- You want visible evidence that students are learning. Many of the ways you evaluate students' learning in literacy are directly applicable.
- For some of the social studies objectives, your visible evidence may be the children's social behaviors.
- You want to gauge the success of your activities, lessons, and overall unit not only by the engagement and responsiveness of your students and by your own sense of satisfaction but also by tangible evidence that the students are learning—that they are mastering the content, skills, and processes on which they will be evaluated at the end of the year in many states and school districts.

READINGS ABOUT INSTRUCTIONAL DESIGN AND THEMATIC APPROACHES TO INSTRUCTION

Allen, D., & Piersma, M. (1995). *Developing thematic units: Process and product.* Albany, NY: Delmar.

Boyer, E. (1995). *The basic school: A community for learning.* Princeton, NJ: Carnegie Foundation for the Advancement of Teaching.

Dorman, Suzanne, & Levine, Joel. (1997). *A practical guide to elementary instruction: From plan to delivery.* Boston: Allyn and Bacon.

Kemp, Jerrold, Morrison, Gary, & Ross, Steven. (1999). *Designing effective instruction* (2nd ed.). Upper Saddle River, NJ: Merrill-Prentice-Hall.

Lewis, A. (1997). Learning our lessons about early learning. *Phi Delta Kappan, 8,* 591–592.

Martin-Kniep, Aiselle. (2000). *Becoming a better teacher: Eight innovations that work.* Alexandria, VA: Association for Supervision and Curriculum Development.

Means, B. (2000/2001). Technology use in tomorrow's schools. *Educational Leadership, 58,* 57–61.

Meinbach, A., Rothlein, L., & Fredericks, A. (1995). *The complete guide to thematic units: Creating the integrated curriculum.* Norwood, MA: Christopher Gordon.

Queen, J. Allen. (1999). The instructional unit. In J. Allen Queen (Ed.), *Curriculum practice in the elementary and middle school* (pp. 217–278). Upper Saddle River, NJ: Merrill-Prentice-Hall.

Queen, J. Allen, Burrell, Jenny, & McManus, Stephanie. (2001). *Planning for instruction: A year-long guide.* Upper Saddle River, NJ: Merrill-Prentice-Hall.

Spann, M. (1992). *Literature-based multicultural activities: An integrated approach.* New York: Scholastic Professional Books.

Sunai, Cynthia, Powel, Deborah, McClelland, Susan, & Rule, Audrey. (2000). *Integrating academic units in the elementary school curriculum.* New York: Holt, Rinehart and Winston.

INTERNET RESOURCES FOR THEMATIC UNITS

Thematic units:
   http://www.proteacher.com/020010.shtml
   http://home.ici.net/~midgef/elres.html#theme
Theme-related resources on the web: http://www.stemnet.nf.ca/CITE/themes.html
Theme units and online activities: http://viking.stark.k12.oh.us/~greentown/grtheme.htm
Theme index: http://teachers.net/lessons/posts/342.html

CHAPTER

11

How do I evaluate my unit and my students' learning?

For better or worse, human beings have been evaluating each others' performance on the job and in school for centuries. This chapter presents perspectives about and strategies for this daunting task, given the integrated purposes of instruction in social studies and literature and with a realistic awareness of district- or state-mandated achievement tests.

Did you know...

- The earliest known form of evaluation occurred over 4,000 years ago in China. During the four Dynasties of Yao and Shun (2357 to 2205 B.C.), Hsia (2205 to 1766 B.C.), and Shung (1766 to 1122 B.C.), examinations were given to all civil servants every three years. After taking the three tests, they were either promoted or dismissed.
- In the United States, evaluation began in the common school. Horace Mann, the father of the common school and the first State Secretary of Education, persuaded the Massachusetts legislature in 1838 to pass an education act that required that a "register" be kept with specific information on each student. Originally, students were evaluated by oral exams, but educators switched to written exams to increase efficiency and specificity of what was being tested. Essay exams became a popular way of evaluating students' knowledge.

Responsibilities for Evaluation

Evaluation is generally considered to be the process of making a judgment, determining effectiveness, or giving value to learners, materials, programs, and processes being assessed. There are several applications of evaluation in schools, with two major, but simple, questions always being the focus:

1. Did we do what we planned to do?
2. Did it work? (Did students learn what they were expected to?)

Curriculum evaluation is the process of collecting and processing data for decision making about the merit of an educational program in a grade level, school, or school district. The two questions become:

1. Was this program implemented as planned?
2. Did the students learn what was expected?

Instructional evaluation, or assessment, is more focused on the individual classroom and particular lessons, units, or periods of instruction. The questions become:

1. Did I implement this lesson/unit as I planned?
2. Did my students learn what I expected?

Student self-evaluation is now more frequently included as a part of both curriculum evaluation and instructional evaluation. As the community demands more student accountability, students are becoming more involved in evaluating their own learning processes, progress, deficits, and achievements. Their questions become:

1. Did I do what the teacher (or I) planned for me to do?
2. What did I learn? Did I learn what was expected?

Let's take a closer look and then point toward ways of bringing evaluation into the everyday life of planning and implementing thematic units. Instructional evaluation, with student self-evaluation, is really at the heart of the matter. Oliva (2001) believes that the evaluation of instruction—that is, the effectiveness of the instructor—occurs through the assessment of student achievement. For example, does the teacher choose the right delivery system? Are the teacher's objectives clear? Has the content been adequately covered? Do test items relate to objectives? How much do students achieve in areas that are assessed? Evaluation of instruction does not answer broader curricular concerns, such as whether the subject matter was the right choice to begin with, whether its content is relevant, whether it meets students' or societal needs, and whether the content has been selected wisely.

Evaluation Questions

To evaluate whether you implemented a unit as planned, there are important questions to ask yourself and your students throughout the planning, implementation, and reflection on the unit when it is completed. The questions should literally begin as you *plan* the unit:

- What *dimensions* of Banks and Banks's model of multicultural education am I targeting in my chosen literature and instructional activities? (See pages 13–14, 17, and 26 in this book.)
- What *levels* of Banks and Banks's model of multicultural education am I planning to approach with the literature I've chosen? (See pages 29–30 in this book.)

- Have I chosen appropriate literature for the unit theme? Are there strong points of integration with two or three NCSS themes? (See Chapter 8.)
- How do I think students and parents will react to this literature?
- Have I planned to evaluate students' learning throughout the unit in a variety of ways?

As you *implement* the unit, you will continue asking questions about whether you are carrying out the lessons and activities as planned (or making appropriate modifications), how your students are responding to the unit, and what your students are learning:

- Is the amount of time planned for the lessons working?
- Is the sequence of lessons/activities working?
- Do the students appear engaged in the content and activities?
- What kind of data am I gathering about students' actual learning? Am I looking at a variety of information? Am I gathering data directly related to the objectives of each lesson and the overall unit?
- Am I making modifications to my instruction because of information gathered from assessing students' learning?

When you have *completed* the unit, you will be asking questions about the overall success of implementation and the overall impact on students' learning:

- Did I implement everything I had planned to do? Did I need to add or delete anything from the unit? How do I know?
- Did I change or need to change the sequence, the length of time spent, or the types of activities? How do I know?
- Do I have data about students' learning related to the overall objectives of the unit? What do I know about their learning from that data?
- Given my experiences in this unit pertaining to multicultural education, NCSS themes, and multicultural literature, what directions do I plan to take next?

Evaluation Strategies for Assessing Students' Mastery of Objectives

There are a wide variety of tools, some of which are more directly related to end-of-the-year types of assessment of students' knowledge/skills gained, and some of which are more related to the teacher's observation of behavior and his or her inferences of students' attitudes/values shifted as suggested by that behavior or as spoken in students' self-reflections and self-evaluations.

- *Traditional Testing:* The traditional testing of students is through various forms of the pencil and paper test. Tests, even in K–4, tend to include objective and essay questions focused on knowledge of content. One strength of this testing is that it can be used as a pretest and posttest to instruction. In these situations, both pretests and posttests should be clearly related to the instructional objectives of the lesson or unit.

- *Performance-Based or Authentic Assessment:*   *Authentic* means "worthy of acceptance or belief, trustworthy" (Engel, 1994, p. 24). Assessments are authentic because they are valuable activities within themselves and involve the performance of tasks that are directly related to real-world problems. The assessments typically take place over time to emphasize the growth of students in the targeted areas of interest, and are often collected in a portfolio.
- *Portfolio*:   A portfolio is a systematic and organized collection of a student's work throughout a unit that measures the student's knowledge and skills and often includes some form of self-reflection by the student. Portfolios may contain creative writing, tests, artwork, exercises, reflective essays, dictated stories, photographs, notes about role plays or performances, and whatever other materials portray growth and achievement.

As you evaluate both the implementation of a thematic unit and the students' learning within that unit, use and adapt the evaluation strategies in our model units freely. Since much of the instruction in social studies, especially social studies with a multicultural education emphasis, is intended to produce permanent changes in behavior and attitude over time, you may also wish to revisit the evaluation of selected objectives throughout the year.

READINGS ABOUT ASSESSMENT

Bean, Thomas. (1998). ReWrite: A music strategy for exploring content area concepts. *Reading Online* (www.readingonline.org).

Bigelow, B. (1999). Why standardized tests threaten multiculturalism. *Educational Leadership, 5,* 37–40.

Engel, B. (1994). Portfolio assessment and the new paradigm: New instruments and new places. *The Education Forum, 59,* 22–27.

Garcia, E., Casimir, M., Iminger, X., Wiese, A., & Garcia, E. (1999). Authentic literacy assessment (ALA) development: An instruction-based assessment that is responsive to linguistic and cultural diversity. *Educators for Urban Minorities, 1,* 48–57.

Ghory, W. J. (1996). Reclaiming evaluation: The Cinderella of school reform. *Equity & Excellence in Education, 29,* 91–96.

Gillespie, G. S., Gillespie, R. D., Ford, K. L., & Leavell, A. G. (1996). Portfolio assessment: Some questions, some answers, some recommendation. *Journal of Adolescent & Adult Literacy, 39,* 480–491.

Halford, J. (1999). A different mirror: A conversation with Ronald Takaki. *Educational Leadership, 56,* 8–13.

Kindsvatter, R., Wilen, W., & Ishler, M. (1996). *Dynamics of effective teaching* (3rd ed.). White Plains, NY: Longman.

Lee, Carol. (1998). Culturally responsive pedagogy and performance-based assessment. *Journal of Negro Education, 67,* 269–279.

National Assessment of Educational Progress (NAEP). (1995). *1994 reading: A first look.* Washington, DC: National Center for Education Statistics.

Nitko, Anthony. (1996). *Educational assessment of students* (2nd ed.). Upper Saddle River, NJ: Prentice-Hall.

Oliva, P. (2001). *Developing the curriculum* (5th ed.). New York: Longman.

O'Neill, J. (2000). Smart goals: Smart schools. *Educational Leadership, 57,* 46–50.

Puckett, Margaret, & Black, Janet. (2000). *Authentic assessment of the young child: Celebrating development and learning* (2nd ed.). Upper Saddle River, NJ: Prentice-Hall.

Ravitch, D. (1995). *National standards in American education: A citizen's guide.* Washington, DC: The Brookings Group.

Sandoval, J., Frisby, C. L., Geisinger, K. F., Scheuneman, J. D., & Grenor, J. R. (Eds.). (1998). *Test interpretation and diversity: Achieving equity in assessment.* Washington, DC: American Psychological Association.

Stiggins, R. J. (1999). Assessment, student confidence, and school success. *Phi Delta Kappan, 81,* 191–198.

Suiter, Mary. (1998). Authentic teaching and assessment in economics education. *Social Studies and the Young Learner, 11,* 22–25.

Swope, K., & Miner, B. (Eds.). (2000). *Failing our kids: Why the testing craze won't fix our schools.* Milwaukee, WI: Rethinking Schools, Ltd.

Theobald, P., & Mills, E. (1995). Accountability and the struggle over what counts. *Phi Delta Kappan, 76,* 462–466.

Tombari, Martin, & Borich, Gary. (1999). *Authentic assessment in the classroom: Applications and practice.* Upper Saddle River, NJ: Merrill-Prentice-Hall.

Wiggins, G. (1993). Assessment: Authenticity, context and validity. *Phi Delta Kappan, 75,* 200–214.

Wolf, D. P., & White, A. M. (2000). Charting the course of student growth. *Educational Leadership, 57,* 6–11.

PART THREE

Exemplar Units

Part Three contains 10 exemplar units, each spanning two suggested grade levels for flexibility of your use. The organizers we have used in developing these units are as follows:

- The thematic focus is broad enough to encompass two or more NCSS themes.
- Literacy objectives for each unit and lesson are drawn from the North Carolina Standard Course of Study; these are state-level curriculum objectives much like those in any state.
- Grade-level recommendations are based on developmental interests and concepts of children, not independent reading level.
- Multiple-book and single-book models are provided. Multiple-book models always include books from several cultural groupings; the six single-book models include selections from four major cultural groups and recommended additional readings that include characters from other groups.
- Activities are based on best practices, with plenty of room for you to modify ideas to fit your students.
- Our predominant choice of books is realistic.
- Our predominant dimension of Banks and Banks's multicultural approaches is decision making and social action. These units do not focus on holidays, celebrations, customs, or contributions of people from various minority groups, although some books of that type appear in Chapter 9's annotated bibliography. Rather, the books often examine problems and difficulties of human beings, with the intention of preparing today's children for an increasingly complex world which they must help to fill with justice and peace.

We hope you find these units useful and effective—and that you don't shy away from the realistic content of these compelling stories. Once you see your students engaged with these powerful ideas, we believe your teaching will continue to move naturally and swiftly into the multicultural educational world of the United States.

Unit No.	Grade Levels	Book(s)	Thematic Focus	Cultural Group(s)	NCSS Strands	Page
1	K–1	Multiple books	Work Is Important!	Multicultural	IV, VI, VII	123
2	K–2	*Thundercake*	Getting Rid of Fears	European American	IV	142
3	1–2	Multiple books	Family Helpfulness	Multicultural	I, IV, VII	151
4	2–3	Multiple books	Overcoming Barriers	Multicultural	II, IV, V	170
5	3–4	*The House on Maple Street*	Cultural Change and Differences	Multicultural	II, III	184
6	3–4	Multiple books	Respecting the Earth	Multicultural	I, III, VIII, IX	199
7	3–4	*Freedom Train*	Courage and Leadership	African American	II, VI	219
8	4–5	*Felita*	Overcoming Prejudice	Hispanic/Latino American	IV, V	234
9	4–5	*Nightjohn*	Courage and Commitment	African American	II, X	240
10	4–5	*Missing May*	People, Places, and Environments	European American	I, II, III	248

Unit 1
Theme: Work Is Important!

Multiple-Book Model: Grades K–1

Related Books, by Subtheme

Work Children Do in the Family
One Night by Cristina Kessler (Mideastern)
Off to School by Gwendolyn Battle-Lavert (African American)
Dumpling Soup by Jama Rattigan (Multiple Asian American)
More than Anything Else by Marie Bradby (African American)

Work Children Do in the Community
A Day's Work by Eve Bunting (Mexican American)
Chicken Sunday by Patricia Polacco (Multicultural)
Peppe the Lamplighter by Elisa Bartone (Italian American)
The Paperboy by Dav Pilkey (African American)

Work Families and Others Do
Mrs. Toggle's Zipper by Robin Pulver (European American)
Mr. Griggs' Work by Cynthia Rylant (European American)
Uncle Jed's Barbershop by Margaree King Mitchell (African American)
The Tangerine Tree by Regina Hanson (Caribbean)
Mama Is a Miner by George Lyon (European American)
Working Cotton by Sherley Williams (African American)
Family Farm by Thomas Locker (European American)
Work Song by Gary Paulsen (Multicultural)
Harvest Year by Cris Peterson (Multicultural)

Rationale

An understanding of the importance of work can lay the foundation for students to develop a strong work ethic, based on a belief in the value of work and an understanding of the relationship among work, goods and services, and the needs and wants of people. However, an understanding of the mistreatment of people in poor working conditions is also important to build children's commitment to fair labor practices for all people. This unit is most aligned with Banks and Banks's transformation approach, as students gain awareness that there are different perspectives on work as well as common values.

Unit Goal

By the end of the unit, all students will express new understandings of the relationship of work, goods and services, needs and wants, fairness, and people of all ages.

NCSS Themes and Performance Standards

IV. Individual Development and Identity

f. Explore factors that contribute to one's personal identity, such as interests, capabilities, and perceptions.
g. Analyze a particular event to identify reasons individuals might respond to it in different ways.

VI. Individuals, Groups, and Institutions

d. Identify examples of tensions between and among individuals, groups, or institutions, and how belonging to more than one group can cause internal conflicts.
e. Identify and describe examples of tension between an individual's beliefs and a government's policies and laws.

VII. Production, Distribution, and Consumption

a. Give examples that show how scarcity and choice govern economic decisions.
b. Distinguish between needs and wants.
c. Identify examples of private and public goods and services.
f. Describe the influence of incentives, values, traditions, and habits on economic decisions.

Literacy Objectives
(Based on NC Standard Course of Study)

a. Follow oral and simple graphic/written instructions.
b. Respond and elaborate in answering what, when, where, and how questions.
c. Discuss and explain response to how, why, and what if questions in sharing narrative and expository texts.
d. Elaborate on how information and events connect to life experiences.
e. Compose a variety of products (e.g., drawings, stories, journal entries, letters, oral retellings).
f. Predict possible events in texts before and during reading.

g. Discuss concepts and information in a text to clarify and extend knowledge.
h. Use new vocabulary in own speech and writing.

Initiating Activity: Work of Children and Grown-Ups

Introduce the unit with a flurry of quick activities involving work, such as cleaning tasks, gardening, picking up litter from the playground, turning in reading logs, and so on, then move into an organized brainstorming activity. Using the first two rows of the two-column chart below, ask children to offer examples of kinds of work that fit in each column. (Refer to work they've just done, if necessary.)

After recording a few quick suggestions in each column, and leaving space for more, create a row under those suggestions that spans across the entire chart. Make a new subheading that applies to both columns: "Important work that takes special skills or tools." Again, invite students to offer examples about children's work and grown-ups' work in each column. Some examples from the first set may be used again. Complete the introduction to the unit by having children draw or cut out examples from magazine pictures and place them into one of the four cells of the chart. If your class is small, children may share with the whole group what they found. If your class is larger, you may wish to provide small groups with a blank preformatted chart so that they can construct their own chart and share easily within the small groups.

Important work that *children* can do	Important work that *grown-ups* can do
■ Example ■ Example ■ Example	■ Example ■ Example ■ Example
Important work that takes *special skills or tools*	
Children: ■ Example ■ Example ■ Example	**Grown-Ups:** ■ Example ■ Example ■ Example

Depending on the children's responsiveness and attention span, you might close the lesson at this point by simply indicating that they are going to learn so much more in this unit about important work that people do, and that they will be surprised at some things they learn! If the children are ready for more, then move right into Lesson One.

Lesson One:
Work can involve services

Book

Mrs. Toggle's Zipper by Robin Pulver

Objectives

> **VII. *Production, Distribution, and Consumption***
> **c.** Identify examples of *services.*

Literacy

> **a.** Follow oral and simple graphic/written instructions.
> **d.** Elaborate on how information and events connect to life experiences.

Introduction

Review the children's ideas about special skills and tools people use in their work. Present a mystery box containing both classroom and custodial tools from the story. As they touch the unseen items in the box, record the children's guesses on the board about what the tools are. Introduce the story by reading the title and asking what kind of work someone might do to use these tools. Record their many predictions about the nature of the book character's work, based on the objects from the box and the title of the story. Do not tell the answer or acknowledge any correct guesses—keep the mystery open a little longer!

Central Activity

As you read this lighthearted story, celebrate the children's discovery that Mrs. Toggle is a teacher who needs help from the school custodian. Help students identify any possible relationships between the custodian's work in the story and the custodian's work at their school as you read the story. Emphasize how helpful the teacher's students tried to be, and that children's work is sometimes helping others. At the end of the story, guide children toward an independent activity about *services* with the simple two-column chart that follows. (If you are using other social studies materials about goods and services, help the students make the connections.)

Skills, Tools, and Services	
A school custodian's skills, tools, and services	**My skills, tools, and services**
■ Class Example	■ Class Example
■ My examples	■ My examples

Develop an example with the children in each column to help them understand the concept of *services being linked to actions that help others,* and that services often require skills and tools. The examples should show the use of a skill and/or tool to provide a service. Then ask the children to draw or find magazine pictures for one or two more examples in each column.

Depending on your assessment of the students' ability to manage this kind of charting task during the introduction to the unit, you may ask them to complete the chart in small groups and/or independently. If they are ready to generalize from school custodian to other adult occupations at school, change the heading of the first column accordingly. When they share results, help the children emphasize the term *services.* Close the lesson by asking the children to think about what services people need and by mentioning that tomorrow's story may surprise them in many ways!

Assessment

The completed charts provide assessment data to determine if the children can define by example the basic concept of *services* and can apply that concept to themselves and the school. The questions to ask in assessing their learning are (1) Did all students provide (in drawing, pictures, or verbal explanation) accurate examples of a custodian's (or other adult's) services using a skill or tool? (2) Were all students able to give examples of services they provide by using a skill or tool?

Lesson Two:
Goods and services children provide in a family (2 days)

Books

> *Dumpling Soup* by Jama Rattigan
> *One Night* by Cristina Kessler

Objectives

IV. Individual Development and Identity
f. Explore factors that contribute to one's personal identity, such as interests, capabilities, and perceptions.

VII. Production, Distribution, and Consumption
b. Distinguish between needs and wants.
c. Identify examples of private and public *goods* and *services.*

Literacy

c. Discuss and explain response to how, why, and what if questions in sharing narrative and expository texts.
e. Compose a variety of products (e.g., drawings, stories, journal entries, letters, oral retellings).
h. Use new vocabulary in own speech and writing.

Introduction to *Dumpling Soup*

Ask students for examples of how they have helped get meals ready at home, or even what they have cooked by themselves to feed someone else. (You may be surprised!) Introduce the idea of "goods" and "services." Make the distinction between the food from the garden, farm, store, or restaurant being the "goods" and cooking or helping someone cook being the "service." Ask students to listen to *Dumpling Soup* to see what goods and services are mentioned. (Again, help children make connections to any other lessons or textual materials about goods and services.)

Central Activity

As you read *Dumpling Soup*, concentrate on the richness of the story first; let the concepts of goods and services, then needs and wants come next. Focus on the desire of the little girl to make dumplings as well as the desire of the older women in the family to do the same, and her grandmother's absolute support of her in that process. Emphasize the family's positive reaction to the girl's delicious but less-than-perfect-looking dumplings. Be ready for children to notice or ignore the multiracial composition of the family.

After you have finished the story, ask the children to name some of the *goods* and *services* in the story. Help them notice that the grandmother was providing a service, too—that of teaching someone to cook. Then introduce the concepts of *needs* and *wants* and help them identify a difference between the *need* to have nutritious food and the *want* to have (or cook) a particular kind of food.

Assessment

Hand out four notecards. Help the children write one term on each card: *good, service, need, want.* Make sure all children can recognize each word, or pair them with another student who can recognize the words. Use the activity, Ready, Set, Show, for assessment. Read the following paired phrases and statements containing concepts about goods, services, needs, and wants, and have the children hold up the word card that identifies the concept. Give emphasis to the underlined words for clues. Help with examples as needed.

  1. I am very hungry. I hope it's time for lunch. (need)
  2. Let's go to McDonald's and get french fries and a milkshake. (want)

  3. I am a farmer. I just sold 400 pounds of potatoes to _____ School. (goods)
  4. I am a school cook. I'm making mashed potatoes for lunch. (service)

  5. I am six years old. I help my father wash the car. (service)
  6. I am a father. I am going to shop for a better car for my family. (good or want)

  7. I am a school custodian. I can't find my vacuum cleaner. I can't do my job! (need)
  8. I am a teacher. I wish the custodian would clean my room first. (want)

  9. I am the school principal. I write letters to parents. (service)
 10. I am in first grade. I buy pencils at the school store. (good)

This is a three-day lesson. Assessment at this point is ongoing and not final. Unless you have been working with other materials and lessons on these four concepts, you will not be assessing individuals closely in this group activity; rather, you will be looking for a general trend toward correct responses. If you are using *Dumpling Soup* to round out and reinforce other lessons, then you may want to treat this assessment as more specific evidence of each child's learning. You might want to skip the next book.

Introduction to *One Night*

Ask the children to think of a time they were afraid to help (provide a service) because what they had to do seemed too hard or frightening. Give an example from your own experience. Invite them to share their examples in pairs or triads. Then introduce the story: "I'm going to read you a story about a boy who stayed outside all night to help his family. What service do you think he could provide that would keep him outside all night?" Entertain guesses, and then read the story.

Central Activity

As you read *One Night,* let the emotions of this story affect your reading and the children's listening. Help them imagine being away from home and alone all night like the boy in the story. Lead them to realize that he was providing a *service* to his family and *wanted* to go home, but decided caring for the *needs* of the animals was more important, since they produced the *goods* the family would sell.

Assessment

Distribute large newsprint paper. Ask the children to fold the paper into four parts. Have them identify with invented spelling or drawings two *needs, wants, services,* and *goods* in their families, in their school, or in the three stories shared so far in this unit.

Lesson Three:
Goods and services children provide in a community (2 days)

Books

> *Chicken Sunday* by Patricia Polacco
> *Peppe the Lamplighter* by Elisa Bartone

Objectives

IV. *Individual Development and Identity*
i. Analyze a particular event to identify reasons individuals might respond to it in different ways.

VI. *Individuals, Groups, and Institutions*
f. Identify examples of tensions between and among individuals, groups, or institutions, and how belonging to more than one group can cause internal conflicts.

VII. *Production, Distribution, and Consumption*
b. Distinguish between needs and wants.
c. Identify examples of private and public goods and services.

Literacy

a. Follow oral and simple graphic/written instructions.
h. Use new vocabulary in own speech and writing.

Introduction to *Chicken Sunday*

Begin this lesson with a prior lesson—one in which children produce an unusual piece of art, not just a simple drawing with pencils or crayons. (If decorating Easter eggs is appropriate in your community, that activity would link to the book very directly, but it is not necessary.) Move from that lesson into this one with the question: "If you thought about your artwork as a *good*, who might *want* it?" The children will probably mention parents, grandparents, or maybe the art teacher who might want it for a display. Expand their thinking about artistic goods people create by asking what music they listen to or what tapes/CDs they've bought, or what concerts, performances, plays, or movies they've seen or heard about. Ask them to imagine what art children could produce that could actually be sold for money. Then introduce the story by saying, "The children in this story solved a problem by doing just that. Listen to hear what the problem was and why they solved it with their art."

Central Activity

As you read this story, pause at appropriate times and invite the students to react to key events, such as the children being accused of stealing, and how the children used their money to buy a *good* for someone else. Explore the conflict in the story between the storekeeper and the children. Continue to reinforce the concepts of goods and services, needs and wants that are embedded in this very warm story. After the story, invite the children to work together, with older student tutors, with parent volunteers, or independently to fill in the following personal story frame. If children want to embellish their writing with illustrations, they should be encouraged to use the extra space to do so.

My Goods and Services

I want to give _____ a present.

A good or service that _____ wants is _____.

It might cost a lot of money. Maybe I could earn the money.

I can offer the service of _____.

Somebody might need or want that service.

I will ask _____.

Maybe I could earn the money a different way.

I can make some goods. I can make _____.

Somebody might need or want those goods.

I will ask _____.

Assessment

To see if the children are continuing to develop understanding of the central NCSS concepts, begin looking for patterns of responses over several activities now. Ask these questions of yourself: (1) Has every child shown an understanding of the concepts of goods and services, wants and needs in at least two ways by this time (drawing, choosing pictures, holding up the right notecard, offering appropriate comments and examples, giving correct responses to concept questions embedded in the story reading, or in writing)? (2) Are the children ready to leave the familiar territory of family? Are they ready for the next story, which takes them back in history, or do I need to create another lesson with *Chicken Sunday* for reinforcement? (A quick reinforcing activity to plan and implement with any of the books so far is to assign the children parts to act out as you reread the story. For many young children, such whole-body involvement is critically important for their learning.)

Introduction to *Peppe the Lamplighter*

Turn off the lights in the room. If you have windows, close the blinds or shades to darken the room as much as possible. Ask the children to explain why light is important. If you have a blind child, and if it's personally appropriate, ask that child to share strategies for use when light isn't important. Tell the children that today's story centers on a community's *need* for light and one young boy's *service* to that community a long time ago. Ask for predictions of what that service might be. Expand predictions conversationally, but do not tell the answer or acknowledge any correct guesses. Then add, "The boy's father did not want him giving this service at all. He was very cross! Let's see how the boy solves two problems—one for his community and the other one with his father."

Central Activity

Read the story and ask the children to discuss, then write or dictate answers to three questions:

1. Why did the community need light?
2. What service did the boy provide to the community?
3. How did the boy solve his problem with his father?

Assessment

Have children read their responses to a partner and/or to the whole class as you listen for understanding and accuracy in identifying the boy's problems and solutions. You could also collect and read students' written responses if you have highly capable writers.

As an enhancement activity, the students could brainstorm a list of other people in the community who respond to community "needs" (e.g., mail carriers: deliver mail; doctors: take care of sick or injured people; police: keep people safe; etc.).

Lesson Four:
Work that families and others do together (Several days)

Books

A Day's Work by Eve Bunting
The Tangerine Tree by Regina Hanson
Mama Is a Miner by George Lyon
Uncle Jed's Barbershop by Margaree King Mitchell

Objectives

IV. *Individual Development and Identity*
j. Explore factors that contribute to one's personal identity, such as interests, capabilities, and perceptions.

VI. Individuals, Groups, and Institutions

g. Identify examples of tensions between and among individuals, groups, or institutions, and how belonging to more than one group can cause internal conflicts.

h. Identify and describe examples of tension between an individual's beliefs and a government's policies and laws.

VII. Production, Distribution, and Consumption

a. Give examples that show how scarcity and choice govern economic decisions.

b. Distinguish between needs and wants.

c. Identify examples of private and public goods and services.

f. Describe the influence of incentives, values, traditions, and habits on economic decisions.

Literacy

e. Compose a variety of products (e.g., drawings, stories, journal entries, letters, oral retellings).

f. Predict possible events in texts before and during reading.

g. Discuss concepts and information in a text to clarify and extend knowledge.

h. Use new vocabulary in own speech and writing.

Introduction to Subtheme of Unit

Briefly review the children's experiences with stories thus far in the unit, and set the stage for the stories in this extended lesson through the use of the KWHL activity. Before the lesson begins, use an overhead transparency, chart, or chalkboard, and make columns, headed with *K, W, H,* and *L.*

Tell the children that they're going to hear several stories in the next few days in which people have many more problems than *Peppe the Lamplighter* or the children in *Chicken Sunday*. Quickly explain the four columns of the KWHL chart: "The *K* column is where we're going to write what we already *know,* then what we *want* to learn in the *W* column, then *how* we want to learn in the *H* column, and, after the stories, what we *learned* in the *L* column.

Help the students construct a journal to keep during this part of the unit—a personalized *L* column, in a sense. Call it their "Important Learning Journal" or something similar that works for you and your students. Explain that at the end of each story, you're going to help them write a sentence or two about what they learned that is really important to them and/or they could illustrate what they learned.

Introduction to *Uncle Jed's Barbershop*

Using the *K* column of the KWHL chart, invite the children to come up with some examples of problems they *know* about that are related to goods and services, needs and wants. Examples could be problems from the previous stories shared in this unit or from their own personal background knowledge and experiences.

Central Activity

Show the cover of *Uncle Jed's Barbershop* and tell just a little about the story—for example, that the story happened a long time ago when there were different laws and rights for blacks and whites, as well as for their goods and services, and that Uncle Jed solved a lot of problems in his life. Moving to the *W* column, ask children to tell you what they *want* to know about the story—what questions do they have? Give an example if necessary, such as, "Whose uncle was Uncle Jed?" or "What kinds of problems did a barber have back then?" Make sure the questions include goods and services, and wants and needs. Finally, ask the children *how* they might learn about these problems, and record their sugestions in the *H* column (e.g., their ideas might be read a book that tells about barbershops long ago or ask your grandfather).

This story may take two days to read and discuss, depending on the children's engagement with it and their attention spans. If they have little background knowledge of some of the historical problems regarding segregation, they might stop you frequently to ask questions. If they don't ask for clarification, perhaps you'll need to intersperse questions and comments to make sure they're understanding the story. Guide the students to direct your use of the *L* column to write the answers to questions they raised, plus other issues of importance they want to record.

After the story, ask the students to make their first entry in their Important Learning Journal. Have them write the title of the story at the top of the page: *Uncle Jed's Barbershop.* Then invite them to spend a few moments talking to a partner about what they learned that's important for them and their lives. If you have an assistant or classroom volunteers, have them help you during the next phase. Ask the children to become quiet again and to decide what to write. Tell them that they may draw first if they want to (since that helps crystallize and cement thinking for some youngsters) or they may begin by writing (assuming the use of invented or temporary spelling), and that you and your assistants will be moving around to help with spelling or ideas.

To manage this period of individualized assistance, you might want to use a signal system other than hands waving in the air while children wait and do nothing. One teacher we know uses a pencil flag system very successfully. The children have a triangular flag attached to a pencil and insert the pencil in a soft clay base when they need help. They're expected to keep on working while the flag is raised, and they know a helper will be there soon.

Close the part of the extended lesson on this book by asking for a few examples from the children's writings and treating the examples quite seriously. Children will be moved by this book and will be unlikely to write trivial comments in their journals.

Assessment

There are two forms of observational assessment to use during the reading of the story: (1) Did each student actively participate in asking and answering questions about the story? (2) Did the students offer accurate and relevant information to write in the *L* column in response to earlier questions raised by the class or to note something else of importance?

The assessment of the journal entry will not pertain to accuracy of spelling or other mechanics for kindergarten and first-graders. Read for content at this time: Did they hear, remember, or draw conclusions about an issue of importance in the story and apply it to their lives?

Possible Extensions

You may wish to extend the investigation into economic difficulties experienced by blacks in days of postslavery segregation by using the following books:

Working Cotton by Sherley Williams
Off to School by Gwendolyn Battle-Lavert
More than Anything Else by Marie Bradby

You might also encourage your students to ask older relatives or friends who grew up in the South during the years of segregation to come to your classroom and talk about their experiences in those days.

Introduction to *A Day's Work*

Pointing to the KWHL chart used for *Uncle Jed's Barbershop,* explain to the children that they're going to keep expanding that chart for three more books. Start a new section or a new chart; to review, ask the children what they now know about problems with goods and services, wants and needs that they want to add to the *K* column. Introduce *A Day's Work* by explaining that sometimes people who come to the United States from other countries can't get regular jobs right away until they learn how to speak English. They look for work that is for one day, and if they're lucky, it might last longer. Add that the boy in this story helps his grandfather find work by translating back and forth from English to Spanish, but there are problems! If you have bilingual children in your classroom, ask about their experiences and problems in translating for someone in their family. Ask if anyone wants to add to the *H* column (this could include ideas outside of class to learn more about these ideas and issues).

Central Activity

After your brief introduction to the story, ask the children to help fill in the *W* column about this story. As before, offer prompting examples if needed, such as "Did the grandfather get just one day's work? Did the boy help him?" Encourage any bilingual children to ask questions reflective of their own experience, perhaps by asking, "Did the boy make any mistakes in translating that created a problem?" As you read the story, help the children identify answers to their questions to write in the *L* column, as well as other information of interest. Weave in references to goods and services, wants and needs as naturally as possible; the story is strong and will illuminate those concepts easily if you draw some attention to them.

As you read, and after finishing the story, give the students time to share reactions. This is a good story for the "What would you have done?" kind of questioning and thinking. It doesn't need a structured activity for closure, just time for some reflective conversation that will lead into the next journal entry. Again, have the students write the title of the story at the top of their journal pages, then think, talk, and decide what they learned that was really important today.

Assessment

Since you are nearing completion of this unit, be watchful for growing mastery of concepts and vocabulary. Do the children now use the terms *goods* and *services, wants* and *needs* in their discussion of the book? If you use these terms, do the children immediately participate in the conversation with you? Are they using the terms in their journal writing?

Possible Extensions

If the children are particularly engaged in learning about the economic problems of temporary jobs and/or Spanish-speaking immigrants, you might wish to support that interest with books such as *Lights on the River* by Jane Thomas.

Introduction to *The Tangerine Tree*

As you begin the continuation of the KWHL, have the children review what they've written in the *L* columns for the last two books. Then say, "In today's story, there isn't even a day's work like in our last book. Jobs are so *scarce* that a little girl's father has to work far away from his family so he can support them. What do you know about that kind of problem that we can put in today's *K* column?" Next, ask them to share ideas of how else they could learn about jobs that are scarce; record their suggestions in the *H* column (e.g., ask parents, call labor office, go on Internet, read other books, etc.).

Central Activity

With no further introduction except to show them the cover picture and explain that the family's home is on an island named Jamaica, move the children directly to the *W* column. They should have questions immediately. *(Note:* Unless you have or can easily imitate a Jamaican accent, be sure you practice this story aloud several times so that you can do justice to the dialect in which it is written.) This story calls for some periodic stopping and asking the students, "How would you feel?"

An important economic concept to be learned through this story pertains to *scarcity*—not of goods, but of jobs. Therefore, the *L* column entries should focus on uncovering children's awareness from the story and from life of the relationship of income (or more simply, money) to jobs, job losses, job changes, layoffs, and so on, to see what they have already learned about problems associated with loss of income. Close with a journal entry as before.

You might ask children if they know of someone (mom, dad, brother, sister, uncle, aunt) who has ever lost a job. Ask them, "How did it make the person feel? How did you feel about it?"

Assessment

Watch for confusion about concepts relating jobs to income. The confusion may relate to specific vocabulary, not the overall concept. Be sure to use and listen for the students' use of various words for income, such as *paycheck, money, check, paying the bills,* and so on. Children's suggestions for the *L* column and their journal entries will reveal their understanding of the importance of jobs to family life and the problem of job scarcity.

Introduction to *Mama Is a Miner*

Review the *L* column from the previous story, with emphasis on the importance of an adult having a job to support the family. Start a new *K* column with the question: "What jobs do you know about that are physically hard and usually get the worker dirty?" Accept any reasonable answers; if you need to give clues, do so.

Central Activity

Show the cover illustration and ask anyone who offered "miner" for the *K* column to tell the class anything he or she knows about that job. If no one suggested that job, make sure the children know basic concepts about the location of mines underground, the purpose of mining, and so forth before moving to the *W* column. With either extensive background or none at all, the review, introduction, brief discussion, book title, and cover illustrations should prompt plenty of questions. Reread the poem aloud, if necessary.

Assessment

Ask the students to discuss things they learned about the various jobs in this extended lesson, and particularly what they learned about why adults have certain jobs in order to support their families (income, pay bills, buy groceries). Students could also list jobs their family members have and why they might have those jobs. They can share what they wrote with a classmate or the teacher.

Culminating and Assessment Activities

In a culminating activity, which will yield assessment data in addition to the all-important journal entries, guide the children in a variation of the game show, "Who Wants to Be a Millionaire?" To involve more than one "contestant," two critical variations are needed: Children rotate onto the contestant's seat after every question and questions increase in dollar value more slowly than on the real show. Two lifelines are made available to the "contestants" because they continue to involve other children: calling a friend (someone in the class) and polling the audience (the class). The four-item multiple-choice format will not be used, so the third lifeline of having two choices removed will not apply. Allow either lifeline to be used at any time to keep the activity lively.

The questions to ask and the associated dollar amounts to allow for 25 participants are as follows:

1. $100 — Is a brand new car a good or a service? (Good)
2. $200 — Is shopping for basic groceries taking care of a need or a want? (Need)
3. $300 — In *Dumpling Soup*, was cooking a good or a service? (Service)
4. $400 — In *Mrs. Toggle's Zipper*, did the teacher want or need his help? (Need)
5. $500 — In *The Tangerine Tree*, did the father want or need a job? (Need)
6. $600 — In *A Day's Work*, if the boy asked his grandfather for a new bike, would that be a want or a need? (Want)
7. $700 — If someone can't get a job, do we say jobs are scary or scarce? (Scarce)
8. $800 — If jobs are scarce, will families have too much money or not enough money? (Not enough)
9. $900 — If families have hard times, like in *Uncle Jed's Barbershop*, which one is most important: wants or needs? (Needs)
10. $1,000 — Were the fancy eggs in *Chicken Sunday* goods or services? (Goods)
11. $5,000 — Did the children in *Chicken Sunday* need or want to buy the beautiful hat? (Want)
12. $10,000 — Did the boy in *Peppe the Lamplighter* provide a good or a service? (Service)
13. $25,000 — What service did the boy *Peppe the Lamplighter* provide for the community? (Any variation of "He lit the streetlights")
14. $50,000 — Why did the father leave home in *The Tangerine Tree*? (Any variation of "To get a job to support his family")
15. $75,000 — In *Mrs. Toggle's Zipper*, did the children try to provide a good or service? Give one example of something they tried to do. (Service)
16. $100,000 — In *Uncle Jed's Barbershop*, what was a service the little girl could not have at first? (Any variation of medical care, hospitalization, operation, medicine, etc.)

17. $200,000   Does the boy in *One Night* provide a good or service for the animals and his family? (Service)

18. $300,000   Does the grandmother in *Dumpling Soup* provide a good or service when she teaches her granddaughter how to make dumplings? (Service)

19. $400,000   Are the dumplings in *Dumpling Soup* a good or a service? (Good)

20. $500,000   What's an example from any story of a service provided by a child?   (Accept any: lighting streetlights, taking care of animals, making dumplings, making Easter eggs, translating for the grandfather, trying to help the teacher get the zipper unstuck, etc.)

21. $600,000   What's an example from any story of a service provided by a grown-up? (Accept any: cooking, teaching, getting the zipper unstuck, any custodial duties mentioned, running a store, running a barbershop, loaning money for the operation, getting a job to support the family, pulling weeds and planting flowers, working in a coal mine, etc.)

22. $700,000   Which story told about an important service job in a poem? *(Mama Is a Miner)*

23. $800,000   Which story told about a child's service as a translator? *(A Day's Work)*

24. $900,000   Which story told about children solving a problem by making goods? *(Chicken Sunday)*

25. $1,000,000 Which story took place on an island far away from the father's new job? *(The Tangerine Tree)*

Closure

Distribute certificates (see example) to everyone in the class: One million dollars worth of success in learning that "Work Is Important!"

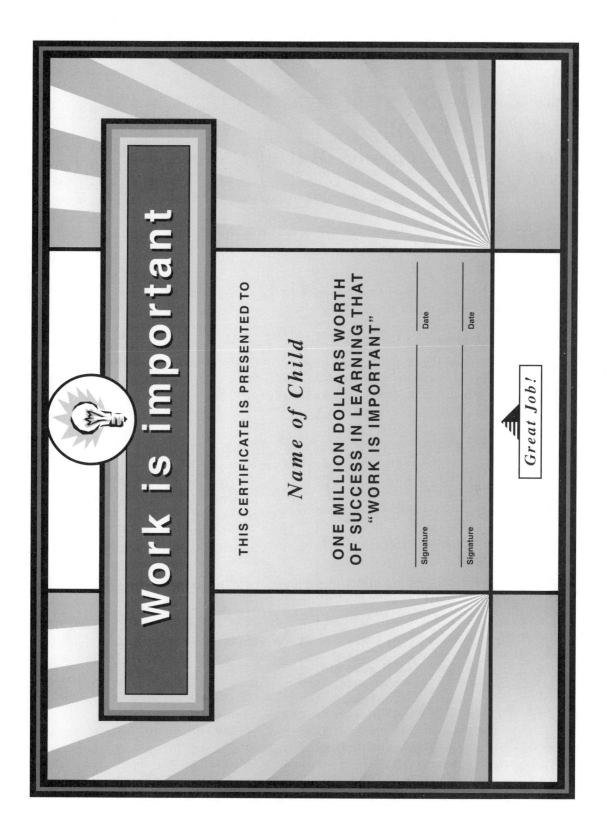

Work is important

THIS CERTIFICATE IS PRESENTED TO

Name of Child

ONE MILLION DOLLARS WORTH
OF SUCCESS IN LEARNING THAT
"WORK IS IMPORTANT"

Signature

Date

Signature

Date

Great Job!

141

Unit 2
Theme: Getting Rid of Fears

Single-Book Model: Grades K–2

Book

Thundercake by Patricia Polacco

Related Books for Expanding the Unit

Storm in the Night by Mary Stolz (African American)
Emma's Rug by Allen Say (Asian American)
Very Last First Time by Jan Andrews (Native American: Innuit)

Rationale

By learning about the commonality of fears and how people help others overcome fears, children can begin to realize the importance of human beings supporting each other, regardless of differences of race, gender, age, language, social class, and so on.

Unit Goal

Students will gain the understanding that everyone has fears and that people can help each other overcome them.

NCSS Themes and Performance Standards

IV. Individual Development and Identity

b. Describe personal connections to place—especially those associated with immediate surroundings.

d. Show how learning and physical development affect behavior.

f. Explore factors that contribute to one's personal identity, such as interests, capabilities, and perceptions.

g. Analyze a particular event to identify reasons individuals might respond to it in different ways.

h. Work independently and cooperatively to accomplish goals.

Literacy Objectives
(Based on NC Standard Course of Study)

   a. Elaborate on how information and events connect to life experiences.
   b. Share personal experiences and response to experiences with text through publishing nonprint texts, discussing interpretations, and/or recording personal responses.
   c. Write and/or participate in writing by using an author's model of language and extending the model.
   d. Demonstrate a sense of story.
   e. Maintain conversation and discussion through attending to oral presentations and through taking turns expressing ideas and asking questions.

Lesson One:
Identifying fears (Whole group/Individual activity, 1 day)

Objectives

   IV. Individual Development and Identity
   d. Show how learning and physical development affect behavior.
   f. Explore factors that contribute to one's personal identity, such as interests, capabilities, and perceptions.
   g. Analyze a particular event to identify reasons individuals might respond to it in different ways.

Literacy

   b. Share personal experiences and response to experiences with text through publishing nonprint texts, discussing interpretations, and/or recording personal responses.
   c. Write and/or participate in writing by using an author's model of language and extending the model.

Introduction

Ask the students if they have ever been afraid; elicit examples. Ask if they think you have ever been afraid; elicit possibilities, then share a specific example. Tell the students that they are going to be working for a few days on a unit about bravery and fear, and that you hope they will discover some new ways to help themselves and others be brave instead of afraid.

Central Activity

Show the following spider map or an age-appropriate variation. Ask the students to brainstorm the kinds of fears that these people might have; write a few suggestions under the left side of each category label. Help the students notice that people have both similar and different kinds of fears at different ages in their lives. Then ask them what these people might do to help themselves be brave instead of afraid. Write those suggestions under the right side of each category label.

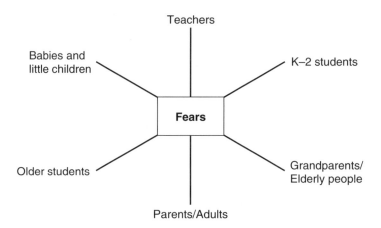

Introduce the book, *Thundercake*, as being about a little girl who was terrified of thunder, and ask for suggestions as to what she might do to stop being so afraid. Make a list of the students' ideas. Read the book (or guide their reading), then ask for reactions to the story's solution, especially reactions that compare any of their ideas from the original spider map or from their list to what actually happened in the story. Also engage students in an evaluative discussion about whether the story's solution would work for them. Revisit the spider map to make changes or additions.

Close the initial lesson with an invitation for students to begin a journal about bravery and fear. Their first entry may be a drawing or a written entry focused on the little girl's fear and bravery in the story and one of their own experiences the story makes them remember.

Assessment

Assess the children's learning by asking (1) Do all students participate in suggesting age-related fears and solutions in the pre- or postreading discussion? (2) Do all students make a journal entry that shows a connection between the story and themselves?

Materials

- Book: *Thundercake*
- Chart paper, marker board, or overhead projector
- Individual drawing paper, folder to begin journal construction

Lesson Two:
Drawing safe places (Group/Individual activity, 1 day)

Objectives

IV. Individual Development and Identity
b. Describe personal connections to place—especially those associated with immediate surroundings.

Literacy

b. Share personal experiences and response to experiences with text through publishing nonprint texts, discussing interpretations, and/or recording personal responses.

Introduction

Review the story of *Thundercake* through discussion, rereading, or read-alouds, with a focus on how the grandmother helped the little girl overcome her fear. Lead the students to identify the importance of the kitchen as a safe place during the storm.

Central Activity

Ask the students to identify a way someone in their family or some other adult has helped them or tried to help them overcome a fear. Expand the discussion to explore the possibility of a special place that, along with the adult, helped them feel braver. Each student will draw, dictate, or write a story about that experience, including the place. Encourage the children to talk with each other as they work, and then have them share their stories with the whole class or in small groups. Display the stories and their illustrations on a roll of paper on the classroom wall, or have the students place the stories in their journals.

Assessment

During discussion and/or in their stories, did all students identify a place that is connected with feelings of safety and bravery in overcoming a fear?

Materials

- Markers
- Roll of paper
- Copy of *Thundercake*

Lesson Three:
Drawing fears away (Individual and group activity, 1 day)

Objectives

IV. Individual Development and Identity
h. Work independently and cooperatively to accomplish goals.

Literacy

e. Maintain conversation and discussion through attending to oral presentations and through taking turns expressing ideas and asking questions.

Introduction

On a special piece of colored construction paper, intentionally torn with ragged edges, you and the students will each draw a picture of a personal fear. It may be one of the same fears identified in earlier lessons or a different one. The fear may be one of their own or one that they would like to help someone else overcome.

Central Activity

Set the conversational context that fears are very normal and that everyone can help themselves and each other by understanding and taking control of fears. Each person will identify the fear in his or her drawing to the class. Students will make suggestions about how to get over the fears. When some students think they can follow (or help someone else follow) the suggestions, they thank their classmates and put the drawings into a magic box labeled "Overcoming Fears." When some students aren't ready, they ask for more suggestions or place the drawing into their journals that day, with the understanding that they may bring this fear back to the group later. When students put fears in the box, they are taking control of those fears. They may decide to make a statement as they put the fear in the box, such as "I'm in charge of my fear" or "I am getting rid of my fear of ____" or "Goodbye, fear! You're out of my life!"

Assessment

To measure assessment, ask (1) Did all students draw a personal fear? (2) Did all students actively participate in the discussion about fears and overcoming them? (3) Did all students place their drawings in the magic box, or do some students need opportunities to bring their fear back to the group?

Materials

- Drawing supplies: markers, crayons, paper, etc.
- Box that is decorated, labeled, and has slot on top for depositing fears

Lesson Four:
Moving fears away (Group activity, 1 day)

Objectives

IV. Individual Development and Identity
h. Work independently and cooperatively to accomplish goals.

Literacy

d. Demonstrate a sense of story.

Introduction

Let the students know the lesson is going to build toward role playing or dramatizing the story of *Thundercake*. Engage students in a review of the story through rereading and/or retelling with students taking as much of the lead as possible. Focus their attention on the physical actions of the characters and invite examples of interpretive movements during the review.

Central Activity

Divide the students into groups so that each group has a full set of "characters": the little girl, the grandma, the hen, the cow, and the thunder. Give each group some time to look through a copy of the book and decide on its actions. Have the groups act out parts while you or they read the story aloud again. Encourage the children to say lines with you that they remember, or you may leave out dialogue and let them improvise their own approximations. An alternative would be to divide the story into logical sections and have each group dramatize one section.

Assessment

For assessment, ask (1) Did the children plan and reenact the story cooperatively? (2) Did each child's movements and/or vocalizations accurately portray his or her character?

Materials

- Multiple copies of *Thundercake*
- Simple props if desired, such as cooking supplies, a table, and a drum to play for the thunder

Lesson Five:
Writing fears away (Group activity, 2 days)

Objectives

IV: Individual Development and Identity

g. Analyze a particular event to identify reasons individuals might respond to it in different ways.

h. Work independently and cooperatively to accomplish goals.

Literacy

c. Write and/or participate in writing by using an author's model of language and extending the model.

Introduction

Ask for the students' ideas about why the grandmother and the little girl felt differently about thunder. Guide the students' attention to the earlier spider map as well as their stories and pictures about fears. Ask why people do not all have exactly the same fears, helping them see that people are individuals, that experiences influence fears, and other such ideas.

Use a large story frame on chart paper, such as the one shown on page 149, with sticky notes for the structural clues in the blanks. Guide the students to create a possible story about one child's fear and another child's helpful understanding. Emphasize thinking about characters and the event so that the difference in responses makes sense. Through modeling aloud and with the students' assistance, move from the structure of a story to a few written sentences that begin the story with more detail and interesting language so that students see how natural it is to elaborate.

Central Activity

In small groups, with a partner, or individually, students will dictate or write a draft of a story about a child's fear and bravery. They may use the story frame and/or beginning of the story created by the class, or their own invention. During the rest of the time allowed and for a period of time the next day, students may revise, complete, and illustrate their stories through conferencing with each other, an older student, or an adult. The entire set of stories may be compiled into a class book.

Assessment

Ask yourself: (1) Did the students work together to create a final version of the class book? (2) Do the students' narratives depict characters whose different reactions to an event are believable?

(Story Title)

Once upon a time in __*(setting)*__, there lived a __*(main character)*__ who loved to __*(character's favorite activity)*__. But there was a problem. *(He/She)* was very afraid of _____.
__*(Main character)*__ wanted to get rid of this fear, so he/she __*(attempt)*__. That didn't work. So he/she tried again. This time, he/she __*(2nd attempt)*__. That didn't work either. Finally, __*(character)*__ asked his/her friend, __*(name of friend)*__, for help. __*(Friend)*__ wasn't afraid of _____ because *he/she* had __*(experience providing the reason for no fear)*__. __*(Friend)*__ had a great idea. __*(Friend)*__ helped __*(main character)*__ by __*(how the friend helped resolve the problem)*__. __*(Main character)*__ got rid of that fear forever!

Materials

- Various kinds of paper for drafting, revising, and preparing final versions
- Writing and drawing tools
- Chart paper or overhead transparency for the story map introductory activities

Culminating and Assessment Activities

The following are suggested activities that may be done by individuals, partners, or small groups. You may want to incorporate variations into earlier lessons, or you may want students to choose one or two as evidence of having met the objectives of the unit. The main assessment question is: *Do children recognize that everyone has fears, and can they offer workable strategies for getting rid of fears?*

- The students may choose a fear shared by many classmates and write a class story about the fear, with the teacher taking dictation on the overhead projector or on chart paper. The students will go around the room, one by one or in pairs, adding on to the story by giving their own creative input. The story will follow a story frame similar to the one in Lesson Five for organization. After any revisions, the story can be made into a big book with students' illustrations at logical places for page breaks.
- Students may dramatize *Thundercake* for another class, ask those students in that class to share their fears, then offer suggestions for how to get rid of them.
- Students may develop skits for their own stories or the class story that demonstrate helping each other get rid of fears.

Unit 3
Theme: Family Helpfulness

Multiple-Book Model: Grades 1–2

Selected Books in Suggested Order of Use

Now One Foot, Now the Other by Tomi DePaola (European American)

Knots on a Counting Rope by Bill Martin, Jr. (Native American)

Allison by Allen Say (Japanese American and European American)

Choice of 3 books from 10 focused on economic issues in families (Multiple cultures)

Choice of any 1 book from 5 focused on family connections (Multiple cultures)

Dandelions by Eve Bunting (European American)

Choice of any 1 book from 14 focused on families creating beauty (Multiple cultures)

Snow Company by Marc Harshman (European American)

Rationale

By studying forms of helpfulness in families, students will gain valuable social knowledge about themselves, families as social and economic units, and families as agents for positive impact on others. This latter possibility allows children to begin to think at the social action level in Banks and Banks's model of multicultural education.

Unit Goal

Students will realize that family helpfulness has many different means of expression.

NCSS Themes and Performance Standards

I. Culture

  a. Explore and describe similarities and differences in the ways groups, societies, and cultures address similar human needs and concerns.

  d. Compare ways in which people from different cultures think about and deal with their physical environment and social conditions.

IV. Individual Development and Identity

  a. Describe personal changes over time, such as those related to physical development and personal interests.

  c. Describe the unique features of one's nuclear and extended families.

  e. Identify and describe ways family, groups, and community influence the individual's daily life and personal choices.

  f. Explore factors that contribute to one's personal identity, such as interests, capabilities, and perceptions.

  g. Analyze a particular event to identify reasons individuals might respond to it in different ways.

  h. Work independently and cooperatively to accomplish goals.

VII. Production, Distribution, and Consumption

  d. Give examples of the various institutions that make up economic systems, such as *families*, workers, banks, labor unions, government agencies, small business, and large corporations.

Literacy Objectives
(Based on NC Standard Course of Study)

  a. Predict and explain what will happen next in stories.

  b. Pose possible how, why, and what if questions to understand and/or interpret text.

  c. Discuss similarities and differences in events and characters across stories.

  d. Make connections to text through the use of oral language, written language, and other means of expression.

  e. Plan and compose a variety of written products in response to text.

Initiating Activity:
How do family members help each other? (Whole class, 1 day)

With an attitude of acceptance, and being prepared for surprises, ask the students what people might be included in a family that lives together in a home and what those people might do together to help each other. Ask student partners or triads to look through magazines and cut out people, then place them into different clusters of family members helping each other. Be sure that the magazines gathered for this activity contain multiethnic pictures, varied settings and activities, and multiple ages of people. Emphasize an expectation of differences in groupings, but help the children see the commonality of different ages of people, especially someone to take care of younger members. Help the children invent categories of helpfulness, or establish a framework for those categories from the ones offered in this unit. Display their findings within the categories of helpfulness on a large chart or rolled paper on a wall of the classroom, then promise that the stories in this family unit will sometimes surprise them, and that they will learn many ways family members help each other.

Lesson One:
Family members help physically (1 day)

Book

Now One Foot, Now the Other by Tomi DePaola

Objectives

IV. Individual Development and Identity
a. Describe personal changes over time, such as those related to physical development and personal interests.

Literacy

d. Make connections to text through the use of oral language, written language, and other means of expression.

Introduction

Ask the children to think of examples of people helping each other in the families in the pictures they grouped, in their own lives, or in stories they've heard or read. Display the following chart on the board, chart paper, or the overhead projector and ask students to decide where their examples belong. Be sure to make the chart large enough to add examples at times throughout the unit. Give examples from your own life or the activities of the classroom or school that would fit the category of "Pretty normal" and "Pretty amazing." (There are no right answers here; the groupings will be based on children's experiences.)

Introduce the book, *Now One Foot, Now the Other*, by saying, "In today's story, I think there are examples of both pretty normal and pretty amazing ways of helping families. I wonder what you will think!"

How Family Members Help Each Other	
Pretty Normal Examples	*Pretty Amazing Examples*

Central Activity

As you read this tender story of a grandfather teaching his young grandson to walk, be prepared to have interruptions when the roles are reversed and the grandson helps the old man learn to walk again after a stroke. Guide the children's understanding of this story at a feeling level by occasionally asking questions such as, "How do you think _____ felt when he helped _____?" or "How would you have felt if you had changed like that as you got older?" Close the first day with this book by having children draw separate pictures of the grandfather helping the very little boy and the older little boy helping the grandfather, then placing those pictures on the chart in the category that makes most sense to them. If time allows, invite the students to share why they placed their pictures where they did, especially if placements vary.

Assessment

For assessment, ask yourself (1) Did the children react with surprise and satisfaction to the help given at different times in this family? (2) Did the children discuss the central idea of age-related changes? (3) Do the children's pictures accurately show the age-related kinds of help being given in the story?

Materials

- Book: *Now One Foot, Now the Other*
- Chart paper or overhead transparency
- Drawing paper

Lesson Two:
Family members help physically (1 day)

Book

> *Knots on a Counting Rope by* Bill Martin, Jr.

Objectives

IV. Individual Development and Identity
   d. Show how learning and physical development affect behavior.

Literacy

   c. Discuss similarities and differences in events and characters across stories.
   d. Make connections to text through the use of oral language, written language, and other means of expression.

Introduction

Ask the children to retell the story of *Now One Foot, Now the Other* as you show them the pictures in the book. Prompt if needed, or let capable students read portions aloud to others. Keep the focus on the theme of helping physically. Reread from the chart the examples of "Pretty normal" and "Pretty amazing" help within families and ask the children to stand each time there is an example read that happened in their family. Encourage selective standing, or young children may want to claim every example as their own! Transition to introducing today's story as being one where another grandfather helps his grandson in a very special way.

Central Activity

As you read *Knots on a Counting Rope* to the students, encourage them to offer comments and reactions about the grandfather's wisdom and the grandson's difficulties, courage, and willingness to learn. Guide the children to identify similarities between yesterday's grandfather's reluctance to overcome his difficulty *(Now One Foot, Now the Other)* and today's grandson's struggle. Partner children and invite them to plan a very short role-play: (1) the physical helpfulness depicted in either story read so far, (2) other physical helpfulness that could happen in the families in either story, and (3) an example of physical helpfulness in their own families. Have three task cards labeled and ready: "Physical helpfulness shown in the story," "Physical helpfulness that could have happened with the people in the story," and "Physical helpfulness between people of different ages in your family." Randomly give a card to each set of partners, who then plan and perform their brief role-play for their classmates. The audience must guess what the example is and where it came from. Close the lesson by having students draw or write one or more examples of how they can help someone in their families.

Assessment

Ask yourself: (1) Are the students fully engaged in the story; can they identify similarities between the characters in the two stories? (2) Are the students fully engaged in the role-play activity? (3) Do the partners depict an accurate example of physical helpfulness? (4) Do the audience members recognize the activity? (5) Can all children identify at least one example of their own physical helpfulness in their family through drawing or writing?

Materials

Book: *Knots on a Counting Rope*
The chart from Lesson One (page 154)
Task cards for the role-play

For Related Reading about Age-Related Changes and Physical Helpfulness

Love You Forever by Robert Munsch (European American)
The Patchwork Quilt by Valerie Flournoy (African American)
Sophie by Mem Fox (African American)
Sachiko Means Happiness (Asian American)

Lesson Three: Families help emotionally (1 day)

Book

Allison by Allen Say (Japanese American and European American)

Objectives

IV. Individual Development and Identity
  e. Identify and describe ways family, groups, and community influence the individual's daily life and personal choices.
  f. Explore factors that contribute to one's personal identity, such as interests, capabilities, and perceptions.

Literacy

  a. Predict and explain what will happen next in stories.
  b. Pose possible how, why, and what if questions to understand and/or interpret text.
  d. Make connections to text through the use of oral language, written language, and other means of expression.

Introduction

Without showing the students the book's cover picture, introduce the idea that today's character doesn't need physical help from her family. She needs emotional help, because she is sad and worried. Invite the children to predict what might make a little girl sad and worried, modeling as needed. List their predictions on the board or chart paper. Beside some (or all) of the predictions, ask them to suggest how a family might give her help for those worries. Write those suggestions to the right of each predicted worry. Keep students focused on multiple ideas for emotional helpfulness, not the right answer to their predictions.

Central Activity

Invite the children to listen to the story to discover Allison's problem and to think about which of their ideas might also have been helpful to her. Read (or guide their reading) with much discussion. Be sensitive to the possibility of adopted children in your class who also don't look like their parents. Encourage the students' questions about why Allison felt this way and why the parents helped the way they did. Intensify the exploration of emotional helpfulness by having the children reread aloud the scenes where Allison's parents try to help, then asking small groups to invent brief role-plays for other possible scenes of helpfulness. Close the activity with a discussion or journal entry of why the children thought the cat helped and why Allison finally felt better.

Assessment

Ask yourself (1) Could the students offer reasonable predictions, then discuss the relationships between their predictions and the actual story? (2) Could the students discuss Allison's transition from upset to contented? (3) Could the students discuss or portray the parents' emotional helpfulness? (4) Could the students interpret why Allison's feelings changed?

Materials

- Book: *Allison*
- Chalkboard or overhead transparency

For Related Reading about Emotional Helpfulness in Families

> *Brave as a Mountain Lion* by Ann Scott (Native American)
> *Amazing Grace* by Mary Hoffman (African American)
> *Willie's Not the Hugging Kind* by Joyce Barrett (African American)

Lesson Four:
Family members help economically (Multiple books, 3–4 days)

Books

A Chair for My Mother by Vera Williams (Latino)
Working Cotton by Sherley Williams (African American)
Chang's Paper Pony by Eleanor Coerr (Asian American)
Coal Mine Peaches by Michelle Dionetti (European American)
Leah's Pony by Elizabeth Friedrich (European American)
The Dream Jar by Bonnie Pryor (European American)
Uncle Jed's Barbershop by Margaree King Mitchell (African American)
A Day's Work by Eve Bunting (Mexican American)
Tangerine Tree by Regina Hanson (Caribbean)
Fly Away Home by Eve Bunting (European American)

Objectives

IV. *Individual Development and Identity*
e. Identify and describe ways family, groups, and community influence the individual's daily life and personal choices.

VII. *Production, Distribution, and Consumption*
d. Give examples of the various institutions that make up economic systems, such as *families*, workers, banks, labor unions, government agencies, small businesses, and large corporations.

Literacy

b. Pose possible how, why, and what if questions to understand and/or interpret text.
d. Discuss similarities and differences in events and characters across stories.
e. Make connections to text through the use of oral language, written language, and other means of expression.
f. Plan and compose a variety of written products in response to text.

Introduction

Choose any of the books listed at the beginning of Lesson Four to read aloud to the students to help them understand the concept of economic problems and economic helpfulness. Introduce the book by asking about allowances, odd jobs they might do at home to earn money, how their parents or older siblings earn money, what families use their money for, and how they help each other economically. Be sure the students can understand the concept of economic helpfulness before you move on. Then tell them what the central problem (economic problem) is in the book you've chosen, ask them to pose questions about how the family in your book might help each other *economically*, and ask them to listen for answers to their questions. Guide them to discuss answers during and after the story.

Central Activity

Let the children know that they are going to choose another book about families having some kind of economic problem and helping each other economically. Give a brief book talk on each of the suggested books or others that you find.

Day One: Help the children form reading groups by interest. Make sure that at least one child in the group can read the story aloud to the others if necessary. If you have only one copy of each book, invite all groups to decide how they're going to read it—taking turns, listening to one or two readers, or all together. Ask each group to write several questions they hope to answer while they read. Tell the students that there will be group activities tomorrow. Give them time to read; monitor for on-task behavior and any need for help. Be sure they respond to some of their original questions. Some groups may need more time to complete the reading than others; therefore, allow ample time and provide other related choices for early completers, such as a money game, learning center activities on economics and mathematics, and so on.

Day Two: Ask the children to move into the same groups as yesterday. Tell them they are going to recommend their book to others with words and pictures. Provide them with a modified story frame such as the following for a guide to introducing the story to their classmates. Invite them to illustrate their story frame with pictures that will make others want to read their book!

(Story Title)

In ____*(Story Title)*____, the family lives in ____*(setting)*____ .

Their economic problem is _____.

You will be surprised to find out how _____*(character)*_____

helps solve this problem!

Day Three: Make multiple copies of the books available for the children to choose and read independently, with a partner, or in small groups. They should make a brief journal entry about what surprised them in this book.

Assessment

On the third or fourth day, depending on the time taken to read another book on Day Three, ask the children to draw and/or write two things: What did they learn about families helping economically that was important to them? What will they do differently to help their own family economically? Students may share their ideas with the whole class or in small groups. Your assessment questions involve whether each student was able to express one or two economic concepts and whether each can identify a helpful economic behavior for himself or herself.

Materials

- Multiple copies of books listed at the beginning of this lesson
- Copies of the story frame
- Drawing paper
- Possible back-up, related independent activities about economics for Day Two

Lesson Five:
Family members stay connected (Multiple texts, 2 days)

Books

Going Home by Eve Bunting (Mexican American)
Sitti's Secrets by Naomi Nye (Mideastern American)
Anna's Athabaskan Summer by Arnold Greise (Native American)
Grandfather's Journey by Allen Say (Japanese American)
Gregory Cool by Caroline Binch (Caribbean)

Objectives

I. Culture
a. Explore and describe similarities and differences in the ways groups, societies, and cultures address similar human needs and concerns.

IV. Individual Development and Identity
c. Describe the unique features of one's nuclear and extended families.

Literacy

c. Discuss similarities and differences in events and characters across stories.
d. Make connections to text through the use of oral language, written language, and other means of expression.

Introduction

This activity will involve interviewing a family member who doesn't live with the student. Provide the children with the following basic interview questions and explain that they may certainly add questions of their own. The interview may be done in person, over the phone, in letters, or by email. Since this interview will take time out of class and will likely involve wait time, you should have children start the interview process earlier in the unit, then come together now for the lesson.

Interview Questions

1. How are you related to me? When did we last see each other?
2. Where do you live?
3. What's it like there? How is it different from where I live?
4. How far away is that from where I live? How long does it take to travel from your home to mine?
5. What is your home like? How is it different from my home?
6. Do you ever help anyone physically or need someone to help you? How?
7. Did you ever help anyone emotionally? How?
8. How do you earn money? Did you ever help anyone economically? How?
9. Did you ever help anyone create beauty? How?
10. Did you ever help someone in some other way? How?

Central Activity

On very large newsprint, have the children create a graphic organizer or map to show their findings. They should depict themselves and their relative some distance apart, then draw or write only the most interesting information they choose to share about this relative and their connections. To pull together some class data that will link to the story, help the students develop a class graph of the range of distances between them and their relatives. Then place push pins on a map of the world to show where the relatives live. (Break here if you need to use two days for this lesson.)

Choose one of the books listed at the beginning of Lesson Five that is likely to have family connections to a place or places most different from those of your students. Introduce the book, a few key illustrations, the characters, and its two settings by using the map and some new push pins of a different color or size. Ask students to look at their work and predict what might be different and what might be similar between their connections and those of the characters in the book. Use the following chart or some variation of it for predicting and then revising or confirming those predictions.

When?	How are the connections different?	How are the connections similar?
Before reading		
After reading		

Close the lesson with the children writing a letter to their relative about their plans to stay connected. Ask them to make connections from two of the stories in the unit so far that makes them think about this relative. For example, you could model:

Dear Grandpa,

We read a story in school this week that made me think of you. There was a little boy whose grandfather helped him learn to walk. Mom said you helped me learn to walk, too.

I'm glad you told me all that stuff about your home and how you have helped people. I like the way you helped my brother economically when he was buying a car. I hope you'll help me like that one day! We read a story about an uncle who used up all his money for his niece's hospital bill and operation. It took him a long time to save up all that money again.

I hope you come to visit soon.

Love,
Chandler

Assessment

Ask yourself (1) Were all the students actively and successful engaged in making comparisons from their data to that of other students and to the information in the story (either verbally or in writing)? (2) Could all the students make connections from stories to their own lives and/or to this relative?

Materials

- One or more of the books listed at the beginning of this lesson
- Large newsprint
- Prepared charts for their prediction and postreading analysis of similarities and differences
- Large world map
- Push pins
- Paper, envelopes, and stamps for letter writing

Lesson Six:
Family members help create beauty (1 day)

Book

Dandelions by Eve Bunting (European American)

Objectives

I. Culture

a. Explore and describe similarities and differences in the ways groups, societies, and cultures address similar human needs and concerns.

d. Compare ways in which people from different cultures think about and deal with their physical environment and social conditions.

IV. Individual Development and Identity

e. Identify and describe ways family, groups, and community influence the individual's daily life and personal choices.

g. Analyze a particular event to identify reasons individuals might respond to it in different ways.

Literacy

d. Make connections to text through the use of oral language, written language, and other means of expression.

Introduction

Over a period of several days (or weeks if gardening is involved), engage the children in bringing flowers of all kinds to the classroom (or growing them if possible) or bringing/finding many pictures of flowers. Create an absolutely flower-drenched display on a bulletin board or table, in a corner, on the windowsills, or wherever best. Encourage the children to smell and touch the flowers and to talk about them. (Coordinate with a science lesson or unit on plants if you can.) Move toward introducing the book, *Dandelions*, by distributing multiple pictures of flowers (or real flowers) from both cultivated and wild plants. Be sure to include dandelions! Ask children in small groups to cluster the flowers into two categories: Very Pretty and Not Very Pretty, or Beautiful and Ordinary, or similar categories that will work for your students. Celebrate the differences among groups! Make the point that people have different ideas about beauty, and that today's story might show them another way to think about beauty.

Central Activity

Show the children the title and cover of the book. Ask them to vote: Do dandelions belong in the Beautiful or the Ordinary category? Encourage them to share their thinking. Celebrate the differences again. Explore why people might have different opinions. Ask the children what other people in their families think about dandelions—for example, have they seen people mow them down when cutting the grass? Then ask the children to listen to decide how dandelions appear to the people in the story—beautiful or ordinary.

Read the story and invite the children to react throughout the story, particularly to the difficulties of the family as they moved westward and to the loneliness of the mother. Elicit or explain the idea that the dandelions looked beautiful because they contrasted with the plain countryside. Help the children see also that the dandelions also looked beautiful to the mother because they were an unexpected and special gift.

Assessment

Close this part of the lesson by asking the children to draw two pictures: one of dandelions appearing beautiful and valuable to the people in the story and one of dandelions appearing as ordinary, or even ugly, to someone else. Invite written or verbal explanations. Note whether children can make distinctions related to the environment, to emotions, to purpose, and so on.

Materials

- *Dandelions* by Eve Bunting
- Variety of flowers or pictures of flowers
- Drawing paper

Lesson Seven:
Family members help create beauty (Multiple books, 1 day)

Books

The Gardener by Sarah Stewart (European American)
The Patchwork Quilt by Valerie Flournoy (African American)

Amazing Grace by Mary Hoffman (African American)
The Last Dragon by Susan Nunes (Chinese American)
Emma's Rug by Allen Say (Asian American)
The Chalk Doll by Charlotte Pomerantz (Caribbean)
Farolitos of Christmas by Rudolfo Anaya (Mexican American)
The Rag Coat by Lauren Mills (European American—Appalachian)
Just Plain Fancy by Patricia Polacco (Religious cultures—Amish)
The Ugly Menorah by Marissa Moss (Religious cultures—Jewish)
Annie's Gifts by Angela Medearis (African American)
Mimi's Tutu by Tynia Thomassie (African American)
Fox Song by Joseph Bruchac (Native American)
The Bat Boy and His Violin by Gavin Curtis (African American)

Objectives

I. Culture

a. Explore and describe similarities and differences in the ways groups, societies, and cultures address similar human needs and concerns.

d. Compare ways in which people from different cultures think about and deal with their physical environment and social conditions.

Literacy

d. Make connections to text through the use of oral language, written language, and other means of expression.

Introduction

Review *Dandelions* and prepare for the next activity by asking the children, "How did the family create beauty in *Dandelions*? How has anyone in your family helped to create beauty? How else do families help create beauty?" Then move the children toward brainstorming about creating beauty in different ways, sometimes because of different circumstances, just like in *Dandelions*. Give situations if necessary to facilitate the brainstorming. Tell the children they are going to have choices again, and that each of the books involves a *problem* and family help in *problem solving with beauty*. Give a brief book talk on each of the books listed at the beginning of this lesson, then have the children choose a book to read with a partner or small group.

Central Activity

As the children read, they should identify the problem and the beauty-filled solution the family helps to create. Each small group of children should design two pictures to place on the large class chart shown here, one rather plain picture depicting the problem and the other one the beauty-filled solution. Make many kinds of art materials available—crayons, tissue paper, construction paper, magazines for collage construction, paint, and so on—so that the pictures on the right side of the chart truly show some beauty. Coordinate this lesson with the art teacher in your school if possible for more unusual and developmentally appropriate art possibilities.

Title of Book	Problem	Solution with Beauty

Close the lesson with a discussion of all the wonderful ways human families have solved problems with beauty in these stories. Encourage the students to share their work and their discoveries that all cultural groups create beauty in some way to solve problems. Ask the children to make a journal entry of how they and their families might solve a problem by creating beauty in the world somewhere.

Assessment

Ask yourself (1) Were all the children actively engaged in reading and discussing the story? (2) Did all the children accurately identify the problem and solution in the story? (3) Did all the children create or contribute to creating the two pictures for the class chart? (4) Were all the children able to identify a possible problem and beauty-filled solution for their families to create?

Materials

- Copies of the books listed at the beginning of this lesson
- Great variety of art supplies
- Large paper for the chart and the children's artwork

Lesson Eight:
Families help others (1 day)

Book

Snow Company by Marc Harshman

Related Books for Possible Extension

The Christmas Menorahs: How a Town Fought Hate by Janice Cohen (Religious cultures)
The Red Comb by Fernando Picó (Caribbean)
Aurora Means Dawn by Scott Sanders (European American)
The Lily Cupboard by Shulamith Oppenheim (Religious cultures)
The Butterfly by Patricia Polacco (Religious cultures)
Smoky Night by Patricia Polacco (Multicultural)

Objectives

IV. Individual Development and Identity

e. Identify and describe ways family, groups, and community influence the individual's daily life and personal choices.
g. Analyze a particular event to identify reasons individuals might respond to it in different ways.

Literacy

b. Pose possible how, why, and what if questions to understand and/or interpret text.
d. Make connections to text through the use of oral language, written language, and other means of expression.
e. Plan and compose a variety of written products in response to text.

Introduction

Depending on your geographic location and the kind of storms that happen, ask children what their family has done when there's a tornado warning, a hurricane, a blizzard, a flood, no electricity, and so on. See if anyone mentions helping other families, too. Introduce the story by telling only that the family in this story mostly helps others during a storm. Put the following three categories of questions on the chalkboard or overhead projector. Tell the students that you and they together are going to ask lots of questions about the story, then read to find the answers. Model how to ask the questions, using any of the examples shown here, then help the children form the same kinds of questions about the story. Write their questions next to your example. Invite each child to choose one question from each category and write it on his or her own paper, then to listen to the story to see if the question can be answered.

What/When/Where? (What kind of storm was it? When did the storm happen? Where were they?)

Why? (Why did people need help? Why did the people come to this family for help? Why was the storm so bad that they needed help? Why did the family decide to help?)

How? (How did the family help? How did the people know to come to this family for help? How did the storm create problems? How did the family know how to help?)

Central Activity

Read this engaging story about a family who takes in people stranded in a blizzard with tones of surprise and amazement in your voice, so that children thoroughly enjoy the problem solving. Invite them to point out the answers they found to their questions, and to record those answers on their papers. Give assistance as needed. After the story, guide the children to ask one more kind of question, then to draw/write/dictate their answers to that, too—be sure they realize that this answer is not in the book, but only in their imaginations.

What if? (What would have happened to the people if the family hadn't helped? What would the family members have felt like if they hadn't helped? What if the people were dangerous? What if the people died?)

Assessment

Can all students generate and answer the four kinds of questions, which tie all objectives together?

Materials

- One copy of *Snow Company*
- Access to the chalkboard or an overhead projector
- Writing/drawing paper

Culminating and Assessment Activities

There are a number of possible activities that are conducive to a final assessment of unit objectives. Choose, modify, or elaborate on any of the following:

- *Family Booklet*. Help the children draw and write about their families relative to each of the ways of helpfulness investigated in the unit.
- *Time Line*. Have the children create a time line about their lives in their families and show each kind of helpfulness at some point along the time line.
- *Time Capsule*. Break the class into groups and ask each group to list the things they believe should be put in a time capsule today for their own children to show the kind of helpfulness that is happening in their families. After listing for a specified amount of time, each group should choose the five most important things on their list to present to the class and be ready to justify their choices.
- *Venn Diagram*. Using a simple Venn diagram, each child could choose any two books from the unit and show two or three similarities in the center, and two or three differences on each side.

Unit 4
Theme: Overcoming Barriers

Multiple-Book Model: Grades 2–3

Selected Books in Suggested Order of Use

Train to Somewhere by Eve Bunting (European American)
Teammates by Peter Golenbock (African American)
Cheyenne Again by Eve Bunting (Native American)
The Bracelet by Yoshiko Uchida (Japanese American)
I Hate English! By Ellen Levine (Chinese American)
The Christmas Menorahs by Janice Cohn (Jewish, Christian)

Related Books for Expanding the Unit

White Socks Only by Evelyn Coleman (African American)
Through My Eyes by Ruby Bridges (African American)
Nim and the War Effort by Milly Lee (Chinese American)
Angel Child, Dragon Child by Michele Maria Surat (Vietnamese American)
Lights on the River by Jane Thomas (Mexican American)
Three Cheers for Mother Jones by Jean Bethel (European American)
The Red Comb by Fernando Picó (Caribbean)
The Butterfly by Patricia Polacco (Jewish)

Rationale

By learning about the many barriers and injustices people have had to overcome, children can become more sensitive to barriers they may pose to others, how they can help others, and what strategies they might use to overcome barriers in their own lives. This unit is most closely aligned with Banks and Banks's decision-making and social action approach.

Unit Goals

Students will be able to describe instances in history, literature, and their own personal lives when people in different cultures and circumstances overcame adversity through their own courage and with the help of others. They will also be able to plan and take action to overcome new barriers and/or to help others overcome them.

NCSS Themes and Performance Standards

II. Time, Continuity, and Change

e. Demonstrate an understanding that people in different times and places view the world differently.

f. Use knowledge of facts and concepts drawn from history, along with elements of historical inquiry, to make informed decisions about and take actions on public issues.

IV. Individual Development and Identity

d. Show how learning and physical development affect behavior.

f. Explore factors that contribute to one's personal identity, such as interests, capabilities, and perceptions.

V. Individuals, Groups, and Institutions

b. Give examples of and explain group and institutional influences—such as religious beliefs, laws, and peer pressure—on people, events, and elements of culture.

d. Identify examples of tensions between and among individuals, groups, or institutions, and how belonging to more than one group can cause internal conflicts.

g. Show how groups and institutions work to meet individual needs and promote the common good, and identify examples of where they fail to do so.

Literacy Objectives
(Based on NC Standard Course of Study)

a. Draw conclusions, make generalizations, and gather support by referencing the text.

b. Respond to fiction, nonfiction, poetry, and drama using interpretive, critical, and evaluative processes.

c. Identify and discuss similarities and differences in events and characters within and across selections and support them by referencing the text.

d. Use text and own experiences to verify facts, concepts, and ideas.

e. Share written and oral products in a variety of ways.

Initiating Activity: That's not fair! (Group activity, 1 day)

Engage your students in playing any familiar game, indoors or outside, but warn them that you're going to change the rules from time to time, and you want to know how they feel about the new rules. Every few minutes or so, change the rules so as to favor different children—either an individual or by some grouping, such as boys, girls, tall, short, blue eyes, brown eyes, dark hair, light hair, and so on. Be very supportive and loving to the children currently in favor, and rather harsh to those out of favor at the moment. Dismiss some children from the game at times. Make the differences very obvious, but don't be so lavish or so harsh as to really upset anyone. Discuss feelings, particularly those of being treated unfairly and being left out. Then introduce the unit as one where you and the children will read many stories about people being treated poorly by some, but helped by others. Indicate that the children will learn how people can work together to overcome barriers of unfairness and injustice.

Lesson One:
Left out (1 day)

Book

Train to Somewhere by Eve Bunting

Objectives

IV. Individual Development and Identity

d. Show how learning and physical development affect behavior.

f. Explore factors that contribute to one's personal identity, such as interests, capabilities, and perceptions.

V. Individuals, Groups, and Institutions

g. Show how groups and institutions work to meet individual needs and promote the common good, and identify examples of where they fail to do so.

Literacy

c. Identify and discuss similarities and differences in events and characters within and across selections and support them by referencing the text.

e. Share written and oral products in a variety of ways.

Introduction

Ask the children how many felt left out sometimes in the game and what that felt like. Ask for examples from their lives of feeling left out at other times. Discuss with the children if they've ever seen someone else feeling that way and helped him or her feel more welcome. Introduce the book, *Train to Somewhere*, by saying that the story is about a very unusual train ride to help orphans find families to adopt them, and that it's based on real events of long ago. Arrange the students' chairs to resemble seats on a train; prepare to act as the conductor, walking up and down the center aisle as you read the story to the passengers. Invite the children to imagine looking for a new family each time the train stops.

Central Activity

As you read, be sure to show the children the amazing illustrations. As a family adopts each child, ask the children if that family looked good to them, and why. Ask how they would be feeling if they were Marianne, and why. Stop before the last station and ask the children to write the ending that would be the best possible for Marianne. Have them share their positive endings with each other, then read the rest of the book. Ask for reactions, comparisons, disappointments, understandings, and so on. Help the children draw positive conclusions about the outcome. Individually, or with partners, have them write about how Marianne and her parents both overcame their barriers and formed a family together, perhaps describing their first few days of getting used to each other.

Assessment

Ask yourself (1) Could the students see that the outcome was positive for both Marianne and her new family? (2) Did their writings about Marianne's life contain positive elements?

Materials

- Copy of *Train to Somewhere*
- Writing paper and pencils

Lesson Two:
Kept out! (1–2 days)

Book

Teammates by Peter Golenbock

Objectives

II. Time, Continuity, and Change

e. Demonstrate an understanding that people in different times and places view the world differently.

f. Use knowledge of facts and concepts drawn from history, along with elements of historical inquiry, to make informed decisions about and take actions on public issues.

IV. Individual Development and Identity

f. Explore factors that contribute to one's personal identity, such as interests, capabilities, and perceptions.

V. Individuals, Groups, and Institutions

b. Give examples of and explain group and institutional influences—such as religious beliefs, laws, and peer pressure—on people, events, and elements of culture.

d. Identify examples of tensions between and among individuals, groups, or institutions, and how belonging to more than one group can cause internal conflicts.

Literacy

b. Respond to fiction, nonfiction, poetry, and drama using interpretive, critical, and evaluative processes.

b. Share written and oral products in a variety of ways.

Introduction

Review the situation in *Train to Somewhere* about Marianne being left out of a family for so long. Explain that in today's story, also based on historical events, a young man is not just *left out*—there are others working hard to *keep him out*. Show the title and cover picture to the children.

Central Activity

Give small groups of students the list of clue words found on page 175 for a story impressions activity. Explain that each group is going to create a prediction about the story by using these words in order. Model and/or help the children create an example of how to use the words in a few sequential sentences to create a possible story fitting your introduction about the young man who has people working hard to keep him out. Intentionally have some parts be right and others be wrong. For example, you might say, "I think the story could be about the times when there were still *segregation laws,* which I think were *unfair.* This *young man* was black, and he was *afraid to challenge* those laws like Rosa Parks did, but he was still a *brave man.* He didn't play sports very well because of all the *abuse and hostility* from white people. Finally, *another brave man* did challenge the laws. He was a teammate, and he *took a stand* against segregation."

Each group should share its prediction, then the children should read and discuss the book in the same small group. Or, you may read the story to them, stopping periodically for the students to discuss the story among themselves. While they read or listen, ask the students to notice if what they predicted really did happen or turned out differently. Don't emphasize right and wrong predictions—keep them thinking!

Clue Words for Story Impressions

Segregation laws
↓
Unfair
↓
Afraid to challenge
↓
Abuse and hostility
↓
Another brave man
↓
Took a stand

Can you use those words in order to write a few sentences about what *Teammates* **might be about?**

Assessment

When they finish the story, give each student writing paper or large newsprint, and have everyone fold their papers in half vertically. Ask them to go back to the text and use the left half of the paper to make a list of every law or behavior that was a barrier to Jackie Robinson. On the right half, have them write what they could do to help change any of those problems if they were still happening today. Ask them also to indicate which laws or behaviors they might be afraid to challenge.

Materials

- Multiple copies of *Teammates*
- Enough copies of the story impressions activity for each group
- Individual writing paper or newsprint

Lesson Three
Two brave men (1 day)

Book

Teammates by Peter Golenbock

Objectives

II. Time, Continuity, and Change

e. Demonstrate an understanding that people in different times and places view the world differently.

f. Use knowledge of facts and concepts drawn from history, along with elements of historical inquiry, to make informed decisions about and take action on public issues.

V. Individuals, Groups, and Institutions

d. Identify examples of tensions between and among individuals, groups, or institutions, and how belonging to more than one group can cause internal conflicts.

Literacy

b. Respond to fiction, nonfiction, poetry, and drama using interpretive, critical, and evaluative processes.

c. Identify and discuss similarities and differences in events and characters within and across selections and support them by referencing the text.

d. Use text and own experiences to verify facts, concepts, and ideas.

e. Share written and oral products in a variety of ways.

Introduction

Have the students participate in read-alouds on key sections of the book—some take the parts of PeeWee Reese, some Jackie Robinson, some the people who wanted to keep Robinson from playing baseball. Model and encourage lots of expression.

Central Activity

Have partners use the following adaptation of Shanahan and Shanahan's "Character Perspective Chart." One partner rereads/rethinks through the story as PeeWee Reese; the other one rereads/rethinks through the story as Jackie Robinson. After answering their individual questions, they collaborate to answer the three questions at the bottom of the chart.

Character Perspective Chart		
Questions for Each Character	*Jackie Robinson*	*PeeWee Reese*
Setting: What were his main settings?		
Problem: What was his major problem?		
Goal: What did he most want to accomplish?		
Attempt: How did he try to accomplish his goal?		
Outcome: What happened because of his attempt?		
Reaction: How did he feel about the outcome?		
Theme: What point did the author want to make?		
What's next for the characters? What might either character do next to help the problems of prejudice disappear?		
What's next for you? What can each of you do to help today's problems of prejudice disappear?		

Source: Adapted from T. Shanahan and S. Shanahan, "Character Perspective Charting: Helping Children to Develop a More Complete Conception of Story," *The Reading Teacher, 50,* 668–677.

Assessment

Ask yourself (1) Could the children see different perspectives of the two characters? (2) Could they add an idea of their own that made sense and would counteract racial prejudice?

Materials

- Several copies of *Teammates*
- Character perspective charts

Lesson Four:
Taken out (1 day)

Book

Cheyenne Again by Eve Bunting

Objectives

II. Time, Continuity, and Change
e. Demonstrate an understanding that people in different times and places view the world differently

IV. Individual Development and Identity
f. Explore factors that contribute to one's personal identity, such as interests, capabilities, and perceptions.

V. Individuals, Groups, and Institutions
b. Give examples of and explain group and institutional influences—such as religious beliefs, laws, and peer pressure—on people, events, and elements of culture.
d. Identify examples of tensions between and among individuals, groups, or institutions, and how belonging to more than one group can cause internal conflicts.
g. Show how groups and institutions work to meet individual needs and promote the common good, and identify examples of where they fail to do so.

Literacy

b. Respond to fiction, nonfiction, poetry, and drama using interpretive, critical, and evaluative processes.
d. Use text and own experiences to verify facts, concepts, and ideas.

Introduction

Tell the children that you hope they will feel some anger during today's lesson. Give them a special piece of "angry paper" to write about those feelings every time they happen. Ask the children to draw on newsprint and talk with each other about all the things they like about their home, their school, their clothes and belongings, their neighborhood, and so on. As they share with each other, suddenly call a halt. Demand that all students tear up their drawings, throw them away, and come back to their seats without a word. Stare at them sternly; see if they write on their "angry papers." If not, you might suggest it.

Central Activity

With no further introduction, read *Cheyenne Again,* a story of a boy who was taken from his home and forced into another mode of life because someone thought that it was better than his own culture. Encourage the children nonverbally with nods and expressions of your own anger as they begin to write on their "angry papers." Ask for some sharing of their comments. Guide a discussion about the story with the following questions: "Have you ever felt anything like this boy? If you had been his classmate, like PeeWee Reese was Jackie Robinson's teammate, how could you have helped?"

Assessment

Ask the children to write a journal entry of their reaction to the story. In their post-reading discussion or in their journal entries, do they show awareness of the differences between that way of thinking about treatment of Native Americans and how people act today? Do they see the injustices?

Materials

- One or more copies of *Cheyenne Today*
- Newsprint
- Unusual paper for "angry papers"

Lesson Five:
Forced in (1 day)

Book

The Bracelet by Yoshiko Uchida

Objectives

II. Time, Continuity, and Change

g. Demonstrate an understanding that people in different times and places view the world differently.

V. Individuals, Groups, and Institutions

d. Identify examples of tensions between and among individuals, groups, or institutions, and how belonging to more than one group can cause internal conflicts.

g. Show how groups and institutions work to meet individual needs and promote the common good, and identify examples of where they fail to do so.

Literacy

b. Draw conclusions, make generalizations, and gather support by referencing the text.

c. Respond to fiction, nonfiction, poetry, and drama using interpretive, critical, and evaluative processes.

d. Use text and own experiences to verify facts, concepts, and ideas.

e. Share written and oral products in a variety of ways.

Introduction

Introduce today's story as also being about a child forced to go somewhere away from home—but along with her family and many others as well. This story, too, is based on historical events and is another example of mistakes made in the past. Provide some background for the students, as needed, about countries in conflict during World War II, and how people from those countries living in the United States were held in suspicion. Randomly assign children to "family groups" and place them in different spots all over the room. Give each family a large card with the country name to hold up for identification. Invite them to imagine that they are a family whose grandparents or great-grandparents came from that country to the United States, and that their family loves this country, works hard, helps others, obeys the law, and practices good citizenship. Then say, "Now we are in a conflict, maybe a war, with _(name of country)_—let's all look at that family with suspicion." Repeat several times so that each group is under suspicion at some time.

Central Activity

Without further introduction, read the story to the students. Allow for reactions, discussion, and questions throughout the reading so that you are sure the children are understanding the story line and getting the full impact of the mistreatment of

Japanese Americans. After the first reading, provide the same family groups with a copy of the book and the following questions for discussion. Children can jot down notes if they choose, but the questions at this point are to stimulate using the text and their own experiences for discussion, not individual written answers.

Discussion Questions

1. What did Emi take along that you would have taken, too? What would you have taken instead? Why?
2. What did Emi remember about her home and friends that you would have too? What would you have remembered instead? Why?
3. What did Emi and her family do to adjust to their new circumstances? What would your family have done? Why?
4. Is there something as important to you as Emi's bracelet? How would you adjust if you were in a prison camp and you lost it?
5. If you were a prison camp guard, what would you worry about? Would you be suspicious of people from other countries? Would you do your job, but be helpful? Would you believe the prison camp was wrong and help people escape?

One question at a time, involve the family groups in sharing their findings and thoughts with the whole class.

Assessment

The group work after the story provides most of the assessment data, but it is highly social, not individual. We suggest one more kind of data that is individual. Invite the children to write a one-page journal entry about their reaction to the lesson. If they need prompting because of the open-endedness of the assignment, you could suggest the following ideas without overfocusing their response:

1. What did you learn or think about in this lesson that is really important to you?
2. What did you learn or think about in this lesson that was a new concept or idea?
3. How would you think, feel, and act if you were suspicious of people from other countries, even if they were completely innocent?
4. How would you think, feel, and act if people were always suspicious of you and your family?

Materials

- Multiple copies of *The Bracelet*
- Multiple copies of the discussion questions
- Cards for country names
- Journals

Lesson Six:
Taking a stand against injustice (1 day)

Book

The Christmas Menorahs by Janice Cohn

Objectives

II. Time, Continuity, and Change

h. Use knowledge of facts and concepts drawn from history, along with elements of historical inquiry, to make informed decisions about and take action on public issues.

V. Individuals, Groups, and Institutions

d. Identify examples of tensions between and among individuals, groups, or institutions, and how belonging to more than one group can cause internal conflicts.

Literacy

b. Draw conclusions, make generalizations, and gather support by referencing the text.

c. Respond to fiction, nonfiction, poetry, and drama using interpretive, critical, and evaluative processes.

d. Identify and discuss similarities and differences in events and characters within and across selections and support them by referencing the text.

e. Use text and own experiences to verify facts, concepts, and ideas.

f. Share written and oral products in a variety of ways.

Introduction

Ask the children to bring religious symbols, or other symbols important to their family, to school for a display. If you have windows, arrange them on a windowsill. If you don't have windows, invent an imaginary window on a table with a large cardboard box or stand-up wooden frame. Invite the children to look through the window at these symbols and admire them. Then ask them to predict which symbols might provoke someone to react in a negative, even dangerous, way. They may have no idea, incorrect ideas, or painfully experiential ideas to share. Take them all respectfully.

Introduce the book as the last in the unit for a group lesson, one in which some people react negatively to a religious symbol. Ask the children to listen (or read) with one question in mind: What would they do?

Central Activity

Read the story, facilitating and allowing time for questions and reactions as you read. Distribute multiple copies of the book to small groups and assign a few pages to each. The groups practice and prepare a dramatic reading or dramatization of their section.

Assessment

Ask children to write a brief journal entry: What would they have done in this situation? Why?

Materials

- Multiple copies of *The Christmas Menorahs*

Culminating and Assessment Activities

The true measure of success of this unit will be the day-to-day behavior of the children that is nonprejudicial and works toward community building. More concrete final activities might include the following:

- Display all the books read in the unit. Place related books nearby in the same display. Have the children volunteer to name the kinds of barriers people overcame in each book. List these barriers on the board or overhead projector. Students may choose any of the following activities related to one or more barriers:
  - Use the Internet to find historical information about that kind of barrier to share with the class.
  - Develop a "promise poster" about barriers they'll not create for themselves or others.
  - Read and prepare a creative book report on one of the related books.
  - Read and prepare a comparison-contrast chart involving one of the related books and one or more of the books studied together in the unit.
- Small groups of children could write and present brief skits centered on a problem of one character and how either that character overcame the barrier or someone else helped him or her overcome it.
- Children could identify various present-day barriers created by other people that they consider unfair or prejudicial. Each child then writes a pledge about what he or she will do to help knock down that barrier each time he or she sees it.
- Small groups of children could prepare "Reader's Theatre" presentations for one of the books studied in the unit or one of the related books.
- The class could identify one school-based or community problem and then design and implement a response that will help reduce the problem or barrier.

Unit 5
Theme: Cultural Change and Differences

Single-Book Model: Grades 3–4

Book

The House on Maple Street by Bonnie Pryor

Rationale

Elementary students must be challenged to understand the evolution of change and how the change process impacts various cultural and racial groups in society. This unit is closely aligned with the transformation approach and the decision-making and social action approach of Banks and Banks.

Unit Goal

By the end of the unit, students will understand the concepts of environmental change and how the environment has influenced various cultures throughout time.

NCSS Themes and Performance Standards

II. Time, Continuity, and Change
a. Demonstrate an understanding that different people may describe the same event or situation in diverse ways, citing reasons for the difference in views.
b. Demonstrate an ability to use correct vocabulary associated with time, such as past, present, future, and long ago; read and construct simple time lines; identify examples of change; and recognize examples of cause-and-effect relationships.
d. Identify and use various sources for reconstructing the past, such as documents, letters, diaries, maps, textbooks, photos, and others.
e. Demonstrate an understanding that people in different times and places view the world differently.

III. People, Places, and Environments

g. Describe how people create places that reflect ideas, personality, culture, and wants and needs as they design homes, playgrounds, classrooms, and the like.

h. Examine the interaction of human beings and their physical environment, the use of land, building of cities, and ecosystem changes in selected locales and regions.

i. Explore the ways that the earth's physical features have changed over time in the local region and beyond, and how these changes may be connected to each other.

Literacy Objectives
(Based on NC Standard Course of Study)

a. Read a variety of texts, including fiction (short stories, novels, fantasies, fairy tales, fables), nonfiction (biographies, letters, articles, procedures and instructions, charts, maps), poetry (proverbs, riddles, limericks, simple poems), and drama (skits, plays)

b. Identify and interpret elements of fiction and nonfiction and support by referencing the text to determine the author's purpose, plot, conflict, sequence, and resolution.

c. Use planning strategies to generate topics and organize ideas (e.g., brainstorming, mapping, webbing, reading, discussion).

d. Focus revision on a specific element, such as word choice, sequence or events and ideas, transitional words, and sentence patterns.

e. Compose a variety of fiction, nonfiction, poetry, and drama selections using self-selected topics and forms (e.g., poems, simple narratives, short reports, learning logs, letters, notes, directions, instructions).

f. Explore technology as a tool to create a written product.

Initiating Activity:
Observation walk (Group activity, 1 day)

Within walking distance of the school, if at all possible, choose an old tree, river, house, or building. Take the students to observe, describe what they see, and speculate about its age, who has played there, what people or animals have been there, what problems have occurred nearby, and so on. Then divide the students into small groups to record their speculations about one question per group, creating either a list or a very rough draft of an imaginative narrative. Questions may be determined by you or the students, but must address the possible history of the selected object. Invite a spokesperson from each group to share his or her ideas.

Tell the students they are going to listen to a book, *The House on Maple Street,* that tells the amazing history of one house. Ask them to notice any comparisons between their ideas and what the author tells in this story and to mark those items on their group paper for later discussion.

Read the book. Invite the students to react to and comment about their comparisons throughout the story. Ask them to bring pictures or items that would help them tell their family's history. You could also ask students to write a letter to their parents, asking the parents to talk to their child about their family history and/or to share pictures with them as part of a school project/assignment.

Lesson One:
Constructing a time line (Small groups, 1 day)

Objectives

II. Time, Continuity, and Change

b. Demonstrate an ability to use correct vocabulary associated with time, such as past, present, future, and long ago; read and construct simple time lines; identify examples of change; and recognize examples of cause-and-effect relationships.

d. Identify and use various sources for reconstructing the past, such as documents, letters, diaries, maps, textbooks, photos, and others.

Literacy

b. Identify and interpret elements of fiction and nonfiction and support by referencing the text to determine the author's purpose, plot, conflict, sequence, and resolution.

c. Use planning strategies to generate topics and organize ideas (e.g., brainstorming, mapping, webbing, reading, discussion).

Introduction

Give small groups of students a single copy of *The House on Maple Street*. Using the overhead projector or chart paper to record their responses, guide them through a review of the book to identify major changes in the area where the maple tree now stands. Introduce the concept of a time line, and show examples from texts or your own construction.

Central Activity

In small groups, have the students construct a simple time line of the events in *The House on Maple Street*, using long rolled paper. Challenge the groups to create a way, such as color coding or the use of a special symbol, to show cause-and-effect relationships in any of the events. Invite groups to share their time lines, and then provide time for students to construct individual time lines, using photographs from home, small sketches, or symbols to represent key events in their family history.

Assessment

Ask yourself (1) Did each group's time line accurately identify examples of change over time in the correct order? (2) Did each group's time line give at least one example of cause and effect? (3) Did each individual student depict some changes in his or her family over time and in the correct order?

Materials

- Rolled paper for time lines

Lesson Two:
Using media center materials (Small groups, 2–3 days)

Objectives

II. Time, Continuity, and Change
a. Demonstrate an understanding that different people may describe the same event or situation in diverse ways, citing reasons for the difference in views.

Literacy

a. Read a variety of texts, including fictions, nonfiction, poetry, and drama.
c. Use planning strategies to generate topics and organize ideas (e.g. brainstorming, mapping, webbing, reading and discussion).

Introduction

In the media center, arouse students' interest in local and state history by showing a tantalizing variety of magazine articles, books, and Internet topics. Work with the media specialist in showing the children how to find a selection on local or state history of interest to them.

Central Activity

Assist the students in finding historical materials of immediate interest, such as gold rushes, pirates, the Westward Movement, development of the Erie Canal or the early railroads, the pollution and reclamation of a river, local urban renewal projects, and so on. Give them time to read, either alone or with a partner, with these guiding questions: "How did your chosen event(s) change the way at least two different people (or groups of people) thought or acted? Why did the same event affect people differently?" Invite the students to talk with each other about their findings. Encourage them to jot down notes from their reading related to the guiding questions. When all students have made choices of materials, read some portions of their selection(s) and jotted notes, and lead a discussion to help them start thinking about pros and cons for groups or individuals affected differently by the same event.

Assessment

This assessment has two parts. First, observe for the answers to these questions: (1) Have all students read materials and jotted down enough notes to assure you that they have been finding answers to the guiding questions? (2) Have they participated responsively in the discussion about pros and cons of an event for different groups or individuals?

When you observe that most students have shown the behaviors desired for questions 1 and 2, begin the next part of the assessment. Give the students an example of a familiar single event that affected people differently in your school or community, such as a new cafeteria. Using large chart paper, guide the students in thinking with you and offer ideas to create a 2 × 2 matrix of pros and cons for each group, such as the following:

The New Cafeteria Example		
	Pros	**Cons**
Students	Tables are nicer. The view is great! There are more choices of food.	The food costs more. It's noisier in the bigger room. Students aren't allowed to go to the salad bar.
Cafeteria Workers	It's cooler in the kitchen. It's easier to cook with the new stoves. It's easier to serve students in the serving line.	Work hours have been cut so the cafeteria ladies make less money. One job was cut.
Teachers	They have a nice area just for teachers. Teachers like the new salad bar.	Teachers worry about the time because students eat too slowly while they are looking around.

After guiding the students in developing this matrix together, ask them to develop the same kind of matrix for their interesting event in history and the people it affected. While the exemplar chart is visually accessible, students may work together or individually on their own matrix. When they are finished, the assessment questions to ask are (1) Could students identify different groups or people affected by an event in history? (2) Could they accurately identify pros and cons for those different groups or people?

Materials

- Books, magazines, newspaper clippings, Internet examples of state and local historical events
- Access to search system in your school or community media center or library
- Chart paper

Lesson Three:
Writing from a time line (Group/Individual activity, several days)

Objectives

II. Time, Continuity, and Change
b. Demonstrate an ability to use correct vocabulary associated with time, such as past, present, future, and long ago; read and construct simple time lines; identify examples of change; and recognize examples of cause-and-effect relationships.

III. People, Places, and Environments
g. Describe how people create places that reflect ideas, personality, culture, and wants and needs as they design homes, playgrounds, classrooms, and the like.

Literacy

c. Use planning strategies to generate topics and organize ideas (e.g., brainstorming, mapping, webbing, reading, discussion).
d. Focus revision on a specific element, such as word choice, sequence or events and ideas, transitional words, and sentence patterns.
e. Compose a variety of fiction, nonfiction, poetry, and drama selections using self-selected topics and forms (e.g., poems, simple narratives, short reports, learning logs, letters, notes, directions, instructions).

Introduction

Guide the students in creating a plausible time line divided into a 100- to 400-year span for their community in relationship to a familiar local place or historical event that no students have already investigated, such as the building of a sports arena downtown or the creation of a protected bird sanctuary. Based on what they learned about other historical events, help them project forward into the future as well as make reasonable guesses about the past. An example follows.

Sugar Creek Parkway			
2100	*2000*	*1900*	*1800*
Children create a playground where an old deserted mill once stood. City planners solve all flooding problems with drainage systems that irrigate crops.	City planners completed a walking mall along its banks, like the River-walk in San Antonio. Floods damaged homes and businesses near the river's banks.	Runoff from mills polluted the river. Industries built dams and generators for the electricity they needed. Floods damaged low-lying cabins.	Catawba Indians fished on the banks of Sugaw Creek. Early settlers renamed it Sugar Creek and built cabins along its banks.

Central Activity

Contact local historical societies, local historians, elderly community members, and others to give an account of how the city or state has changed in 300 years within particular areas of importance. (You could do this yourself or tie this into a writing assignment for the students.) Encourage the children to ask questions, based on their increased awareness of historical changes developed thus far in the unit. Building on the children's interests, expand their earlier categories of historical events and changes to include visitors' information about interaction of human beings with their physical environment—for example, child labor, schooling, pollution, roads, housing patterns, use of natural resources, and technology. As the visitors share information with the students, you and the students may ask questions to fill in any number of time lines similar to the one used in the introduction.

Individual students, partners, or small groups of students choose a time line of interest, then use the resources of the media center, family members, neighbors, or other community resources to add details. They may then expand the time line to draft either an informational or imaginary account of events, with particular emphasis on the interaction of human beings with their physical environment over time.

Assessment

Ask yourself (1) When the students compare the stories brought to them and the various time lines they developed, can they identify differences in perspectives? (2) Can the students summarize information heard or read on the graphic organizers? (3) Do the students' compositions contain historically accurate information presented in the correct sequence?

Materials

- Rolled paper for time lines
- Photographs, tapes, etc., with historical content
- Stories from families, community resources

Lesson Four:
Creating a game (Small group activity, 1–2 days)

Objectives

II. Time, Continuity, and Change

b. Demonstrate an ability to use correct vocabulary associated with time, such as past, present, future, and long ago; read and construct simple time lines; identify examples of change; and recognize examples of cause-and-effect relationships.

d. Identify and use various sources for reconstructing the past such as documents, letters, diaries, maps, textbooks, photos, and others.

Literacy

b. Identify and interpret elements of fiction and nonfiction and support by referencing the text to determine the author's purpose, plot, conflict, sequence, and resolution.

Introduction

You and the students stand in a circle and toss a beach ball to each other. You begin the game by making a statement, such as "I came to work at 8:30 today." Then the group says, "What happened before that?" You then toss the ball to a student who answers the question with his or her own idea. Raising the ball over the head before tossing it is the signal that prompts the class to say again, "What happened before that?" The student then tosses the ball to someone else for a reply, and so on.

Central Activity

The game now moves from the students' own experiences and ideas to the history they know from *The House on Maple Street*. You begin this phase of the game by making a statement, such as, "The child found a piece of cracked pottery in the yard." Again, the group says, "What happened before that?" you toss the ball to a student who must answer that question before raising the ball to toss it to someone else.

A third or alternative phase of the game involves asking historical questions pertaining to any of the material discovered, studied, and shared in the last few days as students pursued areas of interest. In this phase, the student waits for the group to say, "How do you know?" after he or she answers the first question. The student must answer that question by referencing the source of information (book, Internet, newspaper, speaker, etc.) before asking a new question and tossing the ball. Since there is more likelihood of students not knowing answers in this broader-ranging third phase, there should be a signal for the desire to catch the ball as well as for the readiness to toss it.

Assessment

This assessment assumes all students had a turn to participate: (1) Did the students give accurate information about the story and its sequence of events? (2) Did the students give accurate information about local and state historical events and changes in the correct sequence? (3) Are the students becoming more accurate in their use of vocabulary associated with time?

Materials

- Chart with game rules
- Beach ball
- Displays of all time lines created thus far

Lesson Five:
From field trip to newscast (Group activity, 3–4 days)

Objectives

II. Time, Continuity, and Change
b. Demonstrate an ability to use correct vocabulary associated with time, such as past, present, future, and long ago; read and construct simple time lines; identify examples of change; and recognize examples of cause-and-effect relationships.

e. Demonstrate an understanding that people in different times and places view the world differently.

Literacy

c. Use planning strategies to generate topics and organize ideas (e.g., brainstorming, mapping, webbing, reading, discussion).

d. Focus revision on a specific element , such as word choice, sequence or events and ideas, transitional words, and sentence patterns.

Introduction

The class goes on a field trip to a local history museum or library exhibit.

Central Activity

Tell the children that as they view the exhibits, they should make captioned drawings of the artifacts seen. They will then bring to class old textbooks, newspapers, pictures, family stories, and other related articles to represent how people have viewed themselves over the years. (You should screen these treasures before displaying them for the class.)

Using the family treasures and information from the field trip and previous speakers, the students will develop their own individual two-column journal about a particular time period in their state or local community. The first column highlights key events in chronological order, with the effects on different people noted. The second column contains the student's own commentaries from his or her modern perspective, such as, "Didn't they realize that dam would cause flooding?" Ask the children to share this draft with a partner who is responsible for asking three kinds of questions for clarification: "How did _____ affect the different people living there?" "Why did people make that choice (or decision)?" and "What happened before/after that?" Each student then revises for greater clarity the link between order, events, and diverse perspectives of people involved with those events.

Assessment

In the form of a brief newscast, each student tells about one event from his or her study, mentions how that event affected people differently, and shares his or her modern-day perspective on the matter. Based on the journal and the newscast, ask the following assessment questions: (1) Did the student use vocabulary correctly to explain events in chronological order? (2) Did the student identify different perspectives relative to the same event? (3) Was the student able to add his or her own perspective from the present day?

Materials

- Old family treasures
- Notebooks and sketchpads for the field trip
- Mock cardboard box TV, microphone, video camera, or closed-circuit TV for newscast

Lesson Six:
Looking beyond the local area (Group activity, 1–2 days)

Objectives

II. Time, Continuity, and Change
e. Demonstrate an understanding that people in different times and places view the world differently.

Literacy

a. Read a variety of texts, including fiction, nonfiction, poetry, and drama.
c. Use planning strategies to generate topics and organize ideas (e.g., brainstorming, mapping, webbing, reading, discussion).

Introduction

Show a video, film, or CD of a newsworthy event that happened in another part of the country or world during the same time period as one or more of the local/state events studied by the children thus far. Encourage questions and insights, noting similarities and differences of people's responses around the world.

Central Activity

Student teams will choose topics (e.g., child labor, pollution) already shown around the room on time lines or other graphic organizers. They may stay with their same topic or choose another one. Student teams will then engage in research to discover (1) what has happened in other regions of the country and world related to that topic and (2) what the effects were on diverse peoples in those areas.

Assessment

Students will report their findings to the class through the use of some kind of graphic organizer. The assessment questions to ask include (1) Did the students use a variety of materials to investigate their chosen topic? (2) Did the students find differences in how people were affected by historical events around the world? (3) Did the graphic organizer provide a clear identification of main points and their relationship to each other?

Materials

- Variety of informational/historical materials on other states and countries, preferably related to topics of earlier investigation

Lesson Seven:
Compare homes of various cultures (Group activity, 1–2 days)

Objectives

III. People, Places, and Environments

g. Describe how people create places that reflect ideas, personality, culture, and wants and needs as they design homes, playgrounds, classrooms, and the like.

h. Examine the interaction of human beings and their physical environment, the use of land, building of cities, and ecosystem changes in selected locales and regions.

Literacy

e. Compose a variety of fiction, nonfiction, poetry, and drama selections using self-selected topics and forms (e.g., poems, simple narratives, short reports, learning logs, letters, notes, directions, instructions).

Introduction

Using video, pictures, CDs, or the Internet, provide examples that show the relationship of homes to people's environments and cultural patterns. For example, teepees or other forms of tents are best suited for nomadic people because they can pick up their homes and move to a new location. Apartments or condominiums are best suited for people who live and work inside large cities. Invite students to brainstorm other kinds of dwellings and why people might design or choose them.

Central Activity

Ask the students to use drawing and writing paper to sketch and describe how they would design their ideal home or bedroom, showing and writing what they would put in there and why. Have them research different housing situations and determine who lives there, how the environment influences the choice of housing, and if/how/why it reflects something about the dwellers' personalities. The students then revise or simply complete their writing by discussing (1) how their experiences with the environment influenced their choices of an ideal home or bedroom and (2) how their choices do or do not reflect something about their own personalities. (*Note:* Homelessness should be carefully addressed. It may be brought up in the discussions or in the writings. Be prepared to have a social service representative scheduled to speak to the class about this phenomenon.)

Assessment

Ask yourself (1) Have the students written accurately about a linkage between the environment and housing choices? (2) Have the students presented a compelling

argument for the existence or nonexistence of a relationship between their housing choices and their personalities? (3) Have the students written about how their
house is similar and/or different from *A House on Maple Street* (comparison-contrast
activity)?

Materials

- Research materials on housing for different cultures

Lesson Eight
Field trip (science-related) (Group activity, 1–2 days)

Objectives

III. People, Places, and Environments

h. Examine the interaction of human beings and their physical environment,
the use of land, building of cities and ecosystem changes in selected locales
and regions.

Literacy

e. Compose a variety of fiction, nonfiction, poetry, and drama selections using
self-selected topics and forms (e.g., poems, simple narratives, short reports,
learning logs, letters, notes, directions, instructions).

Introduction

Discuss with the class how recycling is a way to interact with the physical environment; elicit examples from the students. Introduce the idea of a field trip to a water
recycling plant. Instruct the students before the trip to pay special attention to the
process for returning water to the streams and lakes in a manner that is safe for the
aquatic life and others that will consume the recycled water. Invite the students to
identify possible problems if water is not recycled safely.

Central Activity

Take the class on a field trip to a water recycling plant. Ask the students to make an
illustrated entry in their journals after returning to class. They may then search the
Internet to see how water is directed from the Colorado River to cities and farms in
southern California, or to find other such recycling systems. The students may use
a variety of graphic organizers to show information found, then write a reaction to
the new problems and possibilities they now understand.

Assessment

Ask yourself (1) Did the students' graphic organizers show the relationship of human beings to their natural and human-made environments through water recycling? (2) Did the students' written reactions indicate a new and positive awareness of water recycling?

Materials

- Research materials on water recycling
- Information on Colorado River or other rivers involved in water recycling projects
- Information on southern California or other parts of the country involved in water recycling projects

Lesson Nine:
Physical features of environment (Group activity, several days)

Objectives

III. People, Places, and Environments
i. Explore the ways that the earth's physical features have changed over time in the local region and beyond, and how these changes may be connected to each other.

Literacy

f. Recognize the power of the media to influence.

Introduction

Use examples from the text, CDs, videos, or the Internet that show the changes in the earth's physical features.

Central Activity

Have the students recall or cite from current news articles that new malls, office buildings, or housing developments are being constructed on or near areas that were previously undeveloped. The students can imagine and write a story about what was there, or how an animal family was forced to move because of the changes. Perhaps they can ask older family members or neighbors what was on the site before the new mall (or office buildings, new houses, etc.). The children may also visit the community library or newspaper office to look through old photos of their community to determine what changes took place in the physical features of the town.

Assessment

Students create a talk show segment to role-play an interview with a character from the book *The House on Maple Street* or from their community (mayor, builder, etc.) to ask about different physical changes in the environment because of what people decided to do. The assessment questions to ask include (1) Can the students describe physical changes accurately? (2) Can the students connect physical changes to needs and wants of humans? (3) Do the students express opinions or cautions about appropriate or inappropriate use of the environment that are based on factual information?

Materials

- Book: *The House on Maple Street*
- Old town newspaper
- Old town photos
- Rules for creating talk show

Culminating and Assessment Activities

The following are suggested activities that may be done by individuals, partners, or small groups. You may want to incorporate variations into earlier lessons, or you may want students to choose one or two as evidence of having met the objectives of the unit.

- Using overhead transparencies, develop a set of overlaid maps showing specific changes in an area chosen from *The House on Maple Street,* the state, or the local community.
- Write to the newspaper or prepare a video segment to send to a local TV station (or use on the school's closed-circuit TV) to argue for or against a proposed development in the community.
- Develop a time-segmented collage about a specific topic (e.g., child labor, water recycling, pollution) that represents changes over periods of time.
- Write a family journal of reactions as a great-grandparent, grandparent, parent, child-self, and future son or daughter chronicling the changes in the world relative to a specific topic of interest, such as housing, technology, transportation, and so on.
- Create a newsletter on water recycling (students could do this in small groups or as a class). Encourage the students to share with classmates, parents, and the media center so that others may learn from it.

Unit 6
Theme: Respecting the Earth

Multiple-Book Model: Grades 3–4

Related Books by Thematic Category
(The *highlighted* book(s) in each category has a lesson plan.)

Reclaiming/Repairing/Rehabilitating the Earth
The River Ran Wild by Lynne Cherry (Multicultural)
There's an Owl in the Shower by Jean Craighead George (European American)
Hawk Hill by Suzie Gilbert (European American)
And Still the Turtle Watched by Sheila MacGill (Multicultural)
Wolves in Yellowstone by Randy Houk (Multicultural)
Red Wolf Country by Jonathan London (Multicultural)

Beautification of the Earth
The Garden of Happiness by Erika Tamar (Multicultural)
Miss Rumphius by Barbara Cooney (European American)
Dandelions by Eve Bunting (European American)
A Day's Work by Eve Bunting (Mexican American)
The Gardener by Sarah Stewart (European American)

Protecting the Environment
Pearl Moscowitz's Last Stand by Arthur Levine (Multicultural)
Death of the Iron Horse by Paul Goble (Native American)
Song of the Trees by Mildred Taylor (African American)
The Great Kapok Tree by Lynne Cherry (South American)
Riverkeeper by George Ancona (European American)
The Tree That Would Not Die by Ellen Levine (Multicultural)
Hawk, I'm Your Brother by Byrd Baylor (Native American)
The Desert Is Theirs by Byrd Baylor (Native American)

Living in Harmony with the Earth
Very Last First Time by Jan Andrews (Native American)
Harvest Year by Cris Peterson (Multicultural)
The Lotus Seed by Sherry Garland (Vietnamese American)

Tanya's Reunion by Valerie Flournoy (African American)
I Have Heard of a Land by Joyce Thomas (African American)
My Two Worlds by Ginger Gordon (Caribbean)
Moonstick: The Seasons of the Sioux by Eve Bunting (Native American)
Sugaring Time by Kathryn Lasky (European American)
The Sacred Harvest: Ojibway Wild Rice Gathering by Gordon Regguinti
(Native American)
Family Farm by Thomas Locker (European American)
All the Places to Love by Patricia MacLachlan (European American)
When the Woods Hum by Joanne Ryder (European American)
Anna's Athabaskan Summer by Arnold Griese (Native American)

Understanding and Surviving Problems in the Environment
How Many Days to America? by Eve Bunting (Caribbean)
Flood by Mary Calhoun (European American)
Kate Shelley: Bound for Legend by Robert San Souci (European American)
Aurora Means Dawn by Scott Sanders (European American)
Summer of Fire by Patricia Lauber (Multicultural)
Steamboat in a Cornfield by John Hartford (European American)
Tikvah Means Hope by Patricia Polacco (Jewish)
The Land of Grey Wolf by Thomas Locker (Native American)
Smoky Night by Eve Bunting (Multicultural)
On Call Back Mountain by Eve Bunting (European American)

Rationale

For students to become concerned about their environment, they must realize the need for many people to care about the earth and its creatures and to act cooperatively with each other and the environment. They must also realize that there are competing concerns regarding many areas of the environment and other social concerns of humans. This unit is most closely aligned with Banks and Banks's decision-making and social action approach. It is a unit that could be easily integrated with science.

Unit Goal

Students will learn both problems and solutions regarding care for the environment and its creatures.

NCSS Themes and Performance Standards

I. Culture
  a. Explore and describe commonalties and differences in the ways groups, societies, and cultures address similar human needs and concerns.
  d. Compare ways in which people from different cultures think about and deal with their physical environment and social conditions.

III. People, Places, and Environments

g. Describe how people create places that reflect ideas, personality, culture, and wants and needs as they design homes, playgrounds, classrooms, and the like.

h. Examine the interaction of human beings and their physical environment, the use of land, building of cities, and ecosystem changes in selected locales and regions.

VIII. Science, Technology, and Society

a. Identify and describe examples in which science and technology have changed the lives of people, such as in homemaking, child care, work, transportation, and communication.

b. Identify and describe examples in which science and technology have led to changes in the physical environment, such as the building of dams and levees, offshore oil drilling, medicine from rain forests, and loss of rain forests due to extraction of resources and alternative uses.

c. Describe instances in which changes in values, beliefs, and attitudes have resulted from new scientific and technological knowledge, such as conservation of resources and awareness of chemicals harmful to life and the environment.

IX. Global Connections

b. Give examples of conflict, cooperation, and interdependence among individuals, groups, and nations.

f. Investigate concerns, issues, standards, and conflicts related to universal human rights, such as the treatment of children, religious groups, and effects of war.

Literacy Objectives (Based on NC Standard Course of Study)

a. Read a variety of texts, including fiction, nonfiction, poetry, and drama.

b. Interact with the text before, during, and after reading, listening, or viewing.

c. Draw conclusions, make generalizations, and gather support by referencing the text.

d. Respond to fiction, nonfiction, poetry, and drama using interpretive, critical, and evaluative processes.

e. Identify and discuss similarities and differences in events and characters within and across selections and support them by referencing the text.

f. Use text and own experiences to verify facts, concepts, and ideas.

g. Compose a variety of fiction, nonfiction, poetry, and drama selections using various topics and forms.

Initiating Activity:
Valuing the earth (1 day)

Investigate the children's existing schemata for this unit by asking students what they think they already know about valuing and taking care of the earth. List their responses on chart paper. Take a count of hands for each value that children have actively done something about—such as picked up litter, recycled, planted trees and flowers, and so on.

Raise the children's awareness of the importance of the earth and problems, changes, and improvements in their environment with any one or more of the following activities:

- Take a nature walk near the school to notice beauty, litter, changes, and so on.
- View and discuss any film or video about the environment.
- View websites concerned with environmental problems and improvements, such as the following:
    http://geogweb.berkeley.edu/GeoImages/BainCalif/subjects/
        NativeEnvironment.html
    http://www.npca.org/flash.html
- Invite an environmental protection agent from your community to visit the classroom and explain his or her job, with many visual examples.

Indicate to the children that they will be reading a number of books about valuing the earth, and that you are going to be very interested in their reactions to these books, especially when they decide to start taking more action on their values than they have in the past.

(*Note:* Each of the lessons in Unit 6 uses a book from the categorical list on the first page of this unit, but suggests extensions for additional lessons on each subtheme. The subthemes may be reordered to align with your intentions and your students' abilities and interests.)

Lesson One:
Reclaiming the earth (1–2 days)

Book

A River Ran Wild by Lynne Cherry

Objectives

I. Culture
d. Compare ways in which people from different cultures think about and deal with their physical environment and social conditions.

III. People, Places, and Environments

h. Examine the interaction of human beings and their physical environment, the use of land, building of cities, and ecosystem changes in selected locales and regions.

VIII. Science, Technology, and Society

a. Identify and describe examples in which science and technology have changed the lives of people, such as in homemaking, child care, work, transportation, and communication.

b. Identify and describe examples in which science and technology have led to changes in the physical environment, such as the building of dams and levees, offshore oil drilling, medicine from rain forests, and loss of rain forests due to extraction of resources and alternative uses.

c. Describe instances in which changes in values, beliefs, and attitudes have resulted from new scientific and technological knowledge, such as conservation of resources and awareness of chemicals harmful to life and the environment.

IX. Global Connections

b. Give examples of conflict, cooperation, and interdependence among individuals, groups, and nations.

Literacy

a. Read a variety of texts, including fiction, nonfiction, poetry, and drama.
c. Draw conclusions, make generalizations, and gather support by referencing the text.
d. Respond to fiction, nonfiction, poetry, and drama using interpretive, critical, and evaluative processes.
g. Compose a variety of fiction, nonfiction, poetry, and drama selections using various topics and forms.

Introduction

Ask the students to listen as you read a true story of something people in the United States almost ruined until one woman cared enough to fight for her values. Read *A River Ran Wild*, pausing for discussion wherever children react. Emphasize change over time in people's values and understandings of the importance of the river and how to take care of it.

Central Activity

Provide multiple copies of the book to three to six small small groups of students, depending on your class size or dynamics. Move those groups to open spaces on the floor. Give them long rolled paper with the directions to use the book for information. One group should draw a beautiful clean river, one a nearly ruined river, and the third a time line of changes to the Nashua River depicted in the book. Each child in a group should draw part of the river and should write one idea with visual details about protecting or ruining the river. Display these mini-murals for the length of the unit.

Assessment

Ask yourself (1) Are the children actively discussing changes in the river over time and how people must be responsible for the care of the earth? (2) Do their murals indicate awareness of human impact on a river? (3) In the beginning of a journal to be kept during the unit, ask the students to react to the question, "What have you learned about respecting the earth that you hadn't thought about before the past two days? So what?"

Possible Extensions

It is likely that this first lesson will not be enough! You may wish to supplement by the following activities:

- Have the children read independently some of the other books about reclaiming the earth and report on what they've found.
- Guide the students through a similar lesson using *And Still the Turtle Watched* by Sheila MacGill to intensify their awareness of efforts to solve environmental problems over time.
- Have the children search the Internet and report about other examples of environmental reclamation.

Materials

- Multiple copies of *The River Ran Wild*
- Long pieces of rolled paper

Lesson Two:
Beautification of the earth (Two books, 1–2 days)

Books

> *Miss Rumphius* by Barbara Cooney
> *The Garden of Happiness* by Erika Tamar

Objectives

I. Culture
d. Compare ways in which people from different cultures think about and deal with their physical environment and social conditions.

III. People, Places, and Environments

g. Describe how people create places that reflect ideas, personality, culture, and wants and needs as they design homes, playgrounds, classrooms, and the like.

h. Examine the interaction of human beings and their physical environment, the use of land, building of cities, and ecosystem changes in selected locales and regions.

Literacy

a. Read a variety of texts, including fiction, nonfiction, poetry, and drama.

d. Respond to fiction, nonfiction, poetry, and drama using interpretive, critical, and evaluative processes.

e. Identify and discuss similarities and differences in events and characters within and across selections and support them by referencing the text.

Introduction

Call the students' attention to their three river murals and the beauty of the one mural. Ask for examples of other aspects of the earth they find beautiful, whether it might be natural environmental beauty or something created by humans. Then direct their attention to a partially prepared long bulletin board or rolled paper stretched across a wall that has two sections: *Natural Beauty of the Earth* and *Human Beautification of the Earth*. Each section has a different yarn outline, one to represent the shape of mountains and valleys, and the other to represent the shape of city buildings.

Give the children magazines with various pictures of the earth's natural and human-made beauty, such as *National Geographic*, travel magazines, *Ranger Rick*, and *Contact*. Ask them each to find one example for each part of the board and paste it on to make a collage. Display this collage near the mini-murals of the rivers. Explain that today's two books focus not on the natural beauty or repair of the natural beauty of the environment but on the further beautification of it by humans. One, *Miss Rumphius*, shows beautification in a number of places around the world, and the other, *The Garden of Happiness*, focuses on beautifying the environment of a city.

Central Activity

The children should choose which book they most want to read. Help group the children for reading with partners or small groups if copies of the books are limited, or if you have readers who will need help. Ask them to pay attention to two things: *Why* did these people work to beautify their environments and *what difference* did they make for others? As the students read, allow independence and conversation. Monitor to be sure that the students are staying focused on those questions, but certainly allow for discussion of other aspects of the two stories.

Beautification of the Earth Why?			
Compare and Contrast	*Miss Rumphius* Why did Miss Rumphius plant flowers?	*The Garden of Happiness* Why did Marisol plant a flower?	**Our connections** Why would we plant flowers?
What's similar?			
What's different?			
What Difference Did It Make?			
Compare and Contrast	*Miss Rumphius* What difference did Miss Rumphius make with her flowers?	*The Garden of Happiness* What difference did Marisol make with her flower?	**Our connections** What difference have flowers made for us?
What's similar?			
What's different?			

If groups finish reading at different times, they may reread favorite parts or continue to discuss their answers to the questions and reactions to the stories. When all groups are ready, distribute or display the following comparison and contrast charts.

To complete the charts, the children must interview each other about the content of the book they didn't read and to make notes in the appropriate cells. Tape a purple paper flower on the *Miss Rumphius* readers and a yellow paper sunflower on the *Garden of Happiness* readers for ease of identification. Set a timer and allow two minutes per interview session. Start with purple interviewing yellow for one minute; then switch roles for one minute. At the end of two minutes, each student must each find a new partner. Allow approximately five sessions, then ask students to return to their seats for a moment. Form new groups of two or three purples and two or three yellows each. Give them a blank copy of the comparison and contrast chart and ask each group to decide on the final contents, based on their interviews and a final rereading of the book. Have groups share when they complete the charts.

Complete the lesson with a personal journal entry in response to the questions, "What does beautification of the earth mean to you? How can you contribute to that beautification?"

Assessment

The assessment questions are straightforward: (1) Did all students use their interview data and books again to construct their group's final comparison and contrast chart? (2) Are there similarities and differences shown on each group's chart? (3) Do the students' journal entries demonstrate understanding of concepts about beautification of the earth?

Possible Extensions

- Actually engage in a school or community beautification project.
- Grow a classroom garden.
- Research the Internet to find out about other students' or communities' beautification projects.
- Write about a fictitious beautification project.
- Read and respond to other books listed for this subtheme.

Materials

- Multiple copies of *Miss Rumphius* and *The Garden of Happiness*
- Prepared bulletin board with landscape and cityscape outlines
- Multiple magazines
- Multiple copies of the comparison and contrast charts

Lesson Three:
Protecting the environment (2–3 days)

Book

Pearl Moscowitz's Last Stand by Arthur Levine

Objectives

III. People, Places, and Environments

g. Describe how people create places that reflect ideas, personality, culture, and wants and needs as they design homes, playgrounds, classrooms, and the like.

h. Examine the interaction of human beings and their physical environment, the use of land, building of cities, and ecosystem changes in selected locales and regions.

VIII. Science, Technology, and Society

a. Identify and describe examples in which science and technology have changed the lives of people, such as in homemaking, child care, work, transportation, and communication.

b. Identify and describe examples in which science and technology have led to changes in the physical environment, such as the building of dams and levees, offshore oil drilling, medicine from rain forests, and loss of rain forests due to extraction of resources and alternative uses.

c. Describe instances in which changes in values, beliefs, and attitudes have resulted from new scientific and technological knowledge, such as conservation of resources and awareness of chemicals harmful to life and the environment.

IX. Global Connections

b. Give examples of conflict, cooperation, and interdependence among individuals, groups, and nations.

Literacy

a. Read a variety of texts, including fiction, nonfiction, poetry, and drama.
b. Interact with the text before, during, and after reading, listening, or viewing.
c. Draw conclusions, make generalizations, and gather support by referencing the text.
d. Respond to fiction, nonfiction, poetry, and drama using interpretive, critical, and evaluative processes.

Introduction

Display on a large chart and read aloud with students the following Navajo poem:

> *Walk on a rainbow trail,*
> *Walk on a trail of song!*
> *And all about you will be beauty.*
> *There is a way out of every dark mist,*
> *Over a rainbow trail.*

Ask the students to imagine what they would like to see on their rainbow trail of beauty. Introduce the picture book, *Pearl Moscowitz's Last Stand,* with this question: "If you were old instead of young and lived in a place that had lost more and more of its beauty with the passing years, what kind of beauty on that rainbow trail would you be willing to fight for?" List suggestions, then provide time for the students to read the story silently or with a partner.

Central Activity

Day One: After eliciting reactions from the students, help them see the comparison between the book and the poem, especially that it is humankind's "song" together that helps create a way out of the dark mist—via a rainbow trail.

For their next journal entry, ask students to create a picture of Pearl Moscowitz's rainbow trail, from the beginning, through the dark mist, and out into the rainbow of beauty again. Ask them to reflect on the "song" created by the diversity of the group around the tree.

Day Two: Ask the students to share their pictures, then emphasize that Pearl's idea of beauty was her personal value. Ask them to revisit the book briefly and try to imagine the ideas of "beauty" others might have had when they changed the look of Pearl's street each time. Tell the students to make a chart identifying each change, the person's possible perception of beauty each time, Pearl's perception of each change, and their personal reaction to each change. This project may be done individually, in partners, or in small groups.

The journal entry after this lesson should focus on the students' reactions to realizing different perceptions of beauty are related to people's experiences, jobs, values, and everyday lives and to the question, "What difference could you make if you fought for beauty *along with* someone who is different from you?"

Assessment

Ask yourself (1) Do the students' pictures of the rainbow trail indicate comprehension of Pearl's point of view? (2) Do the students' charts indicate reasonable inferences about multiple points of view about beauty over a number of years in the city? (3) Do the students' journal entries indicate an awareness that people's different perceptions are related to their jobs, experiences, and values?

Possible Extensions

- Read *The Tree That Would Not Die* for a comparison and contrast activity
- Prepare skits or Reader's Theatre presentations.
- Make posters regarding preservation of certain aspects of their community.
- Engage in a preservation activity with community members.

Materials

- Multiple copies of *Pearl Moscowitz's Last Stand*
- Drawing and writing paper for journal entries
- Navajo poem preprinted on large chart paper

Lesson Four:
Protecting the environment: Justice or injustice? (2 days)

Book

Death of the Iron Horse by Paul Goble

Objectives

I. Culture
a. Explore and describe commonalties and differences in the ways groups, societies, and cultures address similar human needs and concerns.

d. Compare ways in which people from different cultures think about and deal with their physical environment and social conditions.

III: People, Places, and Environments
h. Examine the interaction of human beings and their physical environment, the use of land, building of cities, and ecosystem changes in selected locales and regions.

VIII. Science, Technology, and Society
a. Identify and describe examples in which science and technology have changed the lives of people, such as in homemaking, child care, work, transportation, and communication.

b. Identify and describe examples in which science and technology have led to changes in the physical environment, such as the building of dams and levees, offshore oil drilling, medicine from rain forests, and loss of rain forests due to extraction of resources and alternative uses.

IX. Global Connections

b. Give examples of conflict, cooperation, and interdependence among individuals, groups, and nations.

f. Investigate concerns, issues, standards, and conflicts related to universal human rights, such as the treatment of children, religious groups, and effects of war.

Literacy

b. Interact with the text before, during, and after reading, listening, or viewing.

c. Draw conclusions, make generalizations, and gather support by referencing the text.

d. Respond to fiction, nonfiction, poetry, and drama using interpretive, critical, and evaluative processes.

e. Identify and discuss similarities and differences in events and characters within and across selections and support them by referencing the text.

Introduction

Tell the students that the book you and they will be working with for the next two days contains serious conflict between beauty and progress, much more serious than in the Pearl Moscowitz story, and that they are going to wrestle with ideas of justice and injustice. Make sure they know the meaning of those terms with a request for some examples.

In small groups, have the students list all the examples of injustice they've either seen or experienced firsthand. (You can time them, see which group has the longest list, have them read examples aloud, make comments—keep it fast-paced and lively.) Then have them make a second list related to the first—all the ways they or others have tried to overcome those injustices. Have the students share these lists, too. (The interactions are critically important to hearing lots of different ideas and experiences.)

Central Activity

Day One: Link the children's brainstorming exercise to the story and give a brief introduction to the activity on page 212. For example, you might say, "You have given many examples of injustice and ways people have tried to overcome such injustice. We are going to read a book filled with injustices involving early Native Americans and white soldiers and settlers, but it isn't always easy to decide which people are right and which are wrong in their behavior. Before we read, I want you to talk and think about the following opinions about human rights, and decide if you agree or disagree with each sentence today. You might think differently tomorrow. Use only the first column right now. Write 'Agree' or 'Disagree.'"

Have the students briefly share their opinions in small groups and give reasons for their opinions. Encourage differences of interpretation of the statement

The Statement	My Own Opinion Before Reading	My Group's Prediction	My Group's Interpretation After Reading
1. Humans should never hurt each other unless it's self-defense.			
2. Progress in a country usually means a better sense of justice.			
3. Early Native Americans and the early white settlers and soldiers had a different sense of justice.			
4. It takes enormous courage to fight for justice.			
5. People who fight for justice together usually win.			
6. Violence is never necessary; problems can always be solved in nonviolent ways to achieve justice.			

and differences of opinion. Ask frequently, "Do you see why so-and-so might have that opinion?" Make sure students realize that different experiences may have led classmates to have different opinions.

After the students have completed the first column and shared their ideas in small groups, move them to the next phase. Divide the class randomly into two groups, then cut those groups in half or thirds. Tell half the groups that you want them to take the perspective of the early white settlers and soldiers; the other groups are to take the point of view of the Native Americans for the rest of the lesson.

Give the next directions: "I'm going to tell you a little more about the story, then I want you to use the second column to make predictions. The story focuses on the Cheyenne Indians fighting to keep the railroad from ruining the beautiful earth and their way of life. The white settlers are trying to move westward and create a better life for themselves, and they are fighting to survive, too. Think about what you know about your group of people. Predict what your group's perspective would be in this story for each of these statements. Would they agree or disagree if you asked them? You might think they will have the same or different opinion compared to you. Work with your group to make predictions. Use the second column to write 'Agree' or 'Disagree.'" Have students share their predictions; emphasize differences.

Distribute enough copies of *Death of the Iron Horse* so that the children can share comfortably. Read the introductory message, then let them read the rest independently with only the direction to think about the third column as they read. Ask the students to wait for discussion within their groups until everyone finishes the story. Monitor timing; move the students into discussion as soon as possible. Direct students to fill out the third column in their groups, maintaining their perspective of the Cheyenne or the white settlers and soldiers. Close the lesson with some whole class sharing and a promise of more to come tomorrow. Place the prediction chart into their journals for safekeeping and later reuse. (Or you may break the lesson before they read and continue later if necessary.)

Day Two: Review the events of the previous lesson, the opinions, the interpretations, and the differences in perspectives. Display the predominant interpretations of the "Native Americans" and the "white soldiers and settlers." Ask the students to revisit the first column and see if any of their own personal opinions might have changed because of thinking about this event in history. Ask them to write a short reaction in their journals about their opinions or beliefs about justice and injustice that were influenced by this story. Invite sharing.

Ask the students to rejoin yesterday's small group, but keep their own perspective in thinking about the conflicts between early Native Americans and white soldiers and settlers. On large chart paper, have each group list 5 to 10 questions about changes since that time that they would like to know more about, especially involving respect for the earth and its many peoples. Give an example or two, such as, "What kinds of conflicts still exist today between Native and other Americans about the use of land?" or "Do Native Americans still live in tipis?" After they list questions and display them, allow some time to look through materials in the school library or on the Internet to pursue one or more questions of particular interest to individuals or partners. Ask the students to use their journals as Learning Logs this day, jotting down questions and findings of interest.

Assessment

Ask yourself (1) Could all students give predictions and interpretations from inside an unfamiliar perspective? (2) Could they talk about the reasons for their own opinions, referring to examples of conflict and injustice in the story? (3) Could all students create questions within the framework of the topic?

Possible Extensions

- Write and present a report about historical and current conflicts between Native Americans and others over the use and protection of land.
- Read other materials about the Native Americans' reverence for the earth, such as those listed under this subtheme at the beginning of the unit.

Materials

- Multiple copies of *Death of the Iron Horse*
- Individual copies of the prediction guide for every student
- Large chart paper for groups
- Variety of library materials on Native Americans (past and present)

Lesson Five:
Living in harmony with the earth (1 day)

Book

Very Last First Time by Jan Andrews

Objectives

I. Culture
d. Compare ways in which people from different cultures think about and deal with their physical environment and social conditions.

III. People, Places, and Environments
h. Examine the interaction of human beings and their physical environment, the use of land, building of cities, and ecosystem changes in selected locales and regions.

Literacy

d. Respond to fiction, nonfiction, poetry, and drama using interpretive, critical, and evaluative processes.
g. Compose a variety of fiction, nonfiction, poetry, and drama selections using various topics and forms.

Introduction

Ask the children to identify their various favorite foods and where they get them. Depending on where your school is located, children may respond with a variety of answers (e.g., the grocery store, a farmer's market, their farm or garden, McDonald's and other fast-food restaurants, the river/bayou/lake/ocean, etc.). Ask the children to share the most unusual way they've ever helped get food for themselves or their family. Make a list. Help them make a distinction between buying food and getting it more directly from the environment. Tell the class that this story is about a girl whose method of getting food directly from the environment is probably not like any they've ever known.

Central Activity

Have children fold a piece of newsprint into quarters. Number the sections from 1 to 4. Explain that they are going to be visualizing while you read this story the first time, and that each time you stop reading, they are to sketch briefly what they're imagining the setting looks like. Choose three stopping places within the story for them to make sketches, and make the end of the story the fourth stopping place. Invite the children to walk around the room and look at each other's ideas. Reread the book, showing the children the illustrations throughout and especially at each of your previous stopping places. Ask them to jot down notes about the differences between their imagined settings and the illustrator's work. Emphasize the amazing harmony with their environment that the Innuit women and girls have learned to have.

Assessment

The students' journal entries today should have their sketches attached. Ask them to respond to two questions: "What are some of the most important differences in how this girl gets food and how you do?" and "What thoughts and questions do you have about your own harmony with your environment in relationship to getting food?"

Extension Activities

- Read at least one other book from those listed under this theme.
- Go on a field trip to any kind of unfamiliar setting involving forms of harmony with the environment (e.g., a fish farm, a maple syrup operation, formal gardens, bee farm, ice fishing site, farms focusing on different kinds of produce or animals, etc.).
- Conduct independent research on the Internet and in the library to explore an area of interest stimulated by one of the books in this subtheme.

Materials
- One copy of *Very Last First Time*
- Journals
- Copies of many of the other titles in the list
- Large newsprint sheets for each child

Lesson Six:
Understanding and surviving problems in the environment (2 days)

Book

How Many Days to America? by Eve Bunting

Objectives

I. Culture
d. Compare ways in which people from different cultures think about and deal with their physical environment and social conditions.

III. People, Places, and Environments
h. Examine the interaction of human beings and their physical environment, the use of land, building of cities, and ecosystem changes in selected locales and regions.

VIII. Science, Technology, and Society
b. Identify and describe examples in which science and technology have changed the lives of people, such as in homemaking, child care, work, transportation, and communication.

IX. Global Connections
b. Give examples of conflict, cooperation, and interdependence among individuals, groups, and nations.

Literacy

a. Read a variety of texts, including fiction, nonfiction, poetry, and drama.
b. Interact with the text before, during, and after reading, listening, or viewing.
d. Respond to fiction, nonfiction, poetry, and drama using interpretive, critical, and evaluative processes.
f. Use text and own experiences to verify facts, concepts, and ideas.
g. Compose a variety of fiction, nonfiction, poetry, and drama selections using various topics and forms.

Introduction

Use a KWL graphic organizer entitled "Leave or Stay?" for this last lesson in the unit; guide the whole group or small groups through this process. Activate schemata and review the unit by asking the children what they have learned about how people interact with their environment (e.g., ruining it, reclaiming or repairing it, beautifying it) and why people sometimes fight to protect what they have (e.g., the

Cheyenne in *Death of the Iron Horse*, Pearl Moscowitz in *Pearl Moscowitz's Last Stand*). List some of these examples under the *K* column (*What We Know*).

Introduce *How Many Days to America?* by showing the students the book's cover and letting them know these people were choosing to leave their homes and risking a very dangerous environment to build a new life for themselves somewhere else. Invite them to formulate questions to list under the *W* column (*What We Want to Know*).

Central Activity

Read the book to the students, or have them read independently in small groups or partners, inviting much discussion along the way. List findings in the *L* column (*What We Learned*) after completing the story so as not to diminish the intensity.

Invite additional items for the list that connect to previous lessons if pertinent questions didn't already appear in the *W* column, such as What did people take for their journey? How did people cooperate with each other and the earth to survive?

Add a fourth column—*R (Reactions)*—and elicit the students' reactions to the various findings. From that discussion, either the same day or the next, move into a small group activity of retelling the story through a song (with or without the rhyming element). Have the children brainstorm *simple* tunes they know (e.g., "The Adams Family"; "Old MacDonald Had a Farm"; "Twinkle, Twinkle, Little Star"; "Jingle Bells"; etc.). Show how they can retell *How Many Days to America?* by using one of those tunes by singing and displaying this beginning draft or another example you create:

> *(To the tune of "Home on the Range")*
>
> *O'er the ocean we'll roam.*
> *We must risk all our lives,*
> *For it's hot and dangerous to all.*
> *We must take a chance*
> *For the freedom we need*
> *And work with the sea as we go.*

The children should then spend time in small groups drafting and revising their "songs" to sing to the class. Have some music books available in case students need help choosing a tune to use. The songs may repeat verses in order to tell the whole story. You could also give an option to invent the next phase of these people's lives in America instead of or in addition to retelling the story they read. Complete the lesson by having the children sing their songs.

Assessment

Ask yourself (1) Did the students give examples of conflict and cooperation in the *L* column? (2) Did the students make connections between environmental events and themes in this story and those they had encountered earlier in the unit? (3)

Did the students give personal reactions to this narrative in the *R* column? (4) Did the students' songs retell the story and/or foretell its next phase?

Possible Extensions

- Read more of the books on the list (or students find their own) pertaining to the dangers of the environment, perhaps in categories of wind (e.g., tornado, hurricane, cyclone, duststorm), rain (e.g., hurricane, flood, storms at sea, drought), fire (e.g., forest fire, volcano, brush fire), and earth (e.g., landslide, earthquake).
- Develop booklets about preventive and responsive actions to take when in danger from the environment.
- Study the school plan for fire, tornado, or earthquake drills, then develop an appropriate plan for their homes.

Materials

- Multiple copies of *How Many Days to America?*
- Large chart, transparency, or board space for the KWL activity
- Beginning draft of a song on chart paper or transparency
- A few elementary music books
- Paper and pencil for writing songs

Culminating and Assessment Activities

The following are suggested activities that may be done by individuals, partners, or small groups. You may want to incorporate variations into earlier lessons, or you may want students to choose one or two as evidence of having met the objectives of the unit. Extension activities suggested for each unit may also be modified to become culminating and assessment activities.

- Plant flowers and/or trees on the school grounds or somewhere in the nearby community.
- Work with a neighborhood to decorate all the mailboxes.
- Clean up a local street or park.
- Write letters to the newspaper about improvements needed in the community.
- Create a song, dance, or mural about the environment—take it to a nursing home for beautification.
- Identify ways to be more cooperative with the environment.
- Join community projects about the environment; document activities and learning.
- Develop skits to represent important learnings; present the skits to other classes or parents.

Unit 7
Theme: Courage and Leadership

Single-Book Model: Grades 3–4

Book

Freedom Train by Dorothy Sterling

Rationale

By learning about the remarkable courage and leadership of Harriet Tubman in this powerful book, children should feel encouraged to take action for justice and peace in their own lives, thereby participating in the decision-making and social action approach of Banks and Banks's model of multicultural education.

Unit Goals

Students will develop appreciation for the struggles, courage, and leadership of a major historical figure, Harriet Tubman, during an ugly chapter of American history. From this appreciation, they will also begin to take a stand against modern forms of enslavement.

NCSS Themes and Performance Standards

II. Time, Continuity, and Change

b. Demonstrate an ability to use correctly vocabulary associated with time, such as past, present, future, and long ago; read and construct simple time lines; identify examples of change; and recognize examples of cause-and-effect relationships.

d. Identify and use various sources for reconstructing the past, such as documents, letters, diaries, maps, textbooks, photos, and others.

e. Demonstrate an understanding that people in different times and places view the world differently.

f. Use knowledge of facts and concepts drawn from history along with elements of historical inquiry, to make informed decisions about and take action on public issues.

VI. Power, Authority, and Governance

a. Examine the rights and responsibilities of the individual in relation to his or her social groups, such as family, peer group, and school class.

c. Give examples of how government does or does not provide for the needs and wants of people, establish order and security, and manage conflict.

h. Recognize and give examples of the tensions between the wants and needs of individuals and groups, and concepts such as fairness, equity, and justice.

Literacy Objectives
(Based on NC Standard Course of Study)

a. Use metacognitive strategies to comprehend text and to clarify meaning of vocabulary (e.g., reread the text, consult other sources, ask for help, para-phrase, question).

b. Interact with the text before, during, and after reading, listening, and viewing by setting a purpose using prior knowledge and text information, making predictions, formulating questions, locating relevant information, and mak-ing connections with previous experiences, information, and ideas.

c. Identify and interpret elements of fiction and nonfiction and support by ref-erencing the text to determine the plot, theme, main idea and supporting details, and author's choice of words.

d. Make inferences, draw conclusions, make generalizations, and support one's reasoning by referencing the text.

e. Determine usefulness of information and ideas consistent with purpose.

f. Respond to fiction, nonfiction, poetry, and drama using interpretive, critical, and evaluative processes.

g. Compose fiction, nonfiction, poetry, and drama using self-selected and assigned topics and forms.

Initiating Activity:
Maps of courage (Chapters 1–2, 1 day)

Write the word *COURAGE* on chart paper or an overhead transparency. Circle it. Ask the students to think of other words and ideas related to the word *courage.* Build a concept map by writing the students' suggestions and developing categories as they emerge. (*Alternative:* Start building the concept map together, then break students into small groups to finish their own and share with the class.) Save map(s) to use later in the unit.

Tell the students they are going to read a biography of Harriet Tubman, a woman who escaped from slavery and then returned to lead other slaves to free-dom. Show the cover and read the title. Ask the students for general impressions and predictions about examples of courage they may read about in this book. Read Chapters 1 and 2 aloud, inviting the children to point out examples of courage they hear. Then ask the students what impressions they have of Harriet, particularly focusing on her courage as a young child. Invite additions to the concept map(s).

Ask the children to start a journal of their "journey" with Harriet Tubman. Suggest that their first entry might be a reaction to any of Harriet's ways of showing courage, but allow for related choices.

Lesson One:
Focus on secret behaviors of courage, perceptions of justice
(Chapters 3–4, 1 day)

Objectives

VI. Power, Authority, and Governance
h. Recognize and give examples of the tensions between the wants and needs of individuals and groups, and concepts such as fairness, equity, and justice.

Literacy

a. Use metacognitive strategies to comprehend text and to clarify meaning of vocabulary (e.g., reread the text, consult other sources, ask for help, paraphrase, question).
b. Interact with the text before, during, and after reading, listening, and viewing by setting a purpose using prior knowledge and text information, making predictions, formulating questions, locating relevant information, and making connections with previous experiences, information, and ideas.
d. Make inferences, draw conclusions, make generalizations, and support one's reasoning by referencing the text.
f. Respond to fiction, nonfiction, poetry, and drama using interpretive, critical, and evaluative processes.

Introduction

If possible, play a recording of one of the songs from Chapters 3 and 4, such as "Go Down, Moses" in the chapter titled "School Days," or read the song dramatically. Ask the students to brainstorm what the song might have to do with courage and justice, then have them read to find out.

Central Activity

The students will read or listen to Chapters 3 and 4 ("School Days" and "The Train Whistle Blows") with your guidance, independently, with partners, or in small groups. Ask the students to make a list (individually or in groups) of all the slaves' secret examples of courage as they read. After reading the chapters and discussing the examples they listed, guide the students in choosing one example of conflict between a slavemaster and one or more slaves, and in discussing the different ideas of justice. As a group with one example, then as small groups with their own example, have them think together to comment on ideas of justice on the following chart, followed by sharing their reasons and textual support for their entries.

Conflict situation:		
Justice, according to the slavemaster:	Justice, according to the slave:	Our sense of justice, 170+ years later:

Assessment

Ask yourself (1) Do the entries in the chart indicate that the students can perceive differences in groups' and individuals' sense of justice? Can they back up their interpretations with reasoning and examples based on the story? (2) Ask the students to make individual journal entries related to their own reactions to the historical events in this story, particularly their impressions of what was fair and what wasn't. Do their entries show that each student can perceive differences in what groups and/or individuals consider to be fair, based on this story?

Materials

- Recording of any one of the songs from these chapters, or a similar spiritual with the underlying theme of courage, freedom, escape from bondage, etc.
- Chart paper or overhead transparency for group chart work
- Paper for small group charts
- Students' journals

Lesson Two:
Focus on character motives (Chapter 5, 1 day)

Objectives

II. Time, Continuity, and Change
e. Demonstrate an understanding that people in different times and places view the world differently.

Literacy

a. Use metacognitive strategies to comprehend text and to clarify meaning of vocabulary (e.g., reread the text, consult other sources, ask for help, paraphrase, question).

b. Interact with the text before, during, and after reading, listening, and viewing by setting a purpose using prior knowledge and text information, making predictions, formulating questions, locating relevant information, and making connections with previous experiences, information, and ideas.

d. Make inferences, draw conclusions, make generalizations, and support one's reasoning by referencing the text.

f. Respond to fiction, nonfiction, poetry, and drama using interpretive, critical, and evaluative processes.

g. Compose fiction, nonfiction, poetry, and drama using self-selected and assigned topics and forms.

Introduction

Ask students to brainstorm the kind of events that could upset Harriet so greatly that she would decide to try to escape. (This may be done as a whole group or in a small group, but all students need to have individual copies of the list generated.) Have them put question marks beside those events that a slave with a milder personality might accept and not try to escape. Then have them circle those events that would prompt them to run if they had been a slave.

Central Activity

Read Chapter 5 ("Not Worth a Sixpence") in whatever manner is appropriate for the class, with the purpose of reflecting on the events in this chapter that might make Harriet or them try to escape. After identifying and discussing the precipitating event for Harriet, have the students develop a two-part journal entry about their reaction to that discovery: "Were you surprised about Harriet's reaction? Why or why not?" and "Would that have made you run? Why or why not?"

Assessment

Ask yourself (1) Can the students show, in discussion or journal entry, an understanding of Harriet's reasoning when the master died? (2) Can the students explain their own personal reactions to the situation of the master's death and Harriet's decision to flee?

Materials

- Paper and pencil for documenting the brainstormed list of possibilities
- Students' journals

Lesson Three:
Focus on the events of the journey (Chapters 6–8, 1–2 days)

Objectives

II. Time, Continuity, and Change
d. Identify and use various sources for reconstructing the past, such as documents, letters, diaries, maps, textbooks, photos, and others.

Literacy

b. Interact with the text before, during, and after reading, listening, and viewing by setting a purpose using prior knowledge and text information, making predictions, formulating questions, locating relevant information, and making connections with previous experiences, information, and ideas.

d. Make inferences, draw conclusions, make generalizations, and support one's reasoning by referencing the text.

Introduction

Bring out the concept map(s) created in the initiating activity. Ask the students to suggest new words or phrases to add to the map that would be related to *courage* on the journey Harriet is ready to take.

Central Activity

Ask the children to predict what the story of that journey might be, using a "Story Impressions" activity. After a group-start as a modeling example, the students write a possible story line for Chapters 6 through 8 ("Bound for the Promised Land" through "Riding on the Railroad") in small groups. They create that story around the following key words and phrases from these chapters, to be used in the sequence given:

1. Quaker woman
2. a message
3. going around in circles
4. walked back in silence
5. "Granpa says they going to sell you"
6. dense forest and swampy land
7. waded through the river
8. Harriet remained hidden indoors
9. a graveyard
10. a tiny windowless room
11. free state of Pennsylvania

After sharing their story impressions with the whole class, the students read the three chapters to see what actually occurred (depending on energy levels and interest, they can read them immediately, for homework, or the next day after a brief review). Guide a discussion to summarize the journey, inviting the students to note any predictions they made in "Story Impressions" that matched the actual events.

Make available simple state maps of the territory described; trace with them the general path Harriet took, then have students draw their own interpretive maps of Harriet's first journey north. Display maps and keep for later reuse. Invite journal entries of choice that reflect on Harriet's courage (or theirs under similar circumstances).

Assessment

Ask yourself (1) Can the students draw maps that include several key elements of this first journey? (2) Do the students' journal entries contain inferences and conclusions relating courage to this journey?

Materials

- Maps of Maryland, Delaware, and eastern Pennsylvania
- Drawing paper
- Students' journals

Lesson Four:
Focus on Harriet's courageous leadership
(Chapters 9–12, 2–3 days)

Objectives

IV. Power, Authority, and Governance
a. Examine the rights and responsibilities of the individual in relation to his or her social groups, such as family, peer group, and school class.

Literacy

d. Make inferences, draw conclusions, make generalizations, and support one's reasoning by referencing the text.
g. Compose fiction, nonfiction, poetry, and drama using self-selected and assigned topics and forms.

Introduction

Invite the students to listen to Chapter 9, "In a Strange Land," with this question in mind: "What will Harriet do next?" Stop periodically for predictions, reactions, and discussion.

Central Activity

Given the closing of Chapter 9 and the titles of the next three chapters, "Why Not Every Man?" "Ship of Zion," and "The Old Folks," have the class brainstorm predictions about how Harriet will set people free and who those people will be. In whatever manner is appropriate, the students then read these chapters with much discussion of the relationship between their predictions and what they are finding. To emphasize these critical and dramatic chapters, have the students select and sequence sections of this material to develop into an informal Reader's Theatre presentation to retell the essence of these journeys. (An exemplar script from page 115, where Ben and Old Rit have arrived with Harriet in Burrsville and are preparing to go by train to Thomas Garrett's house, is presented here. Use for modeling if needed.) Complete the study of this section of the book with journal entries that reflect on Harriet's sense of responsibility to her family.

Reader's Theatre Script: pages 115–116
(a scene during Harriet's parents' escape)

HARRIET: Giddy up, you ancient horse. You can't stop. You can rest later. Giddy up. We've got to get to the train station while it's still dark.

BEN: Thank goodness, we're finally here.

OLD RIT: Oh, I need to stretch my legs.

HARRIET: Here are your tickets and your passes. Keep them with you on the train. No one will ask you questions if you show these passes. Now here are the directions to Thomas Garrett's house . . .

BEN: Wait—you're not going with us?

OLD RIT: How can we go on alone? Why can't you go with us? I'm afraid.

HARRIET: Course I can't go with you. They got my picture at every railroad station from Richmond to the Pennsylvania border. You'd be caught sure, traveling with me.

BEN: But . . .

HARRIET: No but's. This is the way it has to be.

OLD RIT: I can't. I can't . . .

HARRIET: No tears. You ride those cars as if you been riding trains all your life. Don't talk to no one, and when you get to Wilmington go straight to Thomas Garrett's. I'll meet you there tomorrow.

Assessment

Ask yourself (1) Do the students reference the text while developing Reader's Theatre scripts in order to keep meaning intact, and are they successful in doing so? (2) Do the students' journal entries represent Harriet's sense of responsibility to her family and her enslaved people?

Materials

- Paper for Reader's Theatre scripts
- Minimal found items for props, if desired (e.g., sunbonnet, shawl, blanket, taped sound of a train whistle)
- Students' journals

Lesson Five:
Focus on the many pathways of the journeys
(Chapters 13–14, 1–3 days)

Objectives

II. Time, Continuity, and Change

b. Demonstrate an ability to use correct vocabulary associated with time, such as past, present, future, and long ago; read and construct simple time lines; identify examples of change; and recognize examples of cause-and-effect relationships.

d. Identify and use various sources for reconstructing the past, such as documents, letters, diaries, maps, textbooks, photos, and others

Literacy

c. Identify and interpret elements of fiction and nonfiction and support by referencing the text to determine the plot, theme, main idea and supporting details, and author's choice of words.

Introduction

Have the students reclaim and reexamine the maps they made earlier. Pose the questions: "What could go wrong with these routes?" "What could go wrong once they reach Philadelphia?" What other routes might there have to be?" List possibilities on the chalkboard or overhead projector; have the students make individual lists of their preferred possibilities for each question.

Central Activity

With students keeping their ideas in mind, read Chapters 13 and 14 ("The Lion's Paw" and "Moses") to them to keep the pace lively. Then, in small groups, have the students reread sections of the text in order to develop a large bulletin-board–sized map of these new routes from the south to Canada. Encourage the inclusion of illustrations of and notations about important places and/or events along the journey, such as Gerrit Smith's mansion, the Utica undertaker's hearse, and the train crossing Niagara Falls. Invite the students to write journal entries reflecting on how reconstructing the past through their illustrated and annotated map helps them understand the events better.

Assessment

Ask yourself (1) Do the maps and their illustrations and annotations accurately reflect the journeys described in the book? (2) Do the students use and reflect on their use of the text to make decisions about their maps, illustrations, and annotations?

Materials

- Text
- Large map to mark routes with magic marker or yarn
- Journals

Lesson Six:
Focus on the courage to fight in a variety of ways
(Chapters 15–18, 2–3 days)

Objectives

II. Time, Continuity, and Change
  e. Demonstrate an understanding that people in different times and places view the world differently
  f. Use knowledge of facts and concepts drawn from history, along with elements of historical inquiry, to make informed decisions about and take action on public issues.

Literacy

  c. Identify and interpret elements of fiction and nonfiction and support by referencing the text to determine the plot, theme, main idea and supporting details, and author's choice of words.

    d. Make inferences, draw conclusions, make generalizations, and support one's reasoning by referencing the text.

    e. Determine usefulness of information and ideas consistent with purpose.

    f. Respond to fiction, nonfiction, poetry, and drama using interpretive, critical, and evaluative processes.

Introduction

Divide the students into small, diverse groups. Ask them to choose the fastest writer in the group, who will list in 30 to 60 seconds all the different ways they can identify to fight injustice (such as slavery). Have the groups share, but keep the pace lively. Then give them another 30 to 60 seconds to list possible outcomes next to each of those ways of fighting. Share again. Then introduce the prediction guide on page 230, saying, "You know from the end of Chapter 14 that Harriet intends to join the Union Army. You've thought of many different ways of fighting injustice. What do you predict Harriet would think of these statements about fighting injustice?"

Central Activity

Use the prediction guide (and its directions) to guide the students' thinking before, during, and after reading or listening to Chapters 15 through 18, ("The Most of a Man" to "Mr. Lincoln's Army"). Conclude with a journal entry about which kinds of fighting they would have been willing to do and why.

Assessment

Ask yourself (1) Can the students use material in the book accurately to support or revise their interpretations of Harriet's positions about the different ways of fighting injustice? (2) Can students take a stand on any of the issues that arise about fighting the injustice of slavery?

Materials

- Text
- Sufficient copies of prediction guide
- Journals

Prediction Guide
What does Harriet Tubman think of fighting?
(Chapters 15–18)

Directions

1. Think about everything you have read so far about Harriet Tubman and her courage.
2. Read each statement below. Do you think Harriet would agree or disagree with each statement about fighting against injustice? Put an *A* in the "Prediction" column if you think she would agree or a *D* if you think she would disagree.
3. Then work with your group to reach consensus about your predictions. You may have to go back to earlier parts of the book to argue for your prediction.
4. Read the chapters to see what Harriet does or doesn't do as a member of the Union Army.
5. Think again about Harriet's opinions about fighting, now that you've read about her activities. Put an *A* in the "Interpretations" column if you now think she would agree with a statement or a *D* if you think she would disagree.
6. Once more, work with your group to reach consensus—this time, you'll work toward consensus about your interpretations. Use Chapters 15 through 18 as evidence to support your interpretations.

Predictions about Harriet's Opinions	Statements about Fighting Against Injustice	Interpretations about Harriet's Opinions
	1. People may have to die in battles against injustice.	
	2. The only way to win over slavery is to go to war.	
	3. There are many ways to fight injustice, and they are all important.	
	4. You can't fight injustice by growing food.	
	5. You can fight injustice by learning to read.	
	6. You can fight injustice by taking care of sick people.	

Lesson Seven:
Focus on courage to make unselfish decisions (Chapter 19, 1 day)

Objectives

II. Time, Continuity, and Change
e. Demonstrate an understanding that people in different times and places view the world differently.

f. Use knowledge of facts and concepts drawn from history, along with elements of historical inquiry, to make informed decisions about and take action on public issues.

IV. Power, Authority, and Governance
a. Examine the rights and responsibilities of the individual in relation to his or her social groups, such as family, peer group, and school class.

c. Give example of how government does or does not provide for the needs and wants of people, establish order and security, and manage conflicts.

Literacy

d. Make inferences, draw conclusions, make generalizations, and support one's reasoning by referencing the text.

e. Determine usefulness of information and ideas consistent with purpose.

f. Respond to fiction, nonfiction, poetry, and drama using interpretive, critical, and evaluative processes.

Introduction

Revisit the first concept map about courage. With the whole group, create another concept map about all the difficult *decisions* Harriet had to make—decisions that demanded courage. Tell the students that she is now faced with more difficult decisions, and that things don't work out well every time.

Central Activity

Ask the students to read Chapter 19 ("Victory") and to use Post-it notes or arrows to mark every part of the chapter where they are surprised by something that happens. After reading, focus the discussion on those surprising parts, especially the last event on the train. Invite the students to speculate about whether Harriet or they would have done anything any differently if she or they could have predicted the outcome before making any of the decisions of interest. Ask for journal entries that reflect on any interesting decision Harriet made and any interesting decision made by the government.

Assessment

Ask yourself (1) Are the students able to discuss Harriet's reasons for her decisions, based on the book? (2) Do the students' journal entries reflect personal reactions to Harriet's and governmental decisions?

Lesson Eight:
Focusing on courage during freedom and peace
(Chapter 20, 1 day)

Objectives

II. Time, Continuity, and Change
e. Demonstrate an understanding that people in different times and places view the world differently.

Literacy

d. Make inferences, draw conclusions, make generalizations, and support one's reasoning by referencing the text.
e. Determine usefulness of information and ideas consistent with purpose.
f. Respond to fiction, nonfiction, poetry, and drama using interpretive, critical, and evaluative processes.

Introduction

Tell the students that in this last chapter, Harriet's mother says to her, "You never did have good sense since you was a child." Ask the students if they can find examples of Harriet's activities in this chapter that make them agree with her mother.

Central Activity

Read the last chapter, seeing if the children "disapprove" of any of Harriet's activities in her final years, why she did them, and what they would have done differently. Suggest that the final journal entry be a reflection of any thoughts the students have about Harriet's courage throughout her whole life, including her last days.

Assessment

Ask yourself (1) Do the students suggest any changes in the quality of Harriet's decisions in her later years? (2) Do they recognize the constancy of her courage throughout her life?

Culminating and Assessment Activities

The following are suggested activities that may be done by individuals, partners, or small groups. You may want to incorporate variations into earlier lessons, or you may want students to choose one or two as evidence of having met the objectives of the unit.

- Develop a collage that represents Harriet's values of freedom, courage, loyalty, and sacrifice.
- Develop an annotated time line of the critical events in Harriet Tubman's life or her major contributions.
- Design a "Visual Biography." Draw a series of pictures to highlight Harriet Tubman's life. Draw pictures to describe her trips, actions, and character.
- Design a postage stamp that would honor the Underground Railroad and the courageous people who made it work. List reasons why the Underground Railroad was important to the development of this country and why it should be commemorated this way. Use that list to write a letter to the U.S. Postmaster General, enclosing the design and giving the reasons why the students think their design should be used.
- Write lyrics to a familiar tune, as the slaves did, to tell the story of Harriet Tubman's courage.

Unit 8
Theme: Overcoming Prejudice

Single-Book Model: Grades 4–5

Book

Felita by Nicholasa Mohr

Rationale

Children experience prejudice, to some degree, in the process of becoming an adult. Learning to recognize prejudice and confronting it with a positive, non-threatening approach is an important skill to learn for attaining and maintaining a healthy self-concept. This unit is closely aligned with Banks and Banks's decision-making and social action approach.

Unit Goal

The major goal of this unit is to prepare students to react appropriately to the negative impact of acts of prejudice.

NCSS Themes and Performance Standards

IV. Individual Development and Identity
c. Describe the unique features of one's nuclear and extended families.
g. Analyze a particular event to identify reasons individuals might respond to it in different ways.

V. Individuals, Groups, and Institutions
a. Identify roles as learned behavior patterns in group situations, such as student family members, peer play group member, or club member.
c. Identify examples of institutions and describe the interactions of people with institutions.
d. Identify and describe examples of tensions between and among individuals, groups, or institutions, and how belonging to more than one group can cause internal conflicts.
g. Show how groups and institutions work to meet individual needs and promote the common good, and identify examples of where they fail to do so.

Literacy Objectives
(Based on NC Standard Course of Study)

   a. Use oral and written language to express ideas clearly and effectively in a variety of oral contexts.
   b. Interact with the text before, during, and after reading, listening, and viewing by making connections with previous experiences, information, and ideas.
   c. Make inferences, draw conclusions, make generalizations, and support by referencing the text.
   d. Summarize major points from fiction and nonfiction text(s) to clarify and retain information and ideas.
   e. Produce work that follows the conventions of particular genres (e.g., personal and imaginative narrative, research reports, learning logs, letters of request, letters of complaint).

Lesson One:
Overcoming prejudice (Chapter 1, 2 days)

Objectives

V. Individuals, Groups and Institutions

   a. Identify roles as learned behavior patterns in group situations, such as student family members, peer play group member, or club member.
   d. Identify and describe examples of tensions between and among individuals, groups, or institutions, and how belonging to more than one group can cause internal conflicts.

Literacy

   a. Use oral and written language to express ideas clearly and effectively in a variety of oral contexts.
   b. Interact with the text before, during, and after reading, listening, and viewing by making connections with previous experiences, information, and ideas.

Introduction

In a general discussion, ask the students, "Have you ever moved to a new neighborhood?" Some students will have experienced moving but be sure to have other students share with them what it may feel like for them to move.

Central Activity

The students will create a Plot Relationship Chart to clarify the problem-solution elements of a selection and the sense of the story. Guide the students to fill in the cells similar to the following example.

Somebody	Wanted	But	So
Mami and Papi	a better life for their family	the new neighbors weren't accepting	they moved back to the old neighborhood

Materials

- Text
- Writing paper
- Presentation paper
- Marking pens

Assessment

Evaluate how the student (or group) designs and presents his or her chart. Check for accuracy.

Lesson Two:
Felita and the new girls (Chapter 2, 2 days)

Objectives

IV. Individual Development and Identity

g. Analyze a particular event to identify reasons individuals might respond to it in different ways.

Literacy

c. Make inferences, draw conclusions, make generalizations, and support by referencing the text.

Introduction

Ask the students if they have ever moved to a different neighborhood, town, or state. After sharing any experiences, direct the students to read Chapter 2. Spend part of the period having students compare any shared moving experiences with the experience Felita had with the new girls.

Central Activity

Reread the selection and produce a comparison and contrast table (see the sample on the next page). Address these questions in small or large groups:

- Would you have played with the new girls?
- Would you have been confident enough to play your best?
- Would you have been mean to the new neighbor? (Felita)

Discuss the choices that characters made, and determine which is most similar to the students' way of thinking. Discuss the differences in their ways of thinking. After a guided class discussion, determine what other solutions were/are possible.

Like Me	Not Like Me	Things to Be Done Differently
Similar experiences, thoughts, ideas, actions		

Materials

- Marking pens
- Rulers
- Text

Assessment

In paired teams or individually, have the students write a paragraph discussing what they would do if a child their age with a different cultural background moved into their neighborhood.

Lesson Three:
Felita and Gigi (Chapters 3–5, 2 days)

Objectives

V. Individuals, Groups, and Institutions
a. Identify roles as learned behavior patterns in group situations, such as student family members, peer play group member, or club member.
d. Identify and describe examples of tensions between and among individuals, groups, or institutions, and how belonging to more than one group can cause internal conflicts.

Literacy

a. Use oral and written language to express ideas clearly and effectively in a variety of oral contexts.
b. Interact with the text before, during, and after reading, listening, and viewing by making connections with previous experiences, information, and ideas.

c. Make inferences, draw conclusions, make generalizations, and support by referencing the text.

Introduction

Friends often argue, as Felita and Gigi do. In a large group, read or have students read Chapters 3–5. Introduce and discuss the words *jealous, envy,* and *greed.* Ask the students to write in their journals about their experiences with jealousy, envy, and greed.

Central Activity

- Produce a knowledge chart of relationship indicators of Felita and Gigi. Ask the children to illustrate these charts by drawing pictures and selecting photographs from magazines.
- Identify three groups to which the girls belong and how the tension of competition affected these groups.

Assessment

In small groups, prepare a list of items that can make people feel jealous. Listen to the children discuss how jealousy can affect relationships.

Materials

- Text
- Writing paper

Lesson Four:
Felita and Abuelita (1 day)

Objectives

IV. Individual Development and Identity
c. Describe the unique features of one's nuclear and extended families.

V. Individuals, Groups, and Institutions
g. Show how groups and institutions work to meet individual needs and promote the common good, and identify examples of where they fail to do so.

Literacy

c. Make inferences, draw conclusions, make generalizations, and support by referencing the text.

> **d.** Summarize major points from fiction and nonfiction text(s) to clarify and retain information and ideas.
> **e.** Produce work that follows the conventions of particular genres (e.g., personal and imaginative narrative, research reports, learning logs, letters of request, letters of complaint).

Introduction

Parents and grandparents often have different opinions about the behavior of children. Make two lists on the board as students share what they may do at grandparents' (or aunts', uncles', etc.) homes that their parents will not allow them to do at home.

Central Activity

Ask the students to write a diary entry in Felita's voice, explaining the unique relationship she and her Grandmother shared.

Assessment

Compare the children's diary entry with responses from the introductory activity. To what degree did students personalize their responses?

Materials

- Text
- Writing paper
- Marking pens

Culminating and Assessment Activities

Elicit from the class, and summarize as necessary, definitions for the terms *discrimination, racism,* and *prejudice.* Focus a discussion on reasons for prejudice. Remind the class that most prejudice is based on ignorance; it is commonplace to dislike or fear something one does not know. If a person takes the time to get to know someone, he or she may find something to like about that person. Since this is a sensitive area, it might be helpful to end the activity with a discussion about ignorance and prejudice. Direct each student to prepare a list of 5 to 10 things he or she can do as a citizen to overcome prejudice, and to develop a specific plan for one of them. After you approve the plans, tell all students to implement that plan for one week and report their findings.

Unit 9
Theme: Courage and Commitment

Multiple-Book Model: Grades 4–5

Focus Book

Nightjohn by Gary Paulsen

Rationale

In order to think globally and make positive social decisions, children must be presented with challenging situations that require them to analyze inappropriate human behavior and take appropriate, responsible actions.

Unit Goal

The goal of this unit is to prepare students to identify and acknowledge their fears and to begin finding meaningful solutions for overcoming the struggles impacting their lives.

Related Books

Because of Winn Dixie by Kate DiCamillo
A Freedom River by Doreen Rappaport
The Friendship by Mildred D. Taylor
The Flunking of Joshua T. Bates by Susan Shreve
Fourth Grade Rats by Jerry Spinelli
Bud, Not Buddy by Christopher Paul Curtis
A Year Down Yonder by Richard Peck
The Story of Sitting Bull by Lisa Eisenberg

NCSS Themes and Performance Standards

II. Time, Continuity, and Change
a. Demonstrate an understanding that different people may describe the same event or situation in diverse ways, citing reasons the differences in views.

b. Demonstrate an ability to use correct vocabulary associated with time, such as past, present, future and long ago; read and construct simple time lines; identify examples of change; and recognize examples of cause-and-effect relationships.

X. Civic Ideals and Practices
b. Identify examples of rights and responsibilities of citizens.

Literacy Objectives
(Based on NC Standard Course of Study)

a. Use oral and written language to express ideas clearly and effectively in a variety of oral contexts.

b. Interact with the text before, during, and after reading, listening, and viewing by making connections with previous experiences, information, and ideas.

c. Make inferences, draw conclusions, make generalizations, and support by referencing the text.

d. Summarize major points from fiction and nonfiction text(s) to clarify and retain information and ideas.

e. Produce work that follows the conventions of particular genres (e.g., personal and imaginative narrative, research reports, learning logs, letters of request, letters of complaint).

f. Compose fiction, nonfiction, poetry, and drama using self-selected and assigned topics and forms (e.g., personal and imaginative narratives, research reports, diaries, journals, logs, rules, instructions).

Initiating Activity
(Prereading activity, 1 day)

As a *prewriting activity,* students will focus and organize their ideas, and compare personal experience to an author's meaning or events in works of literature. As a *prereading activity,* students will be asked to write about either an actual experience that they had or to imagine how they would feel if this situation occurred.

Students will respond to the following:

- Write about what you actually did or what you think you would do if you had to take the punishment for someone else when you were innocent.
- Write about how you felt when someone else took the punishment for you when you were guilty and they were innocent or how you think you would feel if this happened to you.

Lesson One:
Communicating (Chapter 1, Day 1)

Objectives

X. Civic Ideals and Practices

b. Identify examples of rights and responsibilities of citizens.

Literacy

a. Use oral and written language to express ideas clearly and effectively in a variety of oral contexts.

Introduction

Review the prereading activities and conduct a survey of how the students feel about fairness and punishment. Initiate a student discussion on the purpose of communication and the variety of ways people communicate in society today. Conclude the discussion with these questions:

- How can people communicate without telephones, radio, television, and/or computers?
- How can people communicate if they cannot read? (teacher-directed discussion)

Central Activity

Divide the students into small groups of three or four and ask each child to develop a secret code through special symbols, nonsense words, or body language to send a simple message to other members in the group. Once all of the groups have planned what they will communicate, direct each group to send its message and allow the other groups to break the code and learn the message. All students return to the large group to listen to you read Chapter 1 to the entire class. Ask them to predict, in writing, their opinions the character Nightjohn is going to play in the book.

Assessment

Read the students' predictions to confirm that the predictions make sense. The students may orally share their predictions with classmates.

Materials

- Journal notebook

Lesson Two
Keeping a secret (Chapters 2–5, Days 2 and 3)

Objectives

X. Civic Ideals and Practices
b. Identify examples of rights and responsibilities of citizens.

Literacy

b. Interact with the text before, during, and after reading, listening, and viewing by making connections with previous experiences, information, and ideas.

Introduction

Tell the students to read Chapters 2 through 5 and to prepare to keep a journal of their personal feelings and written responses to questions that you will assign.

Central Activity

Explain to the students that they are to record their personal reactions to the major events they read in Chapters 2 through 5. Provide several specific questions that solicit the students' written responses. Responses should be honest and thoughtful. Following are a few examples of questions, but you should modify and expand from the list.

- How could you learn if you didn't have books or schools?
- What if you had to keep your learning a secret?
- If you were Sarny, would you continue trying to learn to read?

Assessment

Review the students' journals daily and provide individual direction as necessary. Check to see that each student is giving a focused response that is in alignment with your expectation of individual ability.

Materials

- Journal notebook
- Book: *Nightjohn*

Lesson Three:
A time for change (Chapters 6–7, Days 4 and 5)

Objectives

II. Time, Continuity, and Change

a. Demonstrate an understanding that different people may describe the same event or situation in diverse ways, citing reasons the differences in views.

b. Demonstrate an ability to use correct vocabulary associated with time, such as past, present, future and long ago; read and construct simple time lines; identify examples of change; and recognize examples of cause-and-effect relationships.

Literacy

c. Make inferences, draw conclusions, make generalizations, and support by referencing the text.

d. Summarize major points from fiction and nonfiction text(s) to clarify and retain information and ideas.

Introduction

Use a blank chart (similar to the following example) on the board or on an overhead projector to display character development from the characters in *Nightjohn*. How did each character change from the beginning, middle, and end?

	Beginning	Middle	End
Sarny			
John			
Mother			
Other			

Central Activity

Initiate a student discussion about what the students have learned about the three characters, Sarny, her mother, and John. How did each demonstrate courage? Who demonstrated the most courage? Why?

Assessment

Discuss responses from the class with respect to acts of courage presented. Check for consistency among responses and see if any students state that with courage comes hope, but also risks.

Materials

- Graphic organizer/chart
- Overhead projector/transparencies/pens

Lesson Four:
Taking risks (Day 6)

Objectives

X. Civic Ideals and Practices
b. Identify examples of rights and responsibilities of citizens.

Literacy

e. Produce work that follows the conventions of particular genres (e.g., personal and imaginative narrative, research reports, learning logs, letters of request, letters of complaint).
f. Compose fiction, nonfiction, poetry, and drama using self-selected and assigned topics and forms (e.g., personal and imaginative narratives, research reports, diaries, journals, logs, rules, instructions).

Introduction

Ask the students to determine why Nightjohn risked his own life to help teach slaves to read. What did he have to gain or lose?

Central Activity

Tell the students to write a composition reacting to the following: (1) Nightjohn showed great courage by staying in the South to teach other slaves how to read when he could have stayed away and remained a free man. (2) Nightjohn should not have risked his own life or freedom to help others to read. The students should support their position with specific reasons. Encourage the students to show "courage" in how they feel in their written responses.

Assessment

Develop a rubric or checklist for evaluating how effectively the students support their position.

Materials

- Pencil and paper
- Ruler

Lesson Five: Beyond *Nightjohn* (Days 7–10)

Objectives

X. Civic Ideals and Practices

b. Identify examples of rights and responsibilities of citizens.

Literacy

e. Produce work that follows the conventions of particular genres (e.g., personal and imaginative narrative, research reports, learning logs, letters of request, letters of complaint).

Introduction

Have the students select a book from the list of related books on the first page of this unit plan. (*Note:* Books vary from third- to fifth-grade reading levels. You may need to assist students in selecting a specific book.) Give the students silent reading time in class and/or instructions to complete the book at home.

After all children have read their books, have them prepare to do an "empty chair interview" of a major character from their individual books. You will need to demonstrate the "empty chair interview" approach using a character from the children's last book, *Nightjohn*. Pretend that the character is sitting in an empty chair in front of you. Four or five major questions should be developed for the interview, which is conducted totally in a written format. For example, one might ask this question of Sarny: "How did you feel when you were caught reading?" Sarny's response may be recorded on the chalkboard.

Central Activity

Record the names of major characters from the selected books and divide the class based on the books. For example, all who read *Bud, Not Buddy* are grouped together. Each student then interviews the main character from his or her individual book. Interview questions should lead to description and personal "feelings" of the character. Students share what they wrote within their group. (*Note:* You may let the students work in pairs instead of groups.) After the group activity is completed, each group presents its interview to the class.

Assessment

Direct each child to read his or her written interview to the entire class. Check to see if the student focused on the struggles or fears the main character faced.

Materials

- At least four copies of each book to be used (you may limit the selections to five or six of the nine books)

Culminating and Assessment Activities
(Days 11 and 10)

Probe to see if each student can relate his or her *fear or struggle* with the main character of the selected book and the character(s) in *Nightjohn*. Ask the students to write about a fear or struggle that they have in their lives. Approve each child's fear/struggle prior to presentation to make sure it is appropriate. Encourage non-threatening topics, such as fear of homework, fear of a pet getting lost, fear of getting lost on a trip, fear of doing a good job, and so on. You might want to avoid fears of abandonment, divorce, death, and the like. After they've written their thoughts on paper and you've read them, the children will give a short oral presentation about their fears or struggles. This will be a great way for children to express their fears, which could lead to a meaningful discussion or follow-up activity on problem solving and/or brainstorming ideas about these fears.

Unit 10
Theme: People, Places, and Environments

Single-Book Model: Grades 4–5

Book

Missing May by Cynthia Rylant

Rationale

Encouraging students to think beyond the traditional viewpoints on life and death can assist children in becoming more sensitive to cultural viewpoints other than their own.

Unit Goal

The major goal of this unit is to focus students on the issues of the realities of death and how to gain courage to move forward in the challenges of living within a changed environment.

NCSS Themes and Performance Standards

I. Culture

a. Explore and describe similarities and differences in the ways groups, societies, and cultures address similar human needs and concerns.

b. Give examples of how experiences may be interpreted differently by people from diverse cultural perspectives and frames of reference.

c. Describe ways in which language, stories, folktales, music, and artistic creations serve as expressions of culture and influence behavior or people living in a particular culture.

II. Time, Continuity, and Change

a. Demonstrate an understanding that different people may describe the same event or situation in diverse ways, citing reasons for the differences in view.

b. Demonstrate an ability to use correct vocabulary associated with time, such as past, present, future, and long ago; read and construct simple time lines; identify examples of change; and recognize examples of cause-and-effect relationships.

    d. Identify and use various sources for reconstructing the past, such as documents, letters, diaries, maps, textbooks, photos, and others.

III. People, Places, and Environments

    b. Interpret, use, and distinguish various representations of the earth, such as maps, globes, and photographs.

    c. Use appropriate resources, data sources, and geographic tools such as atlases, databases, grid systems, charts, graphs, and maps to generate, manipulate, and interpret information.

    d. Estimate distance and calculate scale.

    f. Describe and speculate about physical system changes, such as seasons, climate and weather, and the water cycle.

Literacy Objectives
(Based on NC Standard Course of Study)

    a. Use oral and written language to present information and ideas in a clear, concise manner, discuss, interview, solve problems, and make decisions.

    b. Interact with the text before, during, and after reading, listening, and viewing by setting a purpose using prior knowledge and text information, making predictions, formulating questions, locating relevant information, and making connections with previous experiences, information, and ideas.

    c. Use planning strategies to generate topics and organize ideas (e.g., brainstorming, mapping, webbing, reading, discussion).

    d. Compose fiction, nonfiction, poetry, and drama using self-selected and assigned topics and forms (e.g., assume a point of view and develop a composition that consistently addresses an issue or concern from that perspective).

    e. Compose fiction, nonfiction, poetry, and drama using self-selected and assigned topics and forms (e.g., develop an argumentative/persuasive composition that argues for or against an issue, idea, or proposal).

    f. Make oral and written presentations using visual aids with an awareness of purpose and audience.

    g. Conduct research for assigned projects or self-selected projects (with assistance) from a variety of sources through the use of technological and informal tools (e.g., print and nonprint texts, artifacts, people, libraries, databases, computer networks).

Initiating Activity (Group work, Day 1)

For a *large group* activity, introduce the book *Missing May*. Show the students the cover of the book and ask them what they think the book will be about. Do they think May is missing, or is someone missing May? Tell the students the book is set in Deep Water, West Virginia. As a class, locate Deep Water, West Virginia (Fayette County), and your city and state on a map.

For a *small group* activity, divide the class into four groups and give each group an atlas. Have each group find a route from your city to Deep Water. Have them then calculate the time and distance. Which group found the shortest route? (This set of activities, which will be done on the first day, will take an estimated 30 minutes.)

Lesson One:
Time line construction (Chapters 1–2, Day 2)

Objectives

I. Culture
a. Explore and describe similarities and differences in the ways groups, societies, and cultures address similar human needs and concerns.

c. Describe ways in which language, stories, folktales, music, and artistic creations serve as expressions of culture and influence behavior or people living in a particular culture.

III. People, Places, and Environments
b. Interpret, use, and distinguish various representations of the earth, such as maps, globes, and photographs.

c. Use appropriate resources, data sources, and geographic tools such as atlases, databases, grid systems, charts, graphs, and maps to generate, manipulate, and interpret information.

d. Estimate distance and calculate scale.

f. Describe and speculate about physical system changes, such as seasons, climate and weather, and the water cycle.

Literacy

a. Use oral and written language to present information and ideas in a clear, concise manner, discuss, interview, solve problems, and make decisions.

c. Use planning strategies to generate topics and organize ideas (e.g., brainstorming, mapping, webbing, reading, discussion).

Introduction

Read to the class or have the class read Chapters 1 and 2. Begin constructing a time line of events (from the time Ob and May got Summer when she was age 6). The time line should go through several seasons; have the students compare the weather and climate patterns of your state and West Virginia. They can then create a graph at the end of the unit, showing their similarities or differences. This activity will run the length of the book.

Central Activity

For high achievers, point out that several name brands appear in the book (24 to be exact). As each name brand (Johnson's Baby Lotion, Coke, Ruffles, etc.) appears, have the students survey 25 people (the same 25 every time), asking them whether they use or have used this product, store, and so on. Then have the students graph the results. This project will run the length of the book.

For the entire class, after the completion of Chapter 1, have the students discuss what they think the importance of the whirligigs is. Then have them make their own whirligigs.

Assessment

Following this set of activities, the students should be aware of the relationship between the states and their settings in both West Virginia and your state. For another tie-in, have them compare and graph the populations of West Virginia and your state.

Materials

- Several maps/atlases
- Book: *Missing May*
- Graph paper
- Rulers
- Pencils/pens

Lesson Two:
Compare and contrast (Chapter 3, Days 3 and 4)

Objectives

I. Culture
a. Explore and describe similarities and differences in the ways groups, societies, and cultures address similar human needs and concerns.

II. Time, Continuity, and Change
d. Identify and use various sources for reconstructing the past, such as documents, letters, diaries, maps, textbooks, photos, and others.

Literacy

b. Interact with the text before, during, and after reading, listening, and viewing by setting a purpose using prior knowledge and text information, making predictions, formulating questions, locating relevant information, and making connections with previous experiences, information, and ideas.

    c. Use planning strategies to generate topics and organize ideas (e.g., brainstorming, mapping, webbing, reading, discussion).

    e. Compose fiction, nonfiction, poetry, and drama using self-selected and assigned topics and forms (e.g., develop an argumentative/persuasive composition that argues for or against an issue, idea, or proposal).

    f. Make oral and written presentations using visual aids with an awareness of purpose and audience.

    g. Conduct research for assigned projects or self-selected projects (with assistance) from a variety of sources through the use of technological and informal tools (e.g., print and nonprint texts, artifacts, people, libraries, databases, computer networks).

Introduction

As a *large group*, read Chapter 3. Have the students write in their journals about a hobby or something they collect. Then have the students begin collecting pictures for a class collage. Have them bring in their favorite picture and an old family picture. (This project should be ready to put together within two days.)

Central Activity

For a *large group*, have the students discuss the way Ob, Cletus, and Summer spend their Christmas. Then have them compare this with their own experiences. (This will be evaluated through a journal entry.)

    Chapter 3 introduces education into the story. For *small group* work, divide the class into groups of four or five. Assign your state to one-half of the group, and West Virginia to the other half. Have them research the states' education history and compare the results. (When was education established? Was it private or public? What kind of higher education was offered? Transportation?) (This activity will be approximately 30–45 minutes.)

Assessment

Have the students discuss why they think education is important. Have each group come up with its top five reasons why the group feels education is important. Each team will then lead a discussion of these questions in the form of a debate. All other class members will be asked to challenge or debate their reasons. Each team will take a turn being the lead group. This should initiate a lot of thinking and conversation.

Materials

- Posterboard for collages
- Paste
- Scissors
- Books on education history of your state and West Virginia

Lesson Three:
Compare and contrast (Chapters 4–5, Days 5 and 6)

Objectives

I. Culture
  a. Explore and describe similarities and differences in the ways groups, societies, and cultures address similar human needs and concerns.

Literacy

  b. Interact with the text before, during, and after reading, listening, and viewing by setting a purpose using prior knowledge and text information, making predictions, formulating questions, locating relevant information, and making connections with previous experiences, information, and ideas.
  c. Use planning strategies to generate topics and organize ideas (e.g., brainstorming, mapping, webbing, reading, discussion).
  d. Compose fiction, nonfiction, poetry, and drama using self-selected and assigned topics and forms (e.g., assume a point of view and develop a composition that consistently addresses an issue or concern from that perspective).
  g. Conduct research for assigned projects or self-selected projects (with assistance) from a variety of sources through the use of technological and informal tools (e.g., print and nonprint texts, artifacts, people, libraries, databases, computer networks).

Introduction

Cletus Underwood is introduced in Chapter 3. For an individual assignment, tell the student to observe Summer's perception of Cletus and be prepared to compare it with Summer's perception at the end of the book. In Chapter 4, Cletus shares his near-death experience. Ask the student, "How would you feel if you were in his shoes?"

Central Activity

In Chapter 5, Summer talks about May's funeral and how the grief process seemed like a system when outsiders get involved. Compare the funeral/burial rituals of the United States with that of another country or culture. (This will be a research activity. Allow two to three days. Have information on funeral rituals for several cultures in the classroom, then allow the students to make a selection from one of these. The students can work in pairs to create a comparison and contrast chart.)

Assessment

Discuss death and the grief process. Then have the students write a paper about their feelings on death. If appropriate, ask them to share their stories with each other or in small groups.

Materials

- Books or other sources with information on funeral rituals in different cultures

Lesson Four:
Study of different routes on map (Chapters 6–8, Days 7 and 8)

Objectives

III. People, Places, and Environments
c. Use appropriate resources, data sources, and geographic tools such as atlases, databases, grid systems, charts, and maps to generate, manipulate, and interpret information.
d. Estimate distance and calculate scale.

Literacy

e. Compose fiction, nonfiction, poetry, and drama using self-selected and assigned topics and forms (e.g., develop an argumentative/persuasive composition that argues for or against an issue, idea, or proposal).
f. Make oral and written presentations using visual aids with an awareness of purpose and audience.
g. Conduct research for assigned projects or self-selected projects (with assistance) from a variety of sources through the use of technological and informal tools (e.g., print and nonprint texts, artifacts, people, libraries, databases, computer networks).

Introduction

As a group, read Chapters 6 through 8. Locate Charleston, West Virginia, and your city and state on a map. Ask, "What do these two places have in common?"

Central Activity

Divide the class into four groups. Have the first group find a route between two cities in your state, calculating time and distance. Have the second group find a route from Deep Water to Charleston, calculating time and distance. Have the third group find a route from Deep Water to one of the two selected cities in your state, calculating time and distance. Have the fourth group find a route from the other selected city in your state to Charleston, calculating time and distance. Compare the results (45-minute activity).

Chapter 8 has a scene involving bats. Have all the students do some research on bats. Try to bring a bat into the class (if possible for a week or two) and observe its behaviors and record data.

Assessment

In Chapter 7, Cletus talks about newspaper headlines. Divide the class into groups of four or five. Give each group a different newspaper—one from an urban area in your state, one from urban West Virginia, one from a rural area in your state, and one from rural West Virginia. Compare the different headlines. Have the students prepare and present arguments about which area to visit and the best route to take from their home city or state.

Materials

- Various newspapers
- Maps/atlases
- Rulers
- Information on bats (books, films, etc.)

Culminating and Assessment Activities
(Days 9 and 10)

Note: The following activities are examples; you will want to choose more than one in order to obtain final assessment information about all unit objectives.

- Divide the class in half. Have half the students write a journal entry from the perspective of Ob about the trip to the capital of West Virginia. Have the other half write a journal entry from the perspective of Cletus. Have the students compare their entries.
- Upon completion of the book, the students should now finish the time line. Create the graph for the weather and climate patterns.
- Divide the class into pairs. Have half the pairs create brochures for your state capital. Have the other half of pairs create brochures for Charleston, the capital of West Virginia. Brochures should include small scale maps of some useful kind and historical information of interest. (This activity will take some researching to find out about sights of interest, but the final product should be completed in class.)
- Have each student design a booklet including each of the following for both your state and West Virginia: the state bird, flower, tree, seal, flag, license plate, and motto. They can either draw or cut out pictures. Are there any alike? Ideas from the booklet could also be included in the brochure.

INDEX